D1508929

WORK, WORKERS, and WORK ORGANIZATIONS

contributing authors

Sheila H. Akabas
Columbia University

Leon W. Chestang
Wayne State University

Jerome Cohen
University of California

Paul A. Kurzman
Hunter College, C.U.N.Y.

Brenda G. McGowan
Columbia University

Martha N. Ozawa
Washington University

Rino J. Patti
University of Washington

Helen Harris Perlman
University of Chicago

Jack Rothman
University of Michigan

Arthur B. Shostak
Drexel University

WORK, WORKERS, and WORK ORGANIZATIONS

A View from Social Work

edited by

Sheila H. Akabas
Columbia University

Paul A. Kurzman
Hunter College,
City University of
New York

Prentice-Hall Inc., Englewood Cliffs, New Jersey 07632

Library of Congress Cataloging in Publication Data
Main entry under title:

Work, workers, and work organizations.

  Includes bibliographical references and index.
  Contents: Work meanings through Western history /
Arthur B. Shostak—Work and social policy / Martha N.
Ozawa—The client as worker / Helen Harris Perlman [etc.]
  1. Social service—Addresses, essays, lectures.
2. Social work administration—Addresses, essays, lectures.
3. Work—Addresses, essays, lectures. I. Akabas,
Sheila H., 1931–   . II. Kurzman, Paul A.
HV31.W67   361.3   81–13940
ISBN 0-13-965355-X   AACR2

Prentice-Hall Series in Social Work Practice
Neil Gilbert and Harry Specht, eds.

Interior design and editorial/
  production supervision by Chrys Chrzanowski
Cover design by 20/20 Services, Inc.
Manufacturing buyer: John Hall

© 1982 by Prentice-Hall, Inc., Englewood Cliffs, N.J. 07632

All rights reserved. No part of this book
may be reproduced in any form or
by any means without permission in writing
from the publisher.

Printed in the United States of America

10 9 8 7 6 5 4 3 2 1

PRENTICE-HALL INTERNATIONAL, INC., *London*
PRENTICE-HALL OF AUSTRALIA PTY. LIMITED, *Sydney*
PRENTICE-HALL OF CANADA, LTD., *Toronto*
PRENTICE-HALL OF INDIA PRIVATE LIMITED, *New Delhi*
PRENTICE-HALL OF JAPAN, INC., *Tokyo*
PRENTICE-HALL OF SOUTHEAST ASIA PTE. LTD., *Singapore*
WHITEHALL BOOKS LIMITED, WELLINGTON, *New Zealand*

In memory of
Our mentor, colleague, and friend,
Hyman J. Weiner
Advocate for the American worker

Contents

Preface

Students of social work will find in WORK, WORKERS, AND WORK ORGANIZA-TIONS a new perspective for the provision of service and the development of social policy. By introducing a view of the world of work, the volume seeks to enhance understanding both in the core curriculum areas and for those interested in method. Because the practice community has played such an instrumental role in its final form, we hope that practitioners will find it equally useful. We see a day when no student can leave social work school without an appreciation of the significance of work in individual development and functioning; without a sense of the impact of work on social work research, policy, and practice; and without an understanding of the influence of work in the organizing processes of a community.

Attention must be paid to the many whose contribution is represented in these pages, but who are not identified elsewhere. As the reader can imagine, the list is a long one. During the process by which we have arrived at this point, we have been the recipients of generous intellectual, financial and professional assistance.

Our greatest debt is to our immediate family members, Aaron, Myles, Seth, and Miriam Akabas and Margaret, Katherine, and David Kurzman, for their consistent understanding and their constant encouragement. All workers will recognize that these supports are essential to the satisfactory completion of any effort. We are also in debt to Seth Akabas for the editorial assistance he offered on the early draft of our own chapter. We drew, as well, on the advice and editorial talents of Dr. Irving Miller throughout this effort. The Silberman Fund and its representatives provided vision, inspiration, and support without which this effort could never have been undertaken. The Fund has been the mid-wife of this project, and we can only hope that, through our efforts, we have helped to achieve the kind of strong, responsive profession to which the leadership of the Fund is committed. We know that their belief in us, and in the social work profession, has been an unfaltering inspiration. We are particularly grateful to Mr. Samuel Silberman, the Fund's President. Without his wisdom and consistent encouragement we might never have brought this project to fruition. We are appreciative, as well, to the Board of the Johnson Foundation, which joined with the Silberman Fund to support the final meeting of this project at the Wingspread Conference Center in April 1979. Mr. Richard Kinch of the Foundation was an exceedingly helpful project officer and we are in his debt.

We are each fortunate to number among our faculty colleagues an individual who combines the qualities of mentor, critic, and friend. For his knowledge, which is so extensive, his observations, which are so incisive, and his spirit, which is so generous, Sheila Akabas is deeply indebted to Dr. Irving Miller of the Columbia University School of Social Work. Paul Kurzman is equally grateful to Dr. Florence Vigilante of the Hunter College School of Social Work whose unswerving commitment to the field of practice and whose keen ability to discern the meaning of work in the practice dimensions of social work has been a constant source of insight and a guiding light to him. As well, we each owe a special debt to our colleagues at the Industrial Social Welfare Center at Columbia, and the World of Work Program at Hunter, and to Dean Mitchell Ginsberg and Dean Harold Lewis of Columbia and Hunter respectively. They have been a constant sounding board and reservoir of good ideas, support, and good will throughout this effort.

No project could have been more fortunate in its staff support. Ms. Nancy Kolben as the staff representative charged with responsibility for both the Practitioners' Conference and the Wingspread meeting, husbanded our energies by tending to a thousand details while keeping us refreshed with new ideas and informed of all developments. Truly, the process would have been untenable without her. Ms. Adrienne Asch provided important staff support to the development of this book, itself. She maintained close contact with all the contributors and assumed the difficult responsibility of interpreting, and then conveying to them, the thoughts of the practitioners. Her ability to communicate ideas was invaluable to the final product. Her tact, intellect, and suggestions are reflected throughout these pages.

We hope that Ruth Antoniades, Michael Howe, Sheila Menashe, Leo Miller, Beth Silverman, and Carvel Taylor—the team of social work practitioners who shared their experience and advice—will find in these pages enough that reflects their contributions that they will feel rewarded for the time, energy, and thinking that they so abundantly offered to all the authors. We owe them a special debt of gratitude. This gratitude is targeted, as well, at the many groups of practitioners in industrial social welfare whose practice examples have stimulated us throughout the years and at our dedicated students whose questions and interest have been a consistent source of rejuvenation. Finally, we express our gratitude to the group of labor and management representatives who joined us at Wingspread to add the vantage of their worldly experience to our writings. Their names are listed as conference participants.

It was not easy to be a contributor to this volume. The exploration of ideas within a context that would become a complementary whole placed demands on the authors far beyond what might be expected of contributors to a typical collection of essays. They remained involved in the task with a dedication that we might have hoped for, but certainly had no right to expect. We have felt privileged to work with them, and are in their debt for their patience, fortitude, and creative contributions.

Sheila H. Akabas

New York City   *Paul A. Kurzman*

Conference Participants*

Sheila H. Akabas
Associate Professor and Director
Industrial Social Welfare Center
School of Social Work
Columbia University
New York, New York

Ruth Antoniades
Assistant Director
Social Services Department
Amalgamated Clothing and Textile Workers
    Union, AFL-CIO
New York, New York

Adrienne Asch
Staff Associate
Industrial Social Work Conference
New York, New York

Marcus B. Bond
Corporate Medical Director
American Telephone and Telegraph
    Company
Basking Ridge, New Jersey

Leon W. Chestang
Professor
School of Social Work
The University of Alabama
Tuscaloosa, Alabama

Jerome Cohen
Professor
School of Social Welfare
University of California, Los Angeles
Los Angeles, California

Michael W. Howe
Manager
Social Resource Center and Training
Northern States Power Company
Minneapolis, Minnesota

Richard Kinney
Public Affairs Research Manager
J.C. Penney Company
New York, New York

Nancy S. Kolben
Educational Program Specialist
Council on Social Work Education
New York, New York

Paul A. Kurzman
Associate Professor and Chairperson
World of Work Program
School of Social Work
Hunter College
City University of New York
New York, New York

Gary A. Lloyd
Executive Director
Council on Social Work Education
New York, New York

Dale Masi
Associate Professor
School of Social Work
Boston College
Chestnut Hill, Massachusetts

Sheila Menashe
Director of Support Services
Municipal Employees Legal Services Plan
District Council 37, American Federation of
    State, County & Municipal Employees,
    AFL-CIO
New York, New York

Irving Miller
Professor
School of Social Work
Columbia University
New York, New York

*Affiliations and titles at time of Conference.

Joyce D. Miller
President
Coalition of Labor Union Women
Vice President
Amalgamated Clothing and Textile Workers
    Union, AFL-CIO
New York, New York

Leo Miller
Manager
Counseling Department
Polaroid Corporation
Cambridge, Massachusetts

Martha N. Ozawa
Professor
George Warren Brown School of Social
    Work
Washington University
St. Louis, Missouri

Rino J. Patti
Professor
School of Social Work
University of Washington
Seattle, Washington

Helen Harris Perlman
Samuel Deutsch Distinguished Professor
    Emeritus
School of Social Service Administration
University of Chicago
Chicago, Illinois

Jack Rothman
Professor
School of Social Work
University of Michigan
Ann Arbor, Michigan

Samuel Silberman
President
The Lois and Samuel Silberman Fund
New York, New York

Beth Silverman
Director of Personal Services
District 65
Distributive Workers of America
New York, New York

Sam Silverstein
Chairperson
Center for Mental Health Services
Manpower, Research, and Demonstration,
    NIMH
Rockville, Maryland

Cynthia Swain
Editorial Assistant
Gulf & Western Industries, Inc.
New York, New York

Carvel Taylor
Director
Employee Counseling Center
CNA Insurance
Chicago, Illinois

Florence Vigilante
Associate Professor
School of Social Work
Hunter College
City University of New York
New York, New York

Leon J. Warshaw
Deputy Director
Mayor's Office of Operations
New York, New York

Robert B. Young
Vice President
Public Affairs
Security Pacific National Bank
Los Angeles, California

About the Authors

Sheila H. Akabas, Ph.D., is Professor at the Columbia University School of Social Work. An economist, she directs the school's Industrial Social Welfare Center and several national research and training projects in rehabilitation and mental health at the workplace, as well as serving as consultant to numerous trade unions, employing organizations, and community mental health centers. Professor Akabas has written in the leading journals of labor and industrial relations, social welfare, and rehabilitation and is coauthor of *Mental Health Care in the World of Work.*

Leon W. Chestang, Ph.D., is Professor and Dean at Wayne State University School of Social Work, Detroit, Michigan. He has lectured and written and has been consulted widely in the area of socio-cultural influences on behavior and on the significance of race and ethnicity as variables in social work practice. Professor Chestang is coeditor of *The Diverse Society: Implications for Social Policy.*

Jerome Cohen, Ph.D., is Professor at the University of California, Los Angeles, School of Social Welfare. He has considerable policy and practice experience in the mental health arena and was the research and program consultant to a community mental health center serving the retail clerks' union. Professor Cohen has written monographs and articles in the area of practice and research and currently serves as chairperson of the NASW Clinical Social Work Task Force.

Paul A. Kurzman, Ph.D., is Professor at the Hunter College School of Social Work, City University of New York. He is chairperson of Hunter's World of Work Program and principal investigator of a national research study of retired workers who are reentering the workplace. Professor Kurzman has lectured and consulted extensively in the area of industrial social welfare. As well as having written widely for professional journals, he is editor of *The Mississippi Experience: Strategies for Welfare Rights Action* and author of *Harry Hopkins and the New Deal.*

Brenda G. McGowan, D.S.W., is Associate Professor at the Columbia University School of Social Work. She has pursued her particular interest in professional ethical issues and change strategies in teaching, practice, and research, and as consultant to Columbia's Industrial Social Welfare Center. Professor McGowan has lectured and written considerably in the field of family and children's services and is a coauthor of a national study on child advocacy.

Martha N. Ozawa, Ph.D., is Professor at the George Warren Brown School of Social Work, Washington University, St. Louis, Missouri. She is Chairperson of the Social Policy, Administration, and Community Development Concentration and a specialist in the areas of income maintenance, employment, social security, and welfare policy. Professor Ozawa has published many professional articles and has served on the editorial board of several journals of the social work profession.

Rino J. Patti, D.S.W., is Professor at the University of Washington School of Social Work, Seattle, Washington. He has directed research in the areas of organizational behavior, agency management, and social welfare administration. Professor Patti is coeditor of *Change From Within: Humanizing Social Welfare Organizations* and author of the forthcoming *Social Welfare Administration: Program Management in the Human Services*.

Helen Harris Perlman, D. Litt., is Samuel Deutsch Distinguished Professor Emeritus, School of Social Service Administration at the University of Chicago. In addition to teaching, she spent many years as a clinical social work practitioner in family, child guidance, and school social work settings. Professor Perlman is a prolific writer and the author of many books, including *Social Casework: A Problem-Solving Process, Persona: Social Role and Personality*, and *Relationship: The Art of Helping People*.

Jack Rothman, Ph.D., is Professor at the University of Michigan School of Social Work, Ann Arbor, Michigan. As a social worker and social psychologist, he has specialized in the application of social science knowledge to contemporary issues of policy and practice. Professor Rothman is a prolific author; his most recent books include *Planning and Organizing for Social Change, Using Research in Organizations*, and *Social R + D in the Human Services*.

Arthur B. Shostak, Ph.D., is Professor of Psychology and Sociology at Drexel University, Philadelphia, Pennsylvania. As an industrial sociologist he has done research on blue-collar stress, pre-retirement programs, and the impact of plant-closings, and has served as an instructor at the George Meany Center of Labor Studies. Professor Shostak has written widely in the field of labor studies. His many books include *Blue-Collar Life, Blue-Collar Stress*, and *Blue-Collar World*.

1

Introduction

This book represents the culmination of a process, a process that has sought to introduce to social work education a view of work, work affiliation, and social policy around work that parallels the profession's devotion to issues concerned with love and family and social policy around individuals and their needs. Such a process, it was felt, would enrich our profession and its practice, since it would add a new knowledge base and expand the options available as we seek to respond to the needs of individuals and communities.

The process was rooted in the increasing recognition being awarded to industrial social work. Back in the 1950's, Wilensky and Lebeaux referred to this field of practice as being one in a constant state of discovery.[1] Then, almost imperceptibly, the picture changed. What once seemed isolated outposts of experimentation, more likely to disappear than to grow, began, in aggregate, to reach that critical mass that guaranteed their survival and encouraged spin-off into other, not quite so isolated substations. A field of practice began to take form: social work in labor and management settings became a new, exciting, and expanding arena for service, one that was different from, but comparable to, professional practice in settings like health systems, schools, and other host sites. In recognition of this burgeoning activity, the National Association of Social Workers (NASW) and the Council on Social Work Education (CSWE) jointly established (the one financing, and the other staffing), a project to promote study and practice in industrial social welfare.

1

At the same time, representatives of two of the major graduate schools that had developed educational programs in the field (Columbia University School of Social Work and Hunter College School of Social Work) came together and noted that the educational base would be greatly enriched by bringing together the practice experience on a national basis. An approach to the Lois and Samuel Silberman Fund, the one foundation in the United States whose principal interest is the development of social work education and practice, resulted in financial and programmatic encouragement for convening a national conference of industrial social work practitioners. Joining with the already established Industrial Social Work Project of NASW/CSWE, and with generous support from the Silberman Fund, the Industrial Social Welfare Center of Columbia and the World of Work Program of Hunter planned a conference for the spring of 1978 to which 100 social work practitioners in industrial settings would bring their practice wisdom.

The planning for this significant event in our profession's history proceeded, based on the following goals:

- to record practice experience;
- to increase public awareness of developments in industrial social work;
- to consider the educational adaptations necessary to improve preparation of graduates for this field of practice;
- to explore linkages between traditional social work settings and trade unions and employing organizations; and
- to develop guidelines for the improved management of, and practice in, industrial social work settings.

As organizational and technical planning for the conference moved forward, a reality, of which the planning group was well aware from its own experience, consistently surfaced in the comments and registration questionnaire responses from invited participants. The theme: social work education had not prepared those in the labor and industrial arenas for work in these specialized settings; more important, practitioners felt that their experiences confirmed the fact that social work education per se was not sufficiently invested in working populations, work institutions, and work issues. There seemed almost universal agreement that work and employment had not been adequately understood as absolutely critical elements of adult functioning. They pointed out that practice in industrial settings had served to highlight the importance of work and to identify the need for adding more of this component to the social work curriculum.

The specialists pointed out that a specialization was not sufficient. As our colleague Dr. Irving Miller commented: "When social workers do their jobs well, they inevitably disclose or uncover unmet needs and embarrassing gaps between the promises and performance."[2] Thus, the new setting of the workplace made visible problems that were previously invisible. A set of nagging questions plagued us: How are working persons treated in community agencies? How do social policy and planning experts incorporate the impact on workers and their families when they develop new programs? When is the status of worker a significant variable in social research, and how often do social researchers even consider that question? Such prodding led to the idea that we should use the practice conference for more than just an in-gathering of practitioners and practice information. In addition, it could become a first step in working with the educational community. The practice conference could be used as a ground-breaking effort, providing an opportunity to expose some leading social work practitioners and educators to this new field of practice. The hope was that they would see, through the microcosm of one field of practice, how their own specialized areas of social work knowledge could be influenced by a view that gave more attention to the issues that this field of practice illuminated.

Once again, the Silberman Fund proved supportive. The educators represented in this book were recruited, and seven concept papers were commissioned, which would review the array of curriculum content in social work.[3] The contributors began their exposure to industrial social work at the Practitioners' Conference of June 1978.[4] Almost at once they concluded that the insights that seem so obvious as one delves into industrial social work practice had not been used to inform, enlighten, inspire, or affect the social worker in general practice or in specialized practice other than industrial social work. They agreed further that, though not previously conceptualized in that way, most clients are either workers, related to a worker, or suffering from the residual status of being a nonworker; that organizations in the community with power, prestige, and resources inevitably must include trade unions and employing organizations; and that an individual's membership in such entities may affect his or her relationship with other social systems or social policy and research efforts. Confirmed by their contacts with practitioners was the educators' realization that the social work profession and its educational enterprises had too long neglected this most significant dimension in the lives of our clients and in the experiences of our communities. This book is an attempt to reverse that gap. As we note in our last chapter, failure to do so may be to condemn our profession to less than its full potential.

In essence, the educators were asked, in preparing their papers, to review the basic components of their own curriculum areas and to identify gaps with regard to coverage of work, workers, and work organizations in the main content of their specialty while as editors we would undertake to specify the nature of industrial social work practice itself. Once the educators left the Practitioners' Conference, teams of industrial social work practitioners were assigned to provide each one with technical assistance and consultation. As the educators struggled to develop manuscripts which would reflect how their own individual areas of expertise are influenced by the insights of industrial social work, practitioners were ever-handy. The preparatory process of the chapters, therefore, began and proceeded in sight of practitioners who supplied constant feedback. Their reactions were incorporated, and chapters were revised until each reflected the dimensions of practice.

A final step in the preparatory process involved a three-day conference at the Wingspread Conference Center of the Johnson Foundation in Racine, Wisconsin.[5]

There, in the beauty and tranquility of an ideal setting for the exchange of ideas, twenty-six social work practitioners and educators and representatives of trade unions and employing organizations joined the authors in a discussion of the manuscripts. These critical evaluations provided the final context in which ideas were explored and incorporated into this first systematic view of how the work-place exerts its impact on social work education and practice. The drafts were revised once again to reflect advice offered on that occasion, and the chapters of this book are the result. As editors we have added introductory comments for each chapter.

The link that the total process created between practitioners, educators, representatives from labor and industry, and authors was unusual and productive. Each paper has been sifted through the eyes of the doers and should be read carefully with consideration for the new view that the content offers on social work. We hope that its reading will provide new insights to the reader.

Notes

[1] Harold L. Wilensky and Charles N. Lebeaux, *Industrial Society and Social Welfare: The Impact of Industrialization on the Supply and Organization of Social Welfare Services in the United States* (New York: Russell Sage Foundation, 1958).

[2] As recorded in taped comments by Dr. Miller at the Wingspread Conference: "Developing a World of Work Perspective in Social Work Education," April 1-4, 1979.

[3] An eighth paper, the one by Arthur Shostak on "Work Meanings," was commissioned later as a result of a consensus growing out of the Wingspread Conference of April 1979.

[4] Proceedings of the conference were published in Sheila H. Akabas, Paul A. Kurzman, and Nancy S. Kolben, eds., *Labor and Industrial Settings: Sites for Social Work Practice* (New York: Columbia University School of Social Work, Hunter College School of Social Work, and Council on Social Work Education, 1979).

[5] Proceedings of that conference were published in *Meeting Human Service Needs in the Workplace: A Role for Social Work* (New York: Industrial Social Work Project, 1980).

2

Work Meanings Through Western History: From Athens to Detroit and Beyond

Arthur B. Shostak, Ph.D.
Drexel University

A former cancer patient reminisced with a social worker: "I really died twice—once when I got the diagnosis and the second time when my boss heard about it and fired me."* Allow the obvious to be restated: For death and the loss of a job to be synonymous in the mind of a normal adult startles us. Although we have no doubt of the finality of death, we are not accustomed to reading that many adults in the United States require work to define their attachment to meaning, to reality, to life itself.

How did work become so instrumental to self-definition and purposeful existence? It was not always so, and Arthur Shostak provides us with a synopsis of the historical record. He notes that although physical survival may have required that the ancients work, success in Greek and Roman times involved finding someone else to perform the task. The Hebrews conceptualized work as a cooperative effort with God, and hence acceptable to all levels of society. The Church fathers, later, and for their own reasons, censored the denigration of work and thereby reduced its "sordid linkage with slavery." The seesaw between thinking of work as personal fulfillment and work as drudgery, performed to fill the stomach, has rocked back and forth ever since.

**As quoted from Frances Feldman,* Work and Cancer Health History: Study of Blue Collar Workers *(Los Angeles, Calif.: Division of The Cancer Society, 1980).*

The author records how, for a millennium or longer, work was a burden, performed to support survival financially, until the enlightenment of the Renaissance appeared to elevate craftsmanship, providing an early glimmer of Maslow's principle of self-actualization from creative production. The artisan mentality, in turn, gave way to merchant princes, and handicrafts began to be replaced by the products of industrialization. In the Protestant Reformation, work itself became an "honor-worthy form of serving God," and the basic value foundation was fixed for the Industrial Revolution. It was Americans, however, who perfected and refined their dedication to work and their dependence on it.

The participants in early industrial labor were mostly women and immigrants. The need that many sought to meet in work was earning a stake, either to marry or move westward and buy land. Thus in America, unlike Europe, the early concept of factory work held it to be not a permanent status, but a transitory occupation, which resulted in hard and consistent labor from workers.

By the time of the Civil War, industrialization had established itself firmly and irrevocably on the American economy. The transitory, independent labor force gave way to an urban poor, demeaned by a management dedicated to Taylorism, which emphasized scientific management and reduced workers to the significance of replaceable parts. Nonetheless, perhaps because of the rising standard of living that maintained the common notion that individual hard labor promised accomplishment, or perhaps because the government allowed business tactics that kept workers bereft of power, industrial progress continued, as before, until 1929.

According to Shostak, the deprivation of work, experienced by one-quarter of the adult labor force during the great depression of the 1930s, changed the meaning of work and the population's relationship to the workplace. To protect themselves from the all-powerful employers, workers joined labor unions in massive numbers. New labor legislation, drawn from Keynesian economics, shifted the balance of power to unions. In a parallel effort, perhaps based in part on the new sense of unity that came from joining, Americans demanded, even as individual voters, more communal welfare—protection from the slavery of work solely for physical survival. New programs eliminated the nonchoice condition of work or starve. Work now had to meet new needs to attract labor. These changes in values, power balance, and worker needs set the stage for new meanings of work and new demands concerning the workplace.

The World War II experience confirmed that new participants (blacks and women) could work productively. Employers, seeking to maintain wartime productivity, but aware of the new power of organized labor and the new expectations fostered by the floor provided by the income maintenance system, which separated physical survival from work, devised the human relations approach to labor force management.

This neo-paternalistic promotion of the happy, productive worker faced pressure from all sides: organized labor suspected that management was using it to manipulate workers; young workers demanded more than just good treatment, such as positions that allowed for personal development and career movement; new participants—women, minorities, and the disabled—became "assertive" and confronted the "beleaguered white males." In response, writes Shostak, the role of work broadened again. Indeed, work has always been—and it seems as if it will always be—a concept in transition.

From this historical analysis, Shostak derives four crucial variables that will influence the course of the meaning of work and the significance of the workplace in the decade of the 1980s: (1) the power distribution among various workers and between them and unions, management, government, and consumers; (2) the needs that the workplace succeeds in satisfying and those that it does not satisfy; (3) participant roles, including those of women entering the labor force, minorities and the disabled asserting their rights, and white men resisting provisions for affirmative action and non-discrimination in employment; and (4) values emphasized as a reflection of economic and social trends.

Shostak offers examples of these variables: the power distribution will be affected by the struggles of organized labor and the instigating effect of managements that carefully monitor and respond to worker demands in the interest of keeping trade unions out. In the area of needs satisfaction, workers increasingly will seek not just permanent jobs, but jobs that meet the individualized needs of an educated labor force. The composition of that force, along with participant roles, will change as more and more groups value and seek entry into the workplace not for the interest of particular jobs, but because they view labor force participation as an entitlement. Finally, the value of worker safety, both mental and physical, is gaining supporters in society.

In a laboratory setting, these four variables, which have shaped the development of work, might predict (as physics equations can tell when the moon will eclipse the sun) the future of work in America. In the social world, however, unknowns enter the formula. Shostak mentions some of these unknowns—technology, computers, energy—which make the future uncertain. Nevertheless, concludes the author, the meaning of work must necessarily evolve from the legacy of its past.

> The true history of a nation can never be known unless we know about the work and lives of the laboring population—for . . . the quality of the lives of these working men and women are the primary measure of the success of a democratic society.
>
> Eli Ginzberg and Hyman Berman, *The American Worker in the Twentieth Century* (New York: Free Press, 1963), p. 4.

Seeking to help explain the work of contemporary Americans he had interviewed in the early 1970s, Studs Terkel urged appreciation of the search that goes on "for daily meaning as well as daily bread, for recognition as well as cash, for astonishment rather than torpor; in short, for a sort of life rather than a Monday through Friday sort of dying." Another writer, Barbara Garson, after recently spending two years studying work across this country, concluded that "real work is a human need, perhaps right after the need for food and the need for love. . . . *People passionately want to work.*" At the same time, however, the longshoreman-philosopher Eric Hoffer has argued that "revulsion from work is a fundamental component of human nature. It is natural to feel work as a curse."[1]

Centerpiece of our daily effort to enhance our lives and to justify fundamental human needs ("Perhaps immortality, too, is part of the quest"), work has also been derided as the "worst thing you can do for your health," a "form of nervousness," the "curse of the drinking class," and "one of the processes by which A acquires property for B."[2] Yet certain of the ancient sages, deeply impressed by its self-actualizing and enabling potentialities, taught centuries ago that a "man at work is the equal of the most learned," and that "men at work are not obliged to stand up when a sage passes by."[3]

This sort of bewildering controversy is compounded by the vexing omission of any discussion of work from otherwise authoritative and complete sources like the *Encyclopedia Americana*, the *Encyclopaedia Britannica*, and the *Encyclopedia of the Social Sciences*. Contrariwise, in the matter of defining the term itself (first used in the ninth century), the profusion of available meanings threatens to overwhelm one: *Webster's International Dictionary*, for example, offers over twenty different definitions of "work" as a noun and over thirty as a verb.[4]

Drawing on the pioneering scholarship of psychologist Walter Neff, a cogent and revealing definition of the term can be used to begin to sort through the furor.

> Work is an instrumental activity carried out by human beings, the object of which is to preserve and maintain life, which is directed at a planful alteration of certain features of man's environment.[5]

An adult's ability to work—and to shape that work experience in a particular way—appears to be the outcome of a long process of individual development. As well, it may be influenced by all sorts of veiled motives a worker may not be entirely aware of or care to readily acknowledge. Work arouses both positive *and* negative emotions (satisfaction and enthusiasm in some, restlessness or ennui in others), drawing thereby on affect as well as on perceptual, cognitive, and motor components of our being. Made up of irrational as well as rational components, the work experience is formed by conditions many workers are individually unaware of, as well as by others of which we steadily gain more understanding.

Given the complexity and the broad range of this basic definitional material, reviewing the history of work meanings is a critical first step in addressing contemporary problems and possibilities—that we might thereby also learn more of distinctive value about *ourselves*, as work is "another way of keeping a diary."[6]

The Ancient World: Greece and Rome

An epoch's dominant work meaning is especially responsive to prevailing economic realities, as is well illustrated by the low status of toil during the Greco-Roman domination of early Western culture (circa 400 B.C.E.-500 C.E.).[7] The city-states relegated arduous toil to slaves or lower-class freemen, and thereby freed their upper classes to disdain work as beneath their dignity (the playwright Xenophon, for example, warned that manual labor softened the body, weakened the mind, discouraged sociability, and resulted in a class notorious as "bad defenders of their country").[8] Many high-born citizens also denigrated work for placing one under the humiliating rule of the customer or purchaser of one's labor (scarcely veiled disdain was aimed, in turn, at those merchants or rich entrepreneurs who lived off the labor of others).

To have any moral worth at all, or so the Ancients taught, work had to be done freely to satisfy one's own needs, as when an epic hero like Odysseus built his own boat, or Penelope spun thread and wove cloth. This high regard for effort *only* when expended independently on oneself (especially in politics, study, competitive sports, or in the game of war), lived on for centuries after the society's eclipse and figured prominently in nineteenth-century anxieties about the emergence of a permanent, propertyless, and uprooted proletariat, totally dependent on being hired by others.

As for the common man—the artisan who was freeborn—no records survive to recount what he made of the aristocracy's disdain for his labor. It is known, however, that he had enough self-esteem to join with his peers in protective trade associations, a primitive low-profile precursor of medieval guilds and, centuries later, of our modern labor unions. In addition, long before the Reformation's Protestant Work Ethic linked work results and divine support, the Greek and Roman craftsmen discretely adopted particular gods as totems to safeguard their various occupations and to insure divine intervention on their behalf.

Given upper-class derision of work and working class modesty in its defense, the collective genius of the Empire was left free to focus everywhere else but on the mechanical arts. Persuaded that ideas concerned with primitive technology downgraded the intellect's real powers, Greco-Roman decision-makers permitted work techniques to stagnate for centuries. Considerable progress was achieved, to be sure, in the more respectable realm of "white-collar" labor, with the earliest forms of public administration, personal services occupations, and the precursors of the modern professions (medicine, law, the arts) gaining a healthy start. The lot of the average man, however, suffered for centuries thereafter from the low valuation placed by aristocrats on his "common" labor—a fate always related to a society's regard for the mechanical arts.

Accordingly, the progress in "white-collar" occupations notwithstanding, by the era in which the barbarians came to dominate, the "position of the working man, far from improving, was, on the contrary, tending to deteriorate."[9] An idle and wretched urban mob was newly emerged, pauperism had spread, and the quality of work life plummeted to a new low—prolonged neglect of workplace innovation playing no small part, thereby, in the fall of the Roman Empire. (Fascinating in this connection is the "only example in the entire history of ancient societies of a workers' revolt based upon specific [work] claims," an unsuccessful uprising in the fourth century A.D. of Jewish peasants in Antioch, who demanded the right to discuss their employment conditions with the orator Libanius).[10]

Judeo-Christian Viewpoints

While sharing with the Greeks a view of work as a hard and often painful necessity, ancient Hebrew scholars went on to pose and attempt to answer a metaphysical question which Greek contempt for work had scornfully left open—"Why had man been condemned to toil to begin with?"[11]

In a major departure from the Greek view of work as a meaningless, blind, tragic necessity, Rabbinical literature viewed work as a way which God had chosen to make his bargain with man: through work man could expiate the original sin committed by Adam and Eve—this opportunity thereby providing Hebrew workers with a unique sense of mission. Additional succor came from the related thought that work actually helped man to restore the primal harmony destroyed by the Fall: To work was to cooperate with God in the great purpose of restoring justice and happiness on earth. Accordingly, unlike the Greek sages, the Hebrews took up lowly occupations and toiled, all the better to help man to atone and to reconquer his lost spiritual dignity.

As the Early Christian fathers had been influenced more by contemporaries of Aristotle and Plato than by the Hebraic sages, their approach to work noted only three sources of worth: It was clearly preferable to sin-tempting idleness; it was a promising source of extra income, which could be given as alms to the poor; and, above all, it was a vital source of commercial projects with which to help build churches and monasteries while waiting out the Second Coming.[12]

Work thereby gained a new value, a spiritual dignity of sorts. It was never, however, exalted as anything of value in and of itself: While it had its uses, it was denied any special honor. Specifically, the Church fathers departed from the Rabbinic sages in denying work an ennobling role in shaping a better world in the here and now. They departed as well from the Greco-Roman tradition in that the Holy Fathers reconciled manual labor and the contemplative life (at least within the walls of their own monasteries). Indeed, their major contribution was to undermine earlier aristocratic scorn of toil and thereby pave the way for strategic medieval revisions in work meanings to follow.

Medieval Catholicism

Throughout the so-called Dark Ages, as part of its contribution to Europe's slow recovery from the barbarian invasions and the Black Death, the Church protected the meaning of work from slipping back into a sordid linkage with slavery and degradation.[13] Medieval monastic orders, for example, taught that the obligation to work was a Divine law. Mystical ideal and practical reality alike led bishops and monks to support the renaissance of once-devastated industrial centers, reorganize production in monastic workshops, promote and help revive trade, pioneer in progressive systems of industrial management, and even take a direct share in organizing it. Above all, the monasteries alone for centuries kept alive hard-earned work techniques of the higher forms of industry (the production of enamel work, porcelain, glasswork, fabrics, and so on).

It was in the Church that there appeared the first signs of pity for the working classes, with leading theologians and preachers proclaiming the social value of the work of the poor and humble and the original equality of serf and freeman before God—provided all were obedient to local clerical authority. Still more historic, however, was the accomplishment of the medieval Church in helping to inaugurate the world's first international economy, one which helped give labor an expansion and freedom hitherto unknown.

The Medieval Guilds

While their exact origins remain a scholarly puzzle, the reappearance in the early Renaissance of the ancient craft guilds was one of the most striking phenomena of the high Middle Ages.[14] Often representing both journeymen and masters, the guilds, like their Greco-Roman predecessors, acted as both benevolent organizations *and* regulatory powers. Their functions included setting wages and prices; adjudicating disputes among members; paying accident, sickness, and death benefits; assisting young journeymen to become independent producers through loans; and promoting and monitoring inventions and improvements. Workers proudly sold products, rather than their own labor, and did not, accordingly, think of themselves merely as lowly wage earners.

Although the guilds took a generally conservative attitude toward technology, they did accept innovation if it did not threaten to favor some members greatly over others or to undermine the quality of a guild product. Accordingly, for perhaps the first time in recorded history, labor-saving devices were actively sought, and, once discovered, were eagerly applied. Innovations also occurred in the guild apprenticeship system, and the craft way of work (and life) reached a peak level of development. Work skills changed rapidly, with some attendant dislocations and social costs, but, overall, the work of common folk gained in stature, complexity, and social significance.

Particular help came here from the Renaissance ideal of work, with its rapt respect for creative craftsmen. The Renaissance ideal directed attention to the transcendental, self-actualizing potential inherent in craftsmanship (as in Maslow's writing, centuries later)—a far cry from earlier preoccupations with work only as a curse, a bane, or a time-making apathetic bore.

When the Middle Ages drew to a close, this brief Golden Age of the Crafts and Guilds foreshadowed troubles that lay ahead, with the industrialization era a mere two centuries away. The regional merchant, developed to meet trade needs beyond a guild's local trade focus, began dictating to the guilds, and even gained ownership of some of them. Guild power and prestige steadily flowed to the new merchant class, and once-proud craftsmen became dependent wage earners once more.

A critical decline in the fortunes of the skilled artisans (the master craftsmen who led the occupational guilds) proved a grim harbinger of the worker's loss of power and self-esteem during the early Industrial Revolution: The victory of the new merchants over handicraft artisans was a subtle and far-reaching change in the organization of work. As often throughout the history of work meanings, this critical shift was brought about not by any tools, techniques, or processes of production, but solely by compelling economic changes in the marketplace.

The Reformation

Until the end of the Middle Ages, markets played only a minor part in the local economic system. From the sixteenth century onward, however, this situation emphatically changed: "Once elaborate machines and plants were used for production in a commercial society, the idea of a self-regulating market was bound to take shape."[15] And with it came the idea of a self-disciplined national supply of able, eager, and docile laborers available for wage employ. The Protestant Reformation was *the* indispensable element in creating this mix, as its ideology helped link the new economic system and the masses, who were being forced off their land by the enclosure movement. So thoroughgoing was the impact of this link that Protestantism "established work in the modern mind as the base and key of life. . . ."[16]

Medieval Catholicism was castigated by Luther and other early Protestant theologians for honoring the work that was done for the Church far more than any done outside. Protestantism taught instead that work anywhere was an honorworthy form of serving God. Accordingly, to accept without question or hope of mobility the occupational class into which one was born and to do most perfectly the work of that class was the one best way of serving God. Every variety of labor was thought thereby to have spiritual dignity, and no one occupation was hailed—as before, under Catholicism—as any more necessary than another to piety and holiness.

This egalitarian re-evaluation of work drew on Luther's principle of justification by faith. Guiding man's focus from its prior fixation on the City of God, it looked in a comparably faith-sanctioned way at the City of Man. The Reformation thereby legitimized a concentration of energies on the material world—in good conscience. Protestantism emancipated economic life from ecclesiastic domination and lifted work from being a taken-for-granted backdrop of life to being a new testing ground for selfhood. "Luther placed a crown on the sweaty forehead of labor. From his hands work came forth endowed with religious dignity."[17]

Calvinism also drew on its thoroughgoing belief in predestination. Workers were challenged as no Western theology had ever done before to seek evidence of their own Divine election through their success at work. People were taught that each possessed a "calling," and that the fulfillment of its obligations, a job quietly and humbly done well, was a divinely imposed duty. Nevertheless, there is no gainsaying the long-run impact on work meanings of the spirit of the Reformation, as summed up in these words—"You think you have escaped from the monastery, but everyone must now be a monk throughout his life."[18]

This view of work and economics, according to Max Weber, helped give rise to the "spirit of capitalism" and, in secularized form, freed of religious motivations and associations, did much to create the modern world as we know it.[19] To be sure, the notion of a worker meekly surrendering to factory servitude *because* of a need to prove himself to God is an interpretation that has not gone without detractors. Typical is Daniel Bell's contention that while the bourgeois entrepreneur was possibly of this mold, it is doubtful whether many workers were similarly disposed. Instead of concern with the "scourging hand of God," workers were more likely goaded by growing hunger, and "much of the early movements of social protest can only be understood with that fact in mind."[20] Be that as it may, Calvinism helped provide the modern entrepreneur with a "fabulously clear conscience" and with the remarkable power to draw employees into cooperating with his exploitation of them by linking servitude with the prospect of eternal salvation.[21]

As long as the Protestant West employed the idea of salvation through dutiful work, and as long as the national state, through the likes of the innovative Speenhamland Law (1795–1832), guaranteed a minimum subsistence to each worker, it was possible for the early industrial working class to grimly accept its lot. With the 1832 repeal of the Speenhamland Law, however, the price of labor became subject to a fluctuating market, and the worker now found himself, despite his protestations, just another commodity.

From this point on, the historic feistiness and the hard-won autonomy of the worker steadily lost ground to the unsparing discipline demanded by the machine requirements of the Industrial Revolution: The tyranny of the clock steadily gained the power to shape the work meanings we now call our own.

The American Industrial Revolution

Switching from industrializing Europe to the intimately-linked situation of the American colonies of the 1700s, we see that our own Industrial Revolution is initially the story of the premier ideology of American republicanism and its distinctive design for the major meaning of work in the new land.[22]

Eager to preserve liberty, order, and virtue, the aristocratic thesis of republicanism urged that early colonialists keep agrarian work Calvinist in character and also avoid the dangers of "satanic mills" and landless male factory hands. Instead, the very first workshops of America were to employ only marginal types of employees (women, children, the aged, and the indigent). Able-bodied males were to remain at either agricultural or craftsman pursuits (masons, cobblers, custom tailors, etc.), as admired by the Jeffersonians and the aristocrats alike.

From the nation's opening experiment with a factory system of production (in 1813, at Waltham, Massachusetts), the young nation's "workshops in the wilderness" were carefully managed to reinforce this republican ideology. In every way posssible they boosted the characteristic qualities of mechanization (regularity, uniformity, subordination, harmony, efficiency, and effectiveness), and urged these attributes as ideals for early American life in general.[23] As the factories were commonly located in the countryside, so as to prevent the rise of a displaced urban mob, the owners often housed their employees in unique company-owned boarding-houses: "Imbued with a completely paternalistic attitude, the manufacturers set absolute standards of behavior and sobriety for their workers,"[24] a form of *in loco parentis* that contributed over the years to regular struggles for freedom by unappreciative adult workers.

Work meanings primarily took their shading from the republican contention that a factory strong in harmony and well-being required the "maintenance of rigid moral standards and the fulfillment of hard work."[25] Respect for labor from 1700 to the 1840s was also profoundly conditioned by its undeniable scarcity: Before the great immigration of the midcentury period, the country lacked an access of available factory hands, and employers were compelled to pay those available far more in wages and in social status than had ever been true abroad. British and European visitors were lavish with their praise for America's early avoidance of the ghastly horrors of industrialization that were common abroad. But nothing could spare the nation the costs that were inherent in the unfolding of the industrialization process itself.

Craftsmen were particularly hard-hit as the steadily-growing availability of factory-produced, cheaper goods undercut the market for their hand-crafted products. Merchant-capitalists, a new economic type, quickly gained control over the once-independent shops of the master craftsmen, the journeymen, and their apprentices:

> The master was compelled in many instances to become a virtual sweatshop operator since his only profit was the difference between the price he received from the capitalist and that which he paid his workers.[26]

Cheaper workers were hired to do skill-less piece work, and the entire apprenticeship system collapsed. Journeymen were no longer paid for the products they made, but instead received daily wages. Those who organized to seek "more" were commonly fired and blacklisted. Little wonder, then, that in the 1830s "craftsmen were the only actively dissatisfied class in the country."[27]

At the same time, a rapidly rising class of new factory hands began to resent and reject the ideology of the "factory-as-republican-school." Charging that tightly-run and repressive workshops were little better than prisons, factory militants demanded that a "secret class war" they saw being waged against them be fought out in the open.[28] Unimpressed by the alleged humanitarian motives of the new industrialists, the dissident laborers charged them with using labor-displacing innovation with no regard at all for those made suddenly jobless or for thousands of others who lived with daily dread of impending job loss.

Republican Whigs retorted by boasting of how much better off the native American factory workers were than their counterparts in the miserable industrial towns abroad. The dissidents chose to focus, however, on unprecedented fluctuations in the new business cycle that left landless workers in a very precarious position. And when the Whigs insisted that transitory workers could readily "go west" and live as nonindustrial farmers if truly aggrieved, the dissidents rejoined much as Alexis de Tocqueville had when, in 1841, he wrote that "when once men have embraced that [industrial] line of life . . . they cannot quit it again, because they soon contract habits of body and mind which unfit them for any other sort of toil."[29]

Even as the related decline in craftsmanship had first diminished the worker's sense of creativity and personal satisfaction, the early factories came to threaten the worker's self-esteem and mental health. As early as the 1830s, de Tocqueville had warned that as production became more efficient the worker became less and less a whole person:

> He every day becomes more adroit and less industrious; so that it may be said of him that in proportion as the workman improves the man is degraded. What can be expected of a man who has spent twenty years of his life in making heads for pins?[30]

This animus against excesses in the division of labor was shared by many newly enfranchised workers, and they produced in the 1830s "more labor agitation, more union activity, than had occurred or would occur before the Civil War."[31]

Especially revealing was a steadily-emerging working class reform agenda, emphasizing that workers did not live by bread alone. The chief demand sought a reduction from twelve- or fifteen- to a mere ten-hour working day, as some free time for education was thought by workers to be necessary if they were ever to advance themselves in society. (Employers warned that such an increase in off-work idleness would undoubtedly undermine morals and encourage intemperance.) Unique workingmen's parties (later absorbed into the Jacksonian Party) advocated the extension of free education to mill-working children, the abolition of imprisonment for debt, revision of the militia system, direct election of public officials, greater equality in taxation, and separation of church and state. This broad reform movement, rather than being a movement of labor alone, was led by men who did not consider themselves part of a permanent working class. The "keynote of labor's demands was not a proletarian hatred of capitalist society, but the desire for an equal chance to share the fruits of capitalism."[32]

Unions and strikes, however, were still illegal criminal or radical conspiracies in various states. And ten-hour legislation was not often enforced, even when enacted. Accordingly, by 1850 workers had to rely heavily on an unprecedented alliance with middle-class reformers and the humanitarian movement, if they were to win any gains at all. At least one historian has concluded that, all in all, the "workingman's condition was much better in 1850 than it had been twenty years before,"[33] while another now contends that "workers themselves were increasingly aware that the American ideal of equality was rapidly receding."[34] Still a third student of this remarkable "take-off" period in America's industrialization process believes that the "losses of the industrial worker in the first half of the century were not comfort losses solely, but losses, as he conceived it, of status and independence. And no comfort gains could cancel this debt."[35]

The Mid-Industrial Revolution

With the onset of massive waves of destitute, skill-less, landless European immigrants, beginning with Irish potato famine victims in the late 1840s, the 150-year-old republican dream of workers as a transitory, independent, and land-oriented bloc came to an emphatic end. In its place, a permanent urban proletariat appeared.

By the outbreak of the Civil War, America had a sizable propertyless and pauperized proletariat, for whom work had little connection to the alleged character-enabling training of yore. Instead, work became far more oppressive, more demanding, and more demeaning than ever before in the republic's history. While the incredibly bloody Civil War helped to reduce mid-century unemployment to unprecedented lows and pushed wages and purchasing power to new highs, casualties among working-class soldiers were enormous, working-class racism was meanly exacerbated, and working-class wages soon fell behind the era's run-away inflation.

With the war's end, industrialization intensified in pace, range, and influence. Employers sought fresh gains in productivity from a novel ally—the reorganization of work itself. Taylorism, or scientific management, slowly developed in the early 1900s to help insure the behavior of humans as cogs and levers in the machine. Until this time it had not been supposed that a man could be managed much like a machine part, but Frederick W. Taylor went far toward proving this position, and employers were intrigued with promised rewards in factory discipline, worker servitude, and plant productivity.

Specialists in time-and-motion study were called on to study workers, instruct them in how to move differently, retime their new motions, and see to it that they abandoned their own motions in favor of prescribed puppetlike ways. Efficiency engineers of the Taylorist persuasion abrogated all decision-making power in factories and offices, and workers and clerks were ordered to leave all job-connected thinking to their betters.[36]

Critics warned that this elitist and demeaning approach undermined a worker's invaluable "instinct for craftsmanship" and was of questionable morality in the demands it made on a human being's individuality.[37] Although the subject of a unique investigation in 1914 by a suspicious Congressional Committee, the popularity of "scientific management" grew steadily in employer circles, especially after Henry Ford incorporated it into his novel (high-wage) assembly-line operations in America's remarkable new auto industry.

By the late 1920s, Americans had come to regard industrial work as a hybrid mixture of revised Calvinism and personal calculus, of the old Protestant Ethic emphasis on self-help now secularized both by scientism and by a bleak new view of man-as-a-machine-part (as in Charlie Chaplin's harrowing caricature of a factory hand in "Modern Times").

Between the start of the Civil War and that of the depression in 1932, labor productivity soared, and a worker in 1929 produced, in round numbers, about four times as much as his grandfather had in 1865.[38] The general standard of living gradually increased, even while a relentless media campaign urged a self-help ideology on all. Antagonism against the reduction of employees to the status of compliant, voiceless hands was effectively undercut by the combination of new-found well-being and ad-stirred desires.

The (Not-So-Great) Depression

With the collapse of unregulated capitalism in 1929, the meaning of work in this country lost much of its hard-earned association with expiation (Hebrew and early Christian teachings), aesthetics (Renaissance emphasis), a "calling" (Reformation focus), personal mobility (early American dream), citizenship-training (1850–1900 republican emphasis), and productivity gains (1910–29 Taylorist preoccupation). By 1933, the largest number of jobless Americans ever in the nation's history, well over 15 million exworkers, heard President Franklin Delano Roosevelt use his inaugural address to pledge that "our greatest primary task is to put people to work."[39]

The work experience of the vast majority who retained their jobs throughout the depression years soon resembled a special kind of trial, one that only a nation-wide depression could make a common fate.

> Those whose ability and seniority merited promotion found that better jobs did not exist. Skilled workers bumped down into unskilled jobs. Voluntary turnover dried up. . . . Joblessness sapped the little remaining strength of the labor movement.[40]

A massive experience in individual and collective impotence, the Great Depression "struck American workers with the force of a tidal wave."[41]

Strategic to the meaning of work for the job seeker was a leading "social invention of the 1930s," the Works Progress Administration (WPA). Before it was shut down in 1939, the WPA provided work for more people, over a longer range of time, than had any other single American organization up until that time.[42] Its 200,000 projects helped engender a still-lively national debate over the appropriate role of the public sector in job creation and job training, a debate that reverberates down to the present in the form of an ongoing controversy over whether CETA posts should be temporary or permanent. Critical as well were related WPA questions about the real worth of replacing unemployment with tasks that critics lambasted as "leaf-raking boon-doggles"; this controversy remains alive as young workers in particular press for CETA employment that they can value as "something more than a job."

A New Labor Movement

Industrial unionism emerged at this time to join with the breadline, the job-clinging employee, and the controversial WPA to help reshape the meaning of work in a wounded America.

AFL craft unions had historically restricted themselves to a craft-by-craft mode of operation. While this strategy secured the bargaining power of an elite crafts-man stratum of the working class, it left unorganized many more millions of unskilled and semiskilled workers, factory and office employees alike (except for the availability in the 1920s of employer-sponsored company unions). At issue was a two-tier valuation of work, one that covertly held that craft work "counted," while all other work did not. Ethnic rivalry between native American workers (commonly craftsmen) and newer blue-collarites (both immigrants from abroad and urban migrants from rural areas) further split the working class.

CIO unionization campaigns in the mid-1930s dramatically challenged this situation. During those years, when the self-esteem of workers was threatened as seldom before, CIO "labor wars" helped the working people to assert the human value of *all* wage earners and to win rare affirmation of their collective power to shape history. Thanks in large part to the successful emergence of factorywide industrial unionism, the decade of the '30s, as judged by historian Sidney Fine, proved to be the "most significant in the history of the American labor movement."[43]

The "New Deal" Social Welfare Structure

It became increasingly evident as the Depression persisted that American faith in the "invisible hand" forces of the marketplace was less and less tenable. Likewise, millions questioned anew the Horatio Alger myth that promised that reward would come to the individually worthy soul. In place of both of these time-honored molders of the meaning of work, a new consensus slowly emerged in favor of unprecedented government intervention in the nation's marketplace, along with the unprecedented development of government mechanisms to provide more security than ever before for ordinary citizens. For the first time in American history, general agreement developed in favor of federal responsibility either for work as a "right" or for some form of income-provision in its absence.

Harkening back to the example of the Speenhamland Law (1795-1832), and to Bismarck's nineteenth-century social welfare innovations, the "New Deal" federal government used the Social Security Act of 1935 to guarantee all contributing workers an income on retirement, even while it helped the states substantially to overhaul and improve both their unemployment and their accident and illness compensation plans. In addition, as a critical part of the redirection in workplace norms, the government moved to secure order out of the deadly warfare then raging in union-management relations—passage of the 1935 Wagner Labor Relations Act was pivotal here. Of like significance, though far less controversial, was a related move to put the government squarely in the "business" of helping to match job seekers with job offerers, to research labor market trends, and to test job seekers to help upgrade the entire job-placement process. Creation in the late 1930s of the U.S. Employment Service was a strategic gain.

In all, then, the decade of the depression had impacted on the modern meaning of work as no decade had ever done before. By its end, what with the emergence of industrial unionism and social insurance, the nation reaffirmed its intent to survive not just as a collection of Social Darwinists grinding up all but the most fit, but as a society based on human concern and mutual support. It is little wonder that writer David Cort contends that "probably nobody can understand America, or hence himself, if he does not understand the Great Depression."[44]

The War Years

With the entry of America into the war the nation's unemployment problem rapidly ended, and labor shortages helped to alter work meanings through the affirmation of on-the-job training and the emergence of a "human relations" alternative to both Taylorism and the hard-boiled, "bluster-and-blame" approach to employee supervision.

On-the-job training (O-J-T) was developed to speed the war-plant acclimatization of several million neophytes (women new to nonhousehold jobs, exfarmworkers new to the city *and* to nonfarming jobs, etc.). Its uncontested success made clear the ability of average citizens to prove superior learners and earners when and if a work environment was heartily supportive: O-J-T thereby helped set the stage for equal job-rights struggles in the '60s and '70s. Its demonstration of the ability of minorities and women to effectively master production work was strategic in being both emphatic and nationwide.

A second major impact also had its source in unprecedented demands for productivity. In response to patriotic imperatives, many workers relaxed work rules and output-pegging practices; certain war plants were soon characterized by swashbuckling and highly productive ways. Absenteeism fell, morale soared, and workers in the plant and office cooperated in ways many even now recall with nostalgia and warmth. Workers earned the promotions that were unavailable to many during the Depression. They gained job security with union-based seniority protection. And, above all, many experienced unprecedented job satisfaction from the "win-the-war" exuberance of the times and from the exhilarating notion that involvement in a greater social cause helps invest all of life with special meaning.

The "Human Relations" Approach

Eager to set ever-higher production records, employers grew interested in the pioneering work of industrial sociologist Elton Mayo. His research at the Chicago Hawthorne Works of Western Electric, as reported in two major books in 1933 and 1939, helped launch a "human relations" movement in employee relations.[45] Perfected in use in the World War II airframe industry, the Mayo approach "laid the basis for a needed breakthrough into an entirely new conception of human work."[46] During, and especially after World War II, human relations practitioners counseled managers to help produce a better-informed, a happier, and a better-adjusted employee—the better to win the productivity gains that the human group at work strategically controlled. While research has failed to confirm a causal association between happiness and postwar productivity, such an association was used as a goad to still-future "community"-building efforts at work.

From the very outset, organized labor viewed these efforts of the human relations practitioners with keen suspicion. It was not only that prime company sponsors were commonly nonunion firms but also that certain workers themselves were little impressed (Western Electric's Hawthorne Works was unionized shortly after Mayo-based reforms were initiated). Whatever doubts remained were resolved by the belief that the human relations approach viewed labor unions as an unavoidable result of errors made by management, rather than as a natural, inevitable, and healthy component of a work setting.

Critics within (and outside of) the labor movement have since charged this seemingly sensitive and humanistic approach with old-fashioned elitism and long-familiar manipulativeness. Caricaturing it as neopaternalistic "cow sociology," certain of the critics call instead for a no-frills, collective bargaining relationship between mutually-respectful peers. This remedy, however, would apply only to the nation's one-in-five unionized workers. Left untouched are 80 million nonunion employees, for whom some variation of the Mayo "human relations" approach, as first explored during the second World War, remains even today a major molder of the modern meaning of work.

The Postwar Period

Four issues in particular—those of *power distribution, needs satisfaction, participant roles,* and *value emphasis*—appear especially influential in shaping the last 2,500 years of the Western history of work meanings. As the deliberately selective table below suggests, answers to questions of who is in charge, what needs are being met (or frustrated), whose work lives are central, and what work values are being stressed reveal much of worth about work realities in the epoch under study—and hint at much of likely concern to ensuing historic periods. Using this paradigm, it is possible to condense and order the myriad developments in the American world of work since 1946 and to raise thereby some of the vital questions to be tackled in the 1980s.

Work-Meaning Components

Epoch	Power Distribution	Needs Satisfaction	Participant Roles	Value Emphasis
1. *Greco-Roman* (400 B.C.E.–500 C.E.)	Entirely in hands of slaveowner or purchaser; guilds were weak, slave revolts unsuccessful; technological R&D went largely neglected; innovation was confined to the professions and administrative art skills.	Largely survival in nature; status gains were few and minor; inter-class mobility was unknown; artisans alone may have enjoyed considerable job satisfaction.	Slaves and descendants of slaves; freed men, artisans, small shop owners; early practitioners of the professions.	Toil was disclaimed by the upper classes; work was seen as a curse; artisans, however, promoted their well-being with guilds.
2. *Early American Industrial Revolution* (1700–1830)	Largely in hands of factory owners, backed up by ministers, journalists, and other influentials; Jacksonian era Work Parties linked with social reformers to pursue political gains—generally unsuccessfully. Onset of massive waves of foreign-born laborers upset power gains of the native-born and insured more decades of employer power.	Personal economic and status well-being, as scarcity of labor prior to waves of mass immigration buttressed high levels of earnings; culture of the period applauded "Lowell Girls" approach and enrollees.	Native Americans; women, aged, etc.; males were to stay on the land, though males flocked to the factories as time went on; "uncouth" foreign-born immigrants were discrimination targets, until they overwhelmed.	Toil was valued as moral education; factory discipline was lauded for shaping a mature personality; blue-collar "radicals" led early opposition to corporate paternalism, and republican use of work as a model for life steadily lost plausibility.

1. Power distribution. Critical in this regard has been the consolidation of labor union strength in blue-collar ranks (outside the Sun-Belt states), and the recent signs of fresh union gains in white-collar ranks (government and service workers). Contrariwise, there is the inability of labor to arrest inflation's inroads and the persistence of certain business-sponsored efforts to weaken labor ("Right-to-Work" lobbies). To complicate the picture further, joint labor-business projects are being formed to protect common interests (as with protectionist efforts to limit overseas imports, such as color TVs, shoes, steel, and autos), even while labor and management meet in a "holy war" over the fate of the Occupational Safety and Health Administration and the fate of proposed plant-closing legislation.

It is at the grass-roots level of the factory and office, however, that the contemporary meaning of work has been particularly affected by the postwar rise of labor unionism. Nonunion operations, for example, often expend special effort to promote job satisfaction (through sophisticated personnel practices) and thereby diminish employee openness to union recruitment arguments. This strategy actually vests considerable power, even if of an indirect sort, in millions of nonunion employees, whose needs and wants are carefully monitored and addressed by employers committed to remaining exclusive directors of their own workforce.

Where 20 million unionists are concerned, the power-sharing relationship at work is direct, overt, formal, and bilateral in nature. Work is influenced by sharp governance (shop stewards *and* foremen), the "rule" of labor contract terms, and the availability of tools for collective "leverage" (the grievance process, the slowdown, the "rulebook" strike, the wildcat strike, the authorized strike, and the resort to compulsory arbitration).

Possibly the greatest impact, however, connects to the sense of solidarity that unionization uniquely promotes: The "good and welfare" free-for-all session that traditionally ends a local union meeting is very much to the point.

> The time was largely spent in members airing grievances against management, in protests against union action and/or inaction, and in educating the rest of us from workers' own personal experiences on such matters of common concern as health hazards and discrimination within the plant. This was ... the time that a sense of worker collectively emerged ... when workers talked about what they needed and deserved. This was a time for anger and joy.[47]

Work, in short, appears to be transformed by a local union's presence from a solo to a collective experience; from one dependent on employer goodwill to one recast by hard-nosed, two-party negotiations; and from one turned inward on the workplace alone to one with an entirely separate, status-shaping (and career-building) set of options (as in the status rewards or penalties of being perceived by "significant others" as a proud "brother" or as a "union goon").

In the 1980s, the public, the workforce, and management will help determine whether labor will reverse its postwar losses in labor force strength. If a "Proposition 13" attack on social welfare programs combines with "topless-inflation," plant closings, job loss to overseas inflation, technological displacement, recession-bred unemployment, and OPEC-fueled bankruptcies, the union-organizing effort may dramatically revive. Similarly, if nonunion employers in factories, hospitals, school systems, and elsewhere begin to scrimp on job rewards for the unorganized, they could wind up doing the union organizers' jobs for them.

In one way or another, however, labor has altered the modern American meaning of work by sensitizing all to the humanity of the rank-and-file. And this achievement finally seems to command (nearly) everyone's respect. Even nonunion employers increasingly appreciate that the dignity of adults at work is a precious matter, one requiring sensitive and mature employee relations practices from all—even if that entails revising some traditional management prerogatives.

2. Needs satisfaction. Critical factors here are the rising level of educational attainment and the new value that employees place on nonwork leisure time. Many would substitute family togetherness for work-centric life styles, even while calling for still more challenge from work itself (as from tasks that are free from boredom and routinization).

Stirred by the Human Potential Movement of the 1960s, and especially by the invigorating notion of a "self-actualizing" life-style (as heralded by psychologist Abraham Maslow and his collaborators), the needs-satisfaction issue at work has been dramatically revised since the end of the Vietnam War.[48] To be sure, the time-honored factors—wages, hours, and working conditions—remain firmly entrenched as the workers' highest priorities, but they are closely followed now by nonmaterial issues recently grouped by pollster Daniel Yankelovich under the rubric "Entitlements."[49] Employees, the pollster reports, feel that they are increasingly entitled to more status, more satisfaction, and more selfhood from their work roles than ever before in the nation's mature industrial phase.

As "status," the new needs include such things as a call for equality in workplace facilities (as with the provision of pothole repairs in the general parking area equal to those in the reserved area), and a related upgrading in job titles. Some workers urge a policy of relying on in-plant promotions, the subsidization of job-related, after-work schooling, and access to profit-sharing plans that afford a worker an opportunity to feel himself or herself also a capitalist (as through Employee Stock Ownership Plans).[50]

As for "satisfaction," the new needs include an interest in job enrichment and job enlargement, with certain employees willing to assess the psychic *and* material rewards cited by enthusiastic proponents. New attention is also focused on ways to transfer employees within a unit to minimize boredom, along with the upgrading of auxiliary services (plant cafeterias, game rooms, lounge areas) to enrich nonwork experiences at work. Regular opinion polls of employees to air gripes, rumors, and reform suggestions are championed by some (especially if done collaboratively with labor in organized shops), while others urge consideration of company-subsidized training in human relations skills for both supervisory *and* local union personnel alike.

By "selfhood" the new needs pivot around a call for accommodation to a worker's *individual* circumstances. A flextime arrangement, for example, is championed to allow a worker to vary arrival and leave-taking time with changing personal pressures. Cafeteria fringe benefit schemes also permit a custom-tailored selection of fringes, matched to one's situation and style of life. Job-sharing arrangements, in turn, help a couple alternate in filling one job, while still meeting both home and employer expectations.[51]

In the 1980s, workers, unions, and employers are likely to wrestle anew with "entitlement" issues that are germane in only the most advanced industrial nations (work meanings in Scandinavia, West Germany, and, to a lesser extent, in Japan and the U.K. are being challenged by these issues). If the American economy remains basically strong, and if labor shortages should develop here (older workers may retire earlier even while the numbers of young job seekers prove sparse), the demand at work for status, satisfaction, and selfhood gains may prove ever more formidable.

At present, however, labor appears dubious about the entire matter, preferring with many employers to concentrate on more familiar and more easily managed matters. Ironically, the unorganized 80 percent of the labor force *may* be more effective than the unionized workers in conveying its interest in these entitlements to attentive employers (as suggested by journals read by personnel administrators), though with what substantial effect remains to be seen.

3. Participant roles. If the meaning of paid work is far different from that of twenty-five years ago, much credit is due to the fact that work is now recognized as a *legitimate vehicle for the self-enhancement dreams of all*—whatever their gender, skin color, sexual preference, age, disability history, offender history, or what not. Exactly how this dream will come true and how white males will recoup from apparent work-role setbacks are among the decade's more intriguing questions.

Critical here has been the "discovery" recently of several million illegal immigrants in the bottom-most tier of the labor force and the related "discovery" of the reluctance of many older people to retire early or even when eligible. Both the "undocumented" and these older employees give witness to the centrality of (paid) work in our lives, especially work that rewards better than anywhere else in the Western hemisphere, that helps the workers stay abreast of inflation's toll.

With the advent of the civil rights movement in the 1960s, the feminist movement in the early 1970s, and the Gray Power, Ex-Offender Power, Gay Power, and Handicapped Power movements in more recent years, the issue of the participants' role at work has dramatically altered. A long-unquestioned hegemony of white males over the bastions of labor force privilege (the skilled trades, the "fast-track" managerial slots, the openings in graduate professional schools) has been challenged by law, public opinion, and resolute minority applicants. To be sure, a barely-contained backlash by besieged white males has helped to hold the lid on real gains (women remain less than 2 percent of all building-trade apprentices, are still confined largely to traditional work roles and locations, and continue to earn less than

60 cents for every dollar garnered by comparable male wage earners). Furthermore, the 1970 Nixon veto of federally sponsored day-care centers has not been reversed, and the Bakke and Weber decisions of the Supreme Court have left much that is still unclear about legal support for "benign quotas" at work.

Possibly the greatest impact, however, has been on the "machismo/John Wayne/ Marlboro Country" associations that men have long made with their work. So long as almost all women, and most males of dubious suitability (nonwhites, homosexuals, the handicapped, and the "license plate fabricators" as "jail-birds"), were excluded from or carefully segregated at work, dominant males took much in the way of manhood props and ego-aids from the associated virility and bravado of a "real man's" job. Myths were generated to help protect this sexist cultural design, and merciless harassment greeted front-runners who dared to challenge related workplace norms.

Now, not only do white males stand in the shambles of a shattered myth structure (women *can* do just about any job men presently monopolize; the handicapped require only a reasonable modicum of accommodation; etc.) but they also suspect that there is more still to come, as, for example, with the slowly-surfacing question of the feminization agenda of certain new women workers. When the Coalition of Labor Union Women, for example, calls for employer-subsidized day-care centers at the workplace (such as the nation had during World War II), the expansion of family-centered fringe options (dental care coverage, legal remedy coverage), and the expanded use of O-J-T to enhance female transfer and promotion opportunities, many men swear, disheartened, that the work experience "ain't what it used to be."

An appropriate anecdote was recently told by a reporter about a thirty-five year-old female apprentice electrician:

> At the construction site, the supply trailer was posted with pictures from *Hustler* magazine when Joni walked in.
> Joni thought about raging. She thought about lecturing. She kept quiet.
> Three days later, the posters had disappeared. Instead, there were angels, and bells, and the tinsel of holidays.
> "I like the new decorations," Joni had said to them. "Better than the old ones." And the guys in the hardhats had grinned.

Elsewhere in the story, Joni, who can earn nearly $29 an hour in wages and benefits at the top of her scale, warned other women who would pioneer like her that they "will probably have to work harder, to prove yourself, but not so hard as to be a threat to them. You must not . . . disapprove of what they do—whether it's swearing, or staring while they use the corner lot as a, uh, bathroom".[52]

In the 1980s, the policymakers, the assertive minorities, the beleaguered white male majority, the groping unions, and the groping employers alike will help determine how much of work's most substantial rewards will be fairly shared with new claimants. If the labor market can expand rapidly enough to absorb both new entrants *and* the laid-off victims of unemployment alike, a rapprochement between the sexes and the races may be successfully achieved. Contrariwise, pressure could develop to win superseniority protection to prevent the laying-off of new hires. Or a newly proposed campaign for "comparable-worth" pay might win advocates for its radical effort to close male-female wage differentials. Should either of these controversial prospects materialize, the ensuing workplace turmoil is likely to be devastating.

4. Value emphasis. Critical here is the emergence of heightened unemployment anxiety (as among the Frost-Belt area workers who fear plant closings). In addition, a call exists for better-than-ever job-preparation training (as for urban high schoolers and dropouts). And, furthermore, growing recognition is clearly felt by two-income couples of the necessity of keeping both spouses on a payroll. In this light, work appears a reasonably rewarding, highly desired, and economically critical component of modern lives, albeit one whose underlying value framework remains dramatically in flux.

Typical of the value shifts of greatest consequence is the intensification of concern with health and safety at work. Surveys of sources of job discontent have commonly found this anxiety ranked second only to inadequate compensation, a rank-and-file judgment intimately linked to the work-related deaths annually of over 14,000 wage earners and the permanent incapacitation of 100,000 men and women.[53] Revelations of the "silent violence of occupational diseases" in the 1970s produced not only the passage of the Occupational Safety and Health Act but also considerable intensification of labor and business efforts to prevent and reduce both the fact and the related dread of such diseases.

Linked to this shift is a second major value shift in the meaning of work, that is the newfound recognition of the mental, as well as the physical health hazards related to stress on the job. Teachers, civil servants, salesmen, and others are thought especially vulnerable to "burn-out," a mental and spiritual exhaustion that can leave a person temporarily unfit for continued performance; their representatives are calling for sensitive remedial attention to the stressors. Blue-collarites, in turn, complain of once-ignored work-setting irritants like the incessant cacophony of the roaring, whirring, pounding, and whistling noises that bring lingering tension headaches (and of course, the risk of sustained hearing loss). Still more novel, however, is the fresh interest that employees are showing in gaining help through workplace referrals for the relief of off-work mental stressors (marital problems, in-law problems, child-rearing problems, "substance-abuse" problems, and so on).[54]

Local union officers and company personnel specialists report more and more requests for counseling and social agency referrals for employees newly curious about mental health services.[55] To be sure, progress is hamstrung by the current unavailability of adequate insurance coverage with which to meet counseling and mental treatment costs. Progress, however, is being boosted by intensified efforts at "consciousness-raising" at work:

> What we are talking about here is making a workplace receptive to individual differences and weaknesses; learning compassion; conveying a different kind of atmosphere and message—one which reduces the stigma of mental illness, increases access to service by saying, "We know that people have emotional problems; it is O.K. to have such problems; we want to help do something about them."[56]

Spurred in part, then, by recent court decisions that link work stressors to compensable mental health injuries, progress here is also aided by increased employee curiosity about possible sources of substantial stress relief (AA, Gamblers Anonymous, Parents Anonymous, the Marriage Encounter Movement, the community mental health clinics, the collectively-bargained therapy coverage plans, and so on).

In the 1980s, Americans will help determine how far this ongoing value shift in the meaning of work will continue. The "campaign" here insists that the physical and mental health of 100 million employees can become far more secure, and can be aided anew by workplace personnel, performing either as treatment specialists or as referral resources. Exposed anew as sites of the "silent killers" of occupational disease, and as not-so-silent sources of avoidable and excessive mental stress, workplaces could become something quite different, something far healthier and even health-promoting—providing that this possibility is a clear-cut value preference of work-shaping parties in the years immediately ahead.

Summary

Work in America is a kaleidoscopic and dynamic subject, one which mixes ancient, contemporary, *and* futuristic ideas.

Of late its extraordinary admixture of work meanings has gained fresh input from four ongoing campaigns: One would further democratize employee-employer relations (a question of power relations). Another would address a variety of postaffluent "entitlement" issues (a question of needs). A third would accommodate the agendas of rising minorities (a question of empowering new participants). And a fourth would assess reforms for new anxieties at work (a question of fresh value perspectives on employee health, both physical *and* mental).

Much more is in the offing, of course, as the ever-changing American work scene includes such vexing matters as the following:

1. the possibility that ensuing years of energy "shortfall" could mean plant-closings, prolonged bouts of high unemployment, and persistent inflation; *or* the contrary possibility that ensuing years of energy "shortfall" could

mean the gradual substitution of human labor for fuel-driven processes, a shortage of labor, a return to making hand-crafted items, and a renaissance in the craft level of many workers;

2. the possibility that automation may steadily displace workers at every skill level and, in combination with advances in computer uses, telecommunications, and artificial intelligence, thoroughly revamp contemporary understanding of where work and nonwork matters begin or end; *or* the contrary possibility that automation and "robotics" will continue only to relieve workers of the most boring or hazardous of tasks, upgrade many attendant jobs, and make no special impact on the availability of jobs except to help reduce the average work schedule and boost productivity gains;

3. the possibility that ensuing years may witness a "hardening of the 'industrial arteries,' " whereby labor-management relations will grow fiercer and most costly for all as intransigence, intolerance, and a lack of creative risk-taking increasingly characterize both the local and the national industrial relations scene; *or* the contrary possibility that the need for productivity gains, in combination with the professionalization of management and the "entitlement" needs of new workers, will encourage fresh ventures in labor-management cooperation (Productivity Committees; worker representation on corporate boards, and the like);

4. the possibility that the antiregulation mood of the country may be skill-fully employed, in fact or effect, to curtail profoundly the regulatory effectiveness of the Occupational Safety and Health Administration and to discourage workplace concern with social welfare issues; *or* the contrary possibility that new expenses of the hidden and long-term toll of physical and mental hazards at work will earn enhanced preventive as well as expanded treatment and rehabilitative resources (of both traditional and innovative types).

The list could be continued, of course, but the point by now is obvious: The meaning of work in America tomorrow is being shaped today by a legacy of still-engaging perspectives from the past, a turbulent fourfold set of challenges in the present, and a sweeping range of appropriately unresolved possibilities. Using the powerful tool of these various work meanings, consciously and deliberately brought to the task, we can help ensure "consciousness-raising" about our collective power to make steady progress toward work lives that reward, engage, and honor us all.

Notes

[1] Studs Terkel, *Working: People Talk About What They Do All Day and How They Feel About What They Do* (New York: Pantheon, 1974), p. xi; Barbara Garson, *All the Livelong Day: The Meaning and Demeaning of Routine Work* (New York: Penguin, 1977), pp. xi, xiii (italics in original); Eric Hoffer, "Work and Days: The Labor of Daily Thought: 1974–1975," *Harper's*, 257, no. 1541 (October 1978), 74.

[2] Terkel, *Working*, p. xi; Howard Brubaker, Done Herold, and Oscar Wilde, as quoted in Leonard Louis Levinson, *The Left-Handed Dictionary* (New York: Collier, 1966), p. 248; Ambrose Bierce, *The Devil's Dictionary* (New York: Sagamore, 1957). p. 101.

[3] The Talmud, as drawn from Leo Rosten, *Treasury of Jewish Quotations* (New York: Bantam, 1977), pp. 423–496.

[4] Neff reports that the *Oxford English Dictionary* derives the word "work" from Old English, Old High German, and Old Frisian, and finds its earliest usages in manuscripts dating from the ninth century (c. 850). Walter S. Neff, *Work and Human Behavior* (New York: Atherton Press, 1968), p. 78.

[5] Ibid.; see also pp. 71-86, passim.

[6] Pablo Picasso, as quoted in Leonard Lewis Levinson, *Webster's Unafraid Dictionary* (New York: Collier, 1967), p. 262.

[7] I rely heavily here on Claude Mosse, *The Ancient World at Work* (New York: W.W. Norton, 1969).

[8] From Oeconomicus (IX, 2, 3), by Xenophon, as quoted in Mosse, *The Ancient World at Work*, p. 25. Xenophon called work the painful price the gods charge for the goods of life.

[9] Mosse, *The Ancient World at Work*, p. 113.

[10] Ibid., pp. 29–30.

[11] I draw extensively here on Andriano Tilgher, *Homo Faber: Work Through the Ages* (Chicago: Henry Regnery, 1958), pp. 11–18.

[12] See in this connection Ernst Troelsch, *The Social Teaching of the Christian Churches* (New York: Olive Wyon, 1931), I, pp. 317, 321, 292-95.

[13] I draw here on P. Boissonnade, *Life and Work in Medieval Europe (Fifth to Fifteenth Centuries)* (London: Routledge & Kegan Paul, 1927).

[14] Helpful here is Jean Gimpel, *The Medieval Machine: The Industrial Revolution of the Middle Ages* (New York: Holt, Rinehart and Winston, 1976).

[15] Karl Polanyi, *The Great Transformation: The Political and Economic Origins of Our Time* (Boston: Beacon, 1957), p. 40.

[16] Tilgher, *Homo Faber*, p. 47.

[17] Ibid., p. 50.

[18] Sebastian Franck, as quoted in Max Weber, *General Economic History* (New York: Collier, 1961), p. 268.

[19] Dennis H. Wrong, "The Meaning of Work in Western Culture," *Humanitas*, 7 (1971), 218.

[20] Daniel Bell, *Work and Its Discontents: The Cult of Efficiency in America* (New York: League for Industrial Democracy, 1970), p. 29.

[21] Franck, in Weber's *General Economic History*, p. 269.

[22] I draw heavily in this section on a remarkable book, John F. Kasson's *Civilizing the Machine: Technology and Republican Values in America 1776-1900* (New York: Penguin, 1977).

[23] See, in this connection, Marvin Eisher, *Workshops in the Wilderness: The European Response to American Industrialization, 1830-1860* (New York: Oxford University Press, 1967), p. 14, passim.

[24] Ibid., p. 17.

[25] Kasson, *Civilizing the Machine*, p. 86.

[26] Douglas T. Miller, *Jacksonian Aristocracy: Class and Democracy in New York, 1830-1860* (New York: Oxford University Press, 1967), p. 33.

[27] Carl R. Fish, *The Rise of the Common Man, 1830-1850* (New York: New Viewpoints, 1971), p. 91.

[28] For a remarkably insightful contemporary account of "alienation," the new aristocracy and a new era of class conflict, see Alexis de Tocqueville, *Democracy in America*, 2 vols. (New York: Pablerher, 1841). Most accessible is a two-volume edition edited by G.P. Mayer and Max Lerner in 1966 for Harper & Row.

[29] Ibid., pp. 200–201.

[30] Ibid., 2: 169–70.

[31] Eisher, *Workshops in the Wilderness*, p. 136.

[32] Miller, *Jacksonian Aristocracy*, p. 43.

[33] Fish, *The Rise of the Common Man*, p. 274.

[34] Miller, *Jacksonian Aristocracy*, p. 55.

[35] Norman Ware, *The Industrial Worker, 1840-1860: The Reaction of American Industrial Society to the Advance of the Industrial Revolution* (Chicago: Quadrangle, 1964), pp. x–xi.

[36] Gilman M. Ostrawder, *American Civilization in the First Machine Age, 1890-1940* (New York: Harper & Row, 1972); p. 208.

[37] Veblen's concept cf the "instinct of workmanship," along with his description of the leisure class, is thought to be the "most comprehensive theory of industrial alienation developed in America during [the period 1890–1920]." Veblen did not blame technology for the adverse effects of the division of labor; social and cultural institutions were at fault for distorting the impact of inventiveness on society. See James B. Gilbert, *Work Without Salvation* (Baltimore: Johns Hopkins, 1977), p. 55. See also Thorstein Veblen, *The Institute of Workmanship; and the State of the Industrial Arts* (New York: Augustus M. Kelly, 1964); "Veblen and the Business Culture," in David Riesman, *Individualism Reconsidered* (Glencoe, Ill.: Free Press, 1954), pp. 271–304.

[38] Robert L. Heilbroner, *The Economic Transformation of America* (New York: Harcourt Brace Jovanovich, 1977), p. 145.

[39] As quoted in Irving Bernstein, *The Lean Years: A History of the American Worker, 1920-1933* (Baltimore: Penguin, 1966), p. 512.

[40] Ibid., p. 507.

[41] Ibid., p. 506.

[42] Invaluable here is Grace Adams, *Workers on Relief* (New Haven, Conn.: Yale University Press, 1939).

[43] Sidney Fine, "The History of the American Labor Movement with Special Reference to Developments in the 1930s" in William Haber, ed., *Labor in a Changing America* (New York: Basic Books, 1966), p. 105.

[44] David Cort, "The Money That Money Can't Buy," *New York Times Book Review* (March 24, 1968), p. 38.

[45] Elton Mayo, *The Human Problems of an Industrial Civilization* (New York: Macmillan, 1933); F.J. Roethlisberger and W.J. Dickson, *Management and the Worker* (Cambridge, Mass.: Harvard University Press, 1939).

[46] Neff, *Work and Human Behavior*, p. 25. See also Richard H. Franke and James D. Kaul, "The Hawthorne Experiments: First Statistical Interpretation," *American Sociological Review*, 43, no. 5 (October 1978), 623–43.

[47] Al Nash, "The Local Union: Center of Life in the UAW," *Dissent* (Fall 1978), p. 399. See also Stanley Aronowitz, *False Promises: The Shaping of American Working-Class Consciousness* (New York: McGraw-Hill, 1974); E.E. LeMasters, *Blue Collar Aristocrats: Life Styles at a Working-Class Tavern* (Madison, Wis.: University of Wisconsin Press, 1975).

[48] See, for example, Abraham H. Maslow, *Motivation and Personality*, 2nd ed. (New York: Harper & Row, 1970) and *Toward a Psychology of Being*, 2nd ed. (Princeton, N.J.: Van Nostrand-Reinhold, 1968). See also Colin Wilson, *New Pathways in Psychology: Maslow and the Post-Freudian Revolution* (New York: Taplinger, 1972).

[49] See, in this connection, Daniel Yankelovich, *The New Morality: A Profile of American Youth in the '70s* (New York: McGraw-Hill, 1974). See also Paul Bernstein, "The Work Ethic That Never Was," *Wharton Magazine* (Spring 1980), pp. 19–25.

[50] See the chapter on objective factors and another on subjective factors in blue-collar work, in Arthur B. Shostak, *Blue-Collar Stress* (Reading, Mass.: Addison-Wesley, 1980), pp. 11–70. See also Felix Kaufman, "The Jobs That Nobody Wants," *The Futurist* (August 1979),

pp. 269–74; Rosabeth M. Kanter, "A Good Job Is Hard to Find," *Working Papers* (May-June 1979), pp. 44–50; Jeremy Seabrook, *What Went Wrong: Why Hasn't Having More Made People Happier?* (New York: Pantheon, 1978).

[51] Helpful here is chapter 8, "Producing: Workplace Reforms," and chapter 9, "Producing: Personnel Reforms," in Arthur B. Shostak, *Modern Social Reforms* (New York: Macmillan, 1974), pp. 187–234. See also David W. Ewing, "Employees' Rights," *Society* (November/December 1977), pp. 104–11; Nat Hentoff, "Free Speech in the Workplace," *Inquiry* (November 13, 1978), pp. 4–6; Franklin Wallick, "What Do Workers Want?" *Journal of Current Social Issues* (Fall/Winter 1979), pp. 26–28.

[52] Dorothy Storck, "Not Bad Fellas, Down at the Site," *Philadelphia Inquirer* (February 1, 1980), p. 1–B. See also Mim Kelber, "AFL-CIO—For Men Only?" *The Nation* (November 17, 1979), pp. 490–92; Joanna Foley, "CLUW Convention Reflects Growth," *In These Times* (October 3–9, 1979), p. 4; Graef S. Criptal, "Comparable Worth?" *Wall Street Journal* (November 5, 1979), p. 30.

[53] See, in this connection, Daniel M. Berman, *Death on the Job: Occupational Health and Safety Struggles in the United States* (New York: Monthly Review Press, 1978). See also James S. House and others, "Occupational Stress and Health Among Factory Workers," *Journal of Health and Social Behavior,* 20 (1979), pp. 139–60; Sidney Lens, "Dead on the Job," *The Progressive* (November 1979), pp. 50–52; Nicholas A. Asford, *Crisis in the Workplace* (Cambridge, Mass.: MIT Press, 1976).

[54] Helpful here is Lillian B. Rubin, *Worlds of Pain: Life in the Working-Class Family* (New York: Basic Books, 1976). See also Richard Sennett and Jonathan Cobb, *The Hidden Injuries of Class* (New York: Vintage, 1973); Arthur Kornhauser, *Mental Health of the Industrial Worker: A Detroit Study* (New York: Wiley, 1965).

[55] Relevant material can be had from Alan A. McLean, *Work Stress* (Reading, Mass.: Addison-Wesley, 1979).

[56] Sheila H. Akabas, "Mental Health Program Models: Their Role in Reducing Occupational Stress," in Alan A. McLean, ed., *Reducing Occupational Stress* (Washington, D.C.; HEW, 1977), p. 193.

3

Work and Social Policy

Martha N. Ozawa, Ph.D.
Washington University

Belief in the value of work, Ozawa notes, has bound American society together in the same way in which religion or political ideology has cemented other societies. As a result, even social policy and social welfare programs revolve around the work status of individuals and families. Because most benefits derive from the world of work, the major self-help effort of disadvantaged persons has been to seek entry thereto. The Affirmative Action movements of the past decade confirm this pressure for inclusion. If social distribution is a function of labor force participation, then, as the author points out, access to employment opportunity and to advancement in that status determines not only the obvious economic rewards but also the receipt of social benefits. This system might distribute fairly if all had equal access; they do not.

A review of the labor force substantiates the divergence between ideological assumptions and practice in the domain of work. We assume equality. We have differentials in job opportunity and differentials in rewards between blacks and whites, men and women, and handicapped and able-bodied workers. These differentials are aggravated by the changing composition of the labor force. For our inability to cope with them, Ozawa blames the ambivalence and the contradictions with which American society manages its welfare ideology.

Policies work against policies, because the goals that animate them are often mutually exclusive and poorly defined. We value a healthy family, which often de-

mands an at-home parent; we also value independent accomplishments for women. Throw into this mix a reluctance to discourage labor force participation, and you will see why we have never developed a family allowance system for rewarding at-home work. We allow the old to remain at work, but we promise upward mobility for equal opportunity populations. We assert the right of employment for all handi-capped persons, yet we do not allocate enough money to rehabilitate those with severe disabilities. We force welfare mothers to work, but we do not create struc-tured day-care arrangements, because we believe that mothers should take care of their children in a family context. Even when we do manage to enunciate our values, as in the Full Employment and Balanced Growth Act of 1978, economic realities frustrate our achieving them. We talk about social values, but we work within an economic reality.

The author suggests that we have been fighting a losing battle for our exclusively work-oriented, reward-distrubition mechanism. We seem overly concerned that any incentive that might encourage non–labor-force work will undermine the founda-tion of American society as a community of individuals committed to work. Ozawa reviews the differential treatment that prevails for those unconnected to work as opposed to those who are labor force participants or related to a partic-ipant. These work-related benefits defined elsewhere as the "occupational social welfare system"* or as the "new property"** have been developing for a long time. She notes that the growth of the federal social insurance sector during the de-pression of the 'thirties and of the private social insurance sector during World War II both used labor force status to determine beneficiary rights. Unions have cham-pioned a society oriented toward the social welfare of its members. (She notes the labor movement's contribution not only to the organized but, through example, to the unorganized sector as well, pointing out that the "unions' push for better working conditions has changed the conceptions of the general public. . . .") But this general upgrading of the definition of society's responsibility has darkened the line of distinction between workers and those outside the labor force.

Ozawa points out, as did Shostak in the previous chapter, that "entitlement" rationalizes beneficiary status. It is preferred to the socially stigmatized status of residual claimant. Social legitimacy attaches to benefits derived from work. Non-workers' rights are stigmatized accordingly. Despite high unemployment rates, the author notes, we blame the victim, and the victim acquires a negative self-image. The process keeps everyone producing, everyone consuming, and capitalism rolling. As Ozawa puts it, "nonwork has been damned to glorify work to a point of cultural hysteria."

Ozawa would contend that if we so value labor force work without a commit-ment to full employment and equal access, we lay the seeds for social destruc-tion. Can a society organized around work, where entitlements derive from one's

**Hyman J. Weiner, Sheila H. Akabas, Eleanor Kremen, and John J. Sommer,* The World of Work and Social Welfare Policy *(New York: Industrial Social Welfare Center, Columbia Univer-sity School of Social Work, 1971).*

***Charles A. Reich, "The New Property,"* Public Interest *3 (1966), 57–89.*

status in relation to a labor force participant, survive when it does not offer equality, or equity, or human growth in the structure of that world of work? If not, what can and should be substituted as an organizing principle for such a society?

The author reminds us that the contribution of social work is that it looks at social policy and raises new questions, promotes new values, and factors new variables into its cost/benefit analysis. Americans devote less social policy consideration to the family than do most other countries. Americans have always acted as if benefits and happy families follow from work, and as if everyone can work. We have ignored society's dependence on family apart from work and left unresolved the interdependence of societal need based on family and work. Recognizing that reality is far from the ideal, Ozawa encourages our tendency, as social workers, to ask a new set of questions. If we develop a social policy that values the family, will it automatically deter economic growth? In the long run, might it increase social and economic productivity? She concludes, also, that this emphasis on work follows from a concentration on the quantity made available in American life (that is, the products of affluence). She suggests that we shift to a concern with the quality of life in America—a life that values family, equality, and opportunity, so that everyone, not just those who thrive on the dedication to an imperfect social Darwinism, may prosper. This is the potential breakthrough that we can achieve through a social policy that understands the real meaning of work in America.

More than two hundred years after the people of this country proclaimed their independence from Great Britain, it is said that they have no national identity that can bind them together. Unlike the people of Japan, who know exactly what it is like to be Japanese, the people in the United States do not know what it is like to be Americans. Unlike the situation in Iran, where Islam can bind the nation together for a common cause, there does not seem to be a religion in the United States that can bind the people together for any cause. Unlike the People's Republic of China, where the dominant political ideology can direct anyone to dig ditches with grace and smiles in order to build a nation, the United States seems to be the setting for no coherent political ideology that justifies any national undertaking. In the heterogeneous American society, no one ethnic culture can excite and ignite the energy of the whole nation. With the constant flow of people in and out of the country through immigration and emigration, and with the diverse cultural backgrounds that are represented here, no cause would seem collectively significant enough to unite all of the people unless an enormous crisis occurred, such as an attack by foreign forces.

A nation, however, cannot be developed, let alone prosper, without a common belief in something. What, then, is it in the United States? If there is anything that has strongly linked the people of this country together, it may be the value attached to work. Apparently the United States does not wish to have a dominant religion, a dominant political ideology, or a powerful nationalism that might unite the people. Instead, one of the main foundation stones on which this nation has been built has been the common understanding that work by everyone is valued and will be fairly rewarded. True, work by all was not the *only* idea on which the nation was built. Some people came to this land to escape political or religious persecution, and their chief objective was to build a nation in which people enjoyed political and religious freedom. From the seventeenth century on, many also came to this country to get away from rigid class barriers, and they endeavored to break down these barriers and strive for more equality. But the majority who have come or who have been born in this country, in the early years or later, have embraced the idea that all who are able to work should do so, and that there should be opportunities for employment for all who want to work (albeit not equal access to all jobs). The nation's steady economic growth and relative political stability have been made possible to great degree by a tacit social agreement between the society and each individual. It was agreed that the building of the nation depended on work by everyone, and that, in return, the human faculties of each individual could be cultivated through activities in the world of work—although some would have better "self-actualizing" opportunities than others.

This social agreement has been implemented within the framework of capitalism. Unlike socialism, capitalism is predicated on the value of free enterprise and depends on people's voluntary economic behavior. Yet paradoxically, a nation developed on the basis of voluntary work cannot afford to have people opt for nonwork. Thus, the society has developed elaborate incentive systems, so that the choice between work (no matter how menial, boring, or physically unsafe) and nonwork is invariably made in favor of work. On the one hand, society acknowledges full social membership for those who work, and, on the other hand, it imposes social stigma on those who do not work; this is part of the incentive package. Another part is making available to workers only legitimate sources of non–wage-related income and services through social insurance programs and private employee benefit programs. In short, work, although voluntary, is so important that American society allocates resources according to status in the world of work, degree of attachment to the labor force, and type of occupation. Because factors related to work determine how resources are allocated, no one can afford *not* to work, even though work is not imposed by law.

This social agreement between society and each individual—which sounds fair enough and simple enough to implement—has not operated in the past to everyone's full satisfaction and is not doing so today. Economic forces are one source of constraint. Increasingly the American economy is finding itself unable to provide opportunities for employment to all who want to work. As technology has advanced, the labor market seems to have become increasingly stratified or segmented. Opportunities to obtain decent jobs are disappearing for the uneducated and the unskilled, who constitute a significant part of social work clientele. Constraint stems also from the social stratification within the world of work, where many workers are discriminated against on account of sex, race, age, or physical or mental disability. Still another source of constraint, which inhibits the effective implementing of the social agreement, is the growing gap between what people expect from work and what work provides in terms of human satisfaction. Can the American society sustain the credibility and the excitement that this social agreement provided in the past? That seems to depend on whether it is willing to make the economic game fair for everyone, even by resorting to the development of social policy regarding employment. However, developing and implementing social policy to make the economic game fairer would have to be done with economic limitations in mind, in both short- and long-range terms.

This, then, is the challenge confronting the American nation. Can and will this country effectively implement its social and economic policies and make the rules of the game in the world of work operate more fairly and effectively? Can and will it provide opportunities for employment for all who wish to work—and also encourage conditions of work that make for fuller and satisfying living? Only if these things are done can the American people collectively and individually find the motivation to do "good" in life, because these were the central ideas that the people started with in building this nation, and because Americans have not found strong alternative sources for motivating their activities.

Another challenge facing America is the public's need to recognize the limitations inherent in work as a social value. Since the American people have single-mindedly put very high value on work, social policy and social welfare programs have revolved around the working status of individuals and families. And because this has happened, the American society has deprived itself of finding a positive rationale for dealing with the social problems of families who do not participate in the world of work, or who have not done so in the past.

This chapter looks first at empirical facts and evidence, to see how the world of work is functioning for various groups of workers in terms of earnings, occupational attainment, and so on. Second, it examines the changing composition of the labor force and what the changes imply. Third, it discusses the meanings of work to individuals and to industry. Fourth, it explores how society provides non-wage-related benefits to families with little or no attachment to the labor force. Fifth, it reviews recent legislation to ban discrimination in employment practices. And sixth, it identifies major issues of social policy related to work. These revolve around the allocation of jobs, the interface between economic determinants and concerns of social policy, the individual worker's interests versus society's interests in the role of women, and societal treatment of those outside of the world of work.

The Functioning of the World of Work

A person's sex, race, and occupation predict in the main how that person will fare in the world of work. Male workers earn more than female workers, whites more than nonwhites, and workers in high-skill occupations more than those in low-skill occupations.

The median weekly earnings of women working full time in 1977 was $156, or 62 percent of men's earnings. The proportion changed little during the past decade. Although women have not done well in improving their wage levels in relation to men's, nonwhites have greatly improved their wage levels in relation to those of white workers. The median weekly earnings of full-time, nonwhite workers rose from 69 percent of the earnings by their white counterparts in 1967 to 79 percent in 1977. Improvement has been especially remarkable among nonwhite female workers, who earned 80 percent of the median earnings of white female workers in 1967, but 94 percent in 1977.[1]

Occupations make a difference in predicting achievement in the world of work. Generally, workers in high-skill occupations earn more than those in low-skill occupations. For example, in 1977, the median earnings of professional and technical workers were $277 a week, but those of clerical workers were only $167.[2] Levels of professional earnings vary widely, depending on the type of profession. For example, the professions of medicine, law, and engineering pay much more than the professions of teaching, nursing, and social work. In high-paying professions, white males predominate, and women and minorities are underrepresented. Even within the so-called female professions, men tend to occupy high-paying supervisory and administrative positions.[3]

Why do some persons do better than others in their occupational achievements? A more penetrating question might be this: Why do white males tend to do better than their female or nonwhite counterparts? Can the difference be explained by personal attributes? Or is there room for explanation by structural or discriminatory factors? To what extent is free competition working in the world of work? All these questions are relevant in determining whether social intervention by way of establishing social policy in employment is justified.

Recent literature and research findings shed some light on these questions. Economists generally try to explain the variation in occupational attainment by two basic factors. One deals with so-called "human capital" variables, such as education, postschool training, and experience.[4] The other deals with structural variables, such as union membership, industry, and occupational affiliations. The structural factor also deals with such questions as whether a worker happens to be at the right place at the right time to obtain a job so as to maximize his capabilities and whether industry, because of technological advancement, creates the kind of jobs that enable workers to maximize their industrial talents. Economic conditions also fall in the category of structural phenomena.

The human capital theory states that an individual's resources are considered as a stock of capital, which determines the person's productivity and hence his earnings. Human capital can be further developed by investing in education, postschool training, and experience. Increase in earnings following such investment is considered to be the return on the human capital investment.[5] To the extent that human capital variables can explain the variation in earnings, no one can complain about differential levels, because the level of earnings is the person's own making.

Structural variables explain variation in earnings that human capital variables cannot: that is, the variation that no individual worker can influence with his own productivity. Structural variables include union membership, affiliation in occupational groupings, types of jobs, and ranks within jobs. When various groups of workers with the same level of human capital resources are equally represented—on the basis of sex, race, and so on—in these structural groupings, it can be said that the world of work is functioning democratically. However, when some groups of workers are over- or underrepresented, even though they have the same level of human capital, then the question of discrimination against certain groups can be raised.

What do empirical findings tell us about these questions?

A study by Kalachek and Raines defined human capital variables in the broadest possible terms. Besides the traditional variables of education, training, and experience, they included the following: (1) variables related to the human physical plant, such as health, age, wife's education; (2) variables related to personal characteristics, such as the individual's personality, attitudes, and psychological traits; and (3) variables related to the individual's upbringing, such as the sophistication and the social status of the home environment during formative years, feelings of self-confidence, economic boldness, ambition, and self-discipline. Despite this broad definition, these variables could explain only 41 percent of the variation in earnings. An additional 16 percent was attributed to structural variables. The rest— 43 percent—was left unexplained by either human capital or structural variables.[6]

A study by Halaby relating to the 1960 levels of earnings of management personnel in a California-based utility firm reveals that only 22 percent, or $602 of the $2,726 male-female salary gap, could be explained by human capital variables— that is, schooling, seniority, experience, and previous position. The rest of the gap— 78 percent, or $2,124—was attributed to the structural variables of jobs and ranks. This means that, controlling for human capital variables, women were underrepresented in high-paying jobs or the high ranks within job classifications.[7] In a study supplementing Halaby's findings, Wolf and Fligstein found that women's post–high school education helped female workers obtain positions with responsibilities, but did not help them progress to positions with additional authority. Post–high school education helped men on both counts. This study reports further that the sex gap in authority was due more to employers' attitudes and behaviors than to qualifications, attitudes, and behaviors of female employees.[8]

Leigh's findings in a study using the National Longitudinal Surveys data of 1966 paints a similarly gloomy picture for blacks. Schooling positively influenced the level of earnings by black men in their first job, but did not help increase their earnings through subsequent job changes, although schooling benefited white men on both counts.[9]

These research findings show that mere possession of human capital does not guarantee that a worker will get ahead in the world of work. Numerous structural constraints are at work. Women and minorities tend to be trapped by these constraints—some beyond anyone's control, others the product of discrimination.

In addition to the fact that structural forces are operating to determine occupational attainment, some economists point out that the labor market is segmented into primary and secondary sectors. The primary labor market exists within corporations and other large organizations that depend on highly technical skills of employees. There both employers and employees have a mutual interest in employee training for complex tasks. Also, high remuneration and good prospects for advancement provide incentives for remaining with the same firm. To facilitate the process, many of these organizations largely use internal recruitment of employees for higher positions.

The secondary labor market, in contrast to the primary one, consists of unskilled, low-paying, dead-end jobs, in which workers lack either the protection of a powerful union or the protection that comes from possessing professional or highly technical skills. Employers in the secondary labor market do not need or do not have a vested interest in upgrading the skills of their employees. Thus regardless of employees' long service, one employee is interchangeable with another. Security of employment is not a built-in phenomenon in the secondary labor market. Employees' quitting or being fired can be a daily occurrence.

Indeed, there is a considerable overlap between the workers in the secondary labor market and the traditional social work clientele. Because of lack of job security, workers in the secondary labor market and their families frequently cross the line between the status of working, receiving unemployment insurance benefits, and being on welfare, and back again to the status of working. Some families may find themselves in more than one status. In the process of shifting their status, these families may have to go through both economic and psychological trauma that families with stable employment do not encounter.

Collective bargaining protects union workers for job security and wage increases, even if it does not provide career advancement. The literature seems to put union jobs within the primary labor market, because of the job security that union membership provides.[10]

The theory of the segmented labor market implies that the individual who misses early entry into the primary labor market with its special advantages will find it difficult to get into it later and thus may be trapped in the secondary labor market forever. So far, empirical research findings that prove this point are hard to come by.[11] However, the concept of the segmented labor market does offer a theoretical framework for understanding how the world of work functions, and it seems to supplement the structural theory of the labor market.

Changing Composition of the Labor Force

The composition of the labor force is going through an enormous change. The population aged sixteen and over has gradually increased its rate of labor force participation from 60.2 percent in 1960 to 62.8 percent in 1977. But during the same period the patterns of change in the rates of labor force participation by men and women were quite different. The rate for men decreased from 84.0 percent to 78.3 percent. The rate of decline for nonwhite men was especially marked: from 83.0 percent to 71.0 percent. There was also a drastic drop in the rate of participation among middle-aged men and men aged sixty-five and over. But the rate for women increased from 37.8 percent to 48.4 percent. Women in all age brackets, except those aged sixty-five years and over, increased their rate of participation, with those in the twenty to twenty-four and twenty-five to thirty-four age brackets showing the greatest relative gain.[12] The increase among women with preschool children was enormous: the rate more than doubled.[13]

The shift in the composition of the labor force by marital status reflects the recent surge in the divorce rate. In the early 1970s, the divorce rate surpassed the record high that occurred right after World War II. The current divorce rate is almost 30 percent.[14] Because of the rising divorce rate, the proportion of men and women in the labor force who were either widowed, divorced, or separated reached 12 percent in 1977, while it was only 10 percent in 1970. The recent increase in the number of young people who stay single is influencing the composition of the labor force. In 1970, 20 percent of the labor force was single; in 1977, 23 percent.[15] Because of the higher divorce rate and larger proportion of singles, more than one out of three persons in the labor force were not married and living with a spouse in 1977.

All these changes are creating far-reaching implications. First, an increasing number of children are adversely affected by marital instability. The number of preschool children in families headed by females increased by 32 percent between 1970 and 1977, even though the total number of preschool children declined by 12 percent. Two and a quarter million preschool children were living in female-headed families in 1977.[16] The other side of this problem is that a growing number of males in the labor force are now living alone because of divorce or separation. Even in intact families, more and more children have mothers who are working out of the home. All this points to the fact that the domains of work and social welfare are rapidly converging. Thus the involvement of many in the world of work can no longer be looked at just as an economic problem, but often must be considered as a social welfare problem. It can be expected that in the future, social workers' clients will increasingly bring to them problems resulting from the maladjusted interface between family living and working out of the home.

Another implication of the increase in the rate of labor force participation among women may be a shift in social and economic relations within the family. That is, as women receive their own earnings, these earnings tend to produce independent effects, and make divorce economically less painful for them.[17] The capabilities of women to earn also may lead to a shift in the power structure at home. As a result, household chores may be divided between wives and husbands more evenly than before. This seems bound to happen, because family members would perceive the implied costs of women's work at home as greater when women receive earnings than when they do not. All this suggests that social workers may be called upon to help families mediate adjustment to the emerging new role and new power of women, which may differ drastically from the problems with which the profession traditionally equipped itself to deal.

The Meanings of Work

In the United States, work seems to be the most important link between individuals and society. Through work, families extract resources from the community to sustain their livelihood. Through work, a person can test his marketable capabilities, and that can give a sense of mastery over certain skills. Work, through its earnings, gives a feeling of continuity in life; the future becomes more secure. Work provides social relationships at the workplace, since a person's functions are inevitably coordinated with those of others in the common endeavor of producing goods and services.[18] In short, work is a cornerstone of life, which helps individuals and families to live both as private and social beings.

What does industry need from individuals? The needs differ according to the nature of the industry. When production of goods and services depends on highly technical equipment or technical knowledge or both, an industry has a great need for skilled and stable workers.[19] Invariably such an industry tends to be run by large-scale monopolistic or oligopolistic corporations. Corporations of this type are likely to be highly profitable, since they can, to a great degree, set the prices of their products in relative freedom from the forces of supply and demand. Because of their profit-making capabilities, large corporations can and do often accede to the demands and needs of their employees, in order to maintain a stable labor force.[20] Large corporations are rapidly finding that laying off their employees is unprofitable because of various expenses associated with layoffs, such as higher rates of unemployment insurance, severance pay, and loss of productivity resulting from employee turnover and the cost of training new employees.[21] It is not an accident that unions thrive when the market for an industry's products is highly concentrated and profits are high, since such an industry may meet much of what the union demands by simply passing the costs on to the consumer.

The needs and responses of highly competitive industries are very different. In such industries, when many relatively small firms produce the same commodity, no one firm can influence, let alone control, prices. When competitive pressure is on, such firms have to lower their prices, even cutting into their normal profits and sometimes incurring losses. This tends to be the case, for example, in the textile, apparel, and cigar-manufacturing industries. Many employees in such industries tend to be low-skilled and do not have the adequate pay, job security, or fringe benefits that large monopolistic or oligopolistic corporations can provide.[22]

Human satisfaction through work is a product of interaction between the individual worker's needs and the employer's needs and responses. Many employees often feel dissatisfaction. What are some of its sources?

According to Maslow's theory, human needs progress from primitive to higher-order needs, starting from the physiological and progressing through safety, love, and esteem to the need for self-actualization.[23] Applying Maslow's theory to the work situation, the worker's needs can be categorized into two groups: (1) life maintenance needs, such as freedom from hunger, freedom from thirst, and safety;

and (2) human growth needs, such as achievement, responsibility, and power.[24] Thus, ideally, the worker wishes to have the opportunity to advance to more interesting, varied, and satisfying work, which also pays better and offers greater recognition than his current job. He desires to do a good job in which he can feel a sense of self-fulfillment.[25]

Unfortunately, what advancing mechanization and the growth of large-scale modern industrial organizations have done to a vast majority of workers seems to be the exact opposite of what meets evolutionary human needs. As industrialization advanced and large organizations came into being, the functional rationality of organizations took precedence over the substantial rationality of individual workers for the sake of organizational efficiency.[26] To compound the problem, unions have felt forced to accept some of the notions of Taylorism in job assignments (that is, assigning jobs through industrial engineering and job simplification), and they have negotiated wage scales for each carefully defined narrow task. Ironically, by taking this action, unions may have increased the job insecurity with which they have been attempting to deal. When jobs are narrowly defined, the possibility is greater that they will be mechanized out of existence; furthermore, union workers are impeded from acquiring skills to do other jobs in their factory.[27]

The workers' lack of opportunity to use their intelligence, the lack of autonomy, and monotony on the job are perhaps the major causes of the growing alienation in America's workplace. A blue-ribbon Special Task Force to the Secretary of Health, Education, and Welfare, created in 1971, reported widespread alienation among American workers. The task force reported that only a small fraction of American workers were satisfied with their jobs—having the satisfaction that comes from a sense of achievement, accomplishment, responsibility, and challenging work.[28] It also reported a high correlation between job dissatisfaction and mental health problems, such as psychosomatic illness, low self-esteem, anxiety, worry, tension, and impaired interpersonal relations.[29]

The gap between what work provides to the worker and what the worker expects from it is widening as new generations of workers come into the labor force with higher educational attainment and heightened expectations about the quality of life. The present generation seems to detest the industrial disciplines that Taylorism imposes and to demand instead autonomous industrial disciplines that the individual may foster on his own. It seems that these young people want to have a more egalitarian organizational life in the workplace and to integrate the emotional aspects of well-being with the economic aspects of work.[30]

And yet American adults do keep working. The rate of absenteeism has not increased.[31] The provision of negative income taxes to working poor families does not appreciably weaken the work incentives of male heads of households, although it tends to decrease the labor supply of wives.[32] Kahn's extensive review of the literature on job satisfaction indicates that the proportion of dissatisfied workers ranges from 10 to 21 percent. It may be reasonable to say, as Kahn does, that few people call themselves extremely satisfied with their jobs, but still fewer report extreme dissatisfaction.[33]

Why do so many persist with a work commitment, and so few drop out of the world of work? True, a lucky few—like university professors and artists—can combine work and play in their professions, and this can give a sense of self-actualization. But to the vast majority of workers, their work is a means of obtaining a livelihood and getting pleasure outside the workplace.

Beyond individually felt needs for work, however, there is another important reason for strong commitment to work, which affects almost everyone. It is this: Participation in the world of work legitimizes the worker's claim to non-wage-related benefits, both in cash and in kind. Granted that these benefits can never satisfy the deep human need for self-actualization through work, they do assure continuity of income and in-kind benefits.

When considering the difference that participation in the world of work makes in claiming non-wage-related benefits through legitimate programs (legitimate in the sense that workers can claim entitlement to benefits), it becomes abundantly clear why the idea of dropping out of the world of work never comes to most workers' minds, although they may complain about the jobs they are holding.

Social Insurance Programs and Private Employee Benefit Programs for Workers and Their Families

Until the 1930s, when this country was hit by a devastating economic crisis, both employers and employees had taken it for granted that boom and bust were inevitable features of the economy. But that depression changed the whole perspective of the economy for politicians, economists, labor, and management. The United States joined the other Western industrialized countries in developing work-related social insurance programs to cushion the adverse effects of the social and economic risks involved in a free economy.

The major social insurance programs that have been developed in this country are these:

- Old-Age, Survivors, and Disability Insurance (OASDI)
- State Unemployment Insurance
- State Workers' Compensation
- Hospital Insurance and Supplemental Medical Insurance (Medicare)
- Temporary Disability Insurance Programs in five states and Puerto Rico

Although OASDI has expanded greatly—at a rate faster than the rate of increase in the gross national product (GNP)—not all social insurance programs have developed adequately. State Unemployment Insurance and State Workers' Compensation programs have lagged far behind OASDI. Temporary Disability Insurance programs are available only in California, Hawaii, New Jersey, New York, Rhode Island, and Puerto Rico.[34]

Private employee benefit programs developed partly as a response to the relatively inadequate development of social insurance programs in this country. The beginning of many of these private programs was seen in the 1940s, followed by rapid expansion in the 1950s and beyond, when legislative gains in the social field became less feasible and tax increases to support them virtually impossible. This occurred at a time of steady economic growth and prosperity. It can be said that the prosperity that made social legislation impossible made private development possible.[35]

There are other reasons why private employee benefit programs have expanded rapidly since the end of World War II. During the war, the National War Labor Board imposed a wage stabilization policy, but it allowed industries to develop non-wage-related programs for their workers. Employers went along with the new policy, on the grounds that employee benefit programs might help to stabilize the work force by reducing turnovers, enhancing the attractiveness of their enterprises to superior workers, improving general morale, and possibly reducing strikes and weakening union appeals.[36] Favorable tax treatment of business expenses for such programs was another powerful incentive to employers for developing them.

Although employers, in developing employee benefit programs, were mainly motivated by their desires to increase the productivity of individual workers, unions pushed for ever-increasing fringe benefits for social purposes. These included cohesion among union rank and file and the collective use of funds for members— for example, to help provide private insurance programs of all types. Another distinction between the motives of management and unions in developing private employee benefit programs was that management tended to look at employee benefits as an investment directed toward future increases in productivity; unions looked at them as deferred wages for work done in the past.[37]

At any rate, once the idea of providing non-wage-related benefits became a norm, the types of programs and the coverage under the various programs expanded rapidly. Nonunion workers began to demand similar benefits. Nonunion employers could no longer get by without providing them. The average annual rate of growth in contributions for private employee benefit programs was 15.6 percent between 1950 and 1960, 12.8 percent between 1960 and 1970, and 12.9 percent during the period 1970-75.[38] In 1975, some $67 billion were contributed for private employee benefit programs for life insurance and death benefits, accidental death and dismemberment benefits, health benefits, and temporary disability benefits (including formal sick leave, supplemental unemployment benefits, and retirement benefits). Contributions are made mainly by employers. In 1974, for example, 92 percent of the total contributions to private pension plans were paid by employers.[39]

Could employee benefit programs have developed as rapidly as they did if there had been no union pressure? Probably not. Although only about one-fourth of American workers belong to unions, the initiative of unions tends to set the tone that nonunionized industries eventually have to follow, if it is economically feasible. In the long run, too, the unions' push for better working conditions has changed the conceptions of the general public regarding what constitutes "acceptable" working conditions.

To measure properly the magnitude of the non-wage-related benefits that workers and their families receive, the benefits provided under social insurance programs must be combined with those under private employee benefit programs. The percentage of wages replaced by Old-Age Insurance is clearly progressive, favoring workers with a record of low earnings over those with a record of high earnings. On the contrary, private pension plans tend to replace a higher percentage of lost wages as levels of earnings increase. When the two types of programs are put together, replacement ratios become almost proportional across wage levels.[40]

The impact of private employee benefit programs may also be assessed by measuring their impact when no comparable social insurance programs exist. A study by Wilder shows that, in states with no publicly developed Temporary Disability Insurance, private plans for short-term illness and disability replace a consistently higher percentage of wages lost as earnings increase.[41]

Another way to measure the net effect of private employee benefit programs is to investigate employee coverage. For example, under private pension plans, coverage tends to be higher for the already economically well off: men over women, whites over blacks, workers in large firms over those in small firms, and high-wage workers over low-wage workers.[42] Similar observation can be made regarding other types of private employee benefit plans.[43]

All these distributive effects point to the fact that families receive non–wage-related benefits in direct proportion to their degrees of attachment to the labor force, their levels of earnings, and their occupational statuses. And these benefits are provided as a matter of entitlement.

The concept of entitlement is important for American workers. The entitlement involved in social insurance and private employee benefit programs clearly distinguishes their philosophical base from that of welfare programs. Families who are entitled to social insurance benefits or private employee benefits or both do not need to go through the income-testing that is required in all welfare programs. Receiving social insurance and private employee benefits does not subject the beneficiary to the suspicion of avoiding work nor to social stigma, as receiving welfare does.

In short, the world of work has become stratified in non–wage-related benefits, just as it has in wage levels. Those who do well in the world of work also receive adequate non–wage-related benefits. Those who do not, receive little and thus may have to resort to handouts from welfare programs with all their negative connotations.

According to Reich, the non–wage-related benefits provided through legislation or government regulations—or indirectly influenced by a special tax treatment or other law—constitute the "new property." These benefits certainly differ from an ordinary return on ordinary private property. Nevertheless, they have the same function of expanding one's economic power beyond what ongoing wages and salaries can provide.[44]

American society's differential treatment of families with current or prior participation in the world of work and those without such participation is expected to get worse for several reasons. First, to respond to workers' ever-increasing demand for a higher quality of life, industries with economic capabilities will use their resources to develop private employee benefit programs. To maintain a stable labor force and growth in production, it would seem that they cannot fail to do so. Ironically, in the age of Proposition 13, it may be found beneficial both for employers and their employees if large corporations use their financial resources internally rather than give them through corporate income taxes or United Way contributions. Second, despite the recent surge in public expenditures for welfare programs, the public evidently wishes to maintain a clear-cut demarcation between welfare programs and work-related programs in philosophy, benefit formulas, and modes of administration. It is not surprising that the United States has never developed such universal programs as old age pensions and children's allowances, which apply to all families regardless of employment status or family income level. These programs, if implemented, would blur the line between the social treatment of families who participate in the world of work and those who do not. Apparently, American people are so committed to the value of work that they do not wish this to happen.

Quest for Full Participation in the World of Work by Women, Minorities, and the Handicapped

As the foregoing sections illustrate, Americans draw prestige, power, and economic benefits from their activities in the world of work. Thus it is natural that disadvantaged persons seek to obtain these assets by becoming part of the world of work. As long as society upholds the value of work as a vital cornerstone of nation-building, it is obligated to make the world of work accessible to all, without discrimination. Recent legislative history is indicative of society's commitment to strive toward this end.

Title VII of the Civil Rights Act of 1964 protects women and minorities against discrimination with respect to any condition of employment.[45]

Executive Order 11246, "Non-Discrimination under Federal Government Contract," protects women and minorities against discrimination in employment by employers who have contracts or subcontracts with the U.S. government in amounts over $10,000. It further requires such employers to develop affirmative action programs to promote opportunities for equal employment.[46]

The Vocational Rehabilitation Act of 1973 requires that any contractor who holds contracts with the federal government in excess of $2,500—or any subcontractor holding contracts in excess of $2,500 with a prime contractor who is covered by the Act—must take affirmative action to employ and advance qualified handicapped individuals.[47] This act also affects all programs in either the public or the private sector that receive federal financial assistance for any purpose.[48] Furthermore, under the Act, employers must make reasonable accommodations for the qualified handicapped person at the workplace. These include job structuring, arranging full- or part-time work schedules to permit medical appointments, acquiring or modifying equipment and devices, providing readers or interpreters, and making all facilities (such as restrooms and drinking fountains) accessible to any handicapped employee.

Establishing public policy to foster equal opportunity for employment has at least two purposes. On the one hand, policymakers recognize the right of access to decent jobs for all qualified workers, regardless of sex, race, or physical or mental handicap. On the other hand, they recognize that the present economic system is not functioning so that it upholds this right adequately. In other words, policymakers aim to change the course of events that have been taking place in the world of work, and this implies the necessity for many employers to change their employment practices. Changes, whatever the reason, always produce pain and controversy.

Public policy in a democratic society is not always consistent with deliberate research on the ramifications of new public policy. For example, although Congress upheld nondiscriminatory employment practices on behalf of women, minorities, and the handicapped, it also passed the 1978 Amendments to the Age Discrimination in Employment Act, which increased the mandatory retirement age to seventy years, with the exception of highly paid employees (who expect to receive an annual retirement benefit of $27,000 or more) and tenured college and university faculty. The Act also eliminated the mandatory retirement age of federal civil service employees.[49]

Enactment of the 1978 Amendments to Age Discrimination in Employment Act can be considered another indication that this society upholds the individual's right to work. However, in reality, given a limited number of opportunities for employment, this Act may set the interests of women, minorities, and the handicapped against the interests of the elderly. Policy issues are bound to arise when the social aspirations embodied in certain legislation come face to face with the economic realities of American society.

Work and Social Policy Issues

Upholding through legislation the individual's right to have access to a decent job as a societal value is relatively simple. Implementing this value fairly is more difficult: (1) because resources and opportunities for implementing it are limited; (2) because this value may conflict with other values held by the society; and (3) because adhering closely to this value may deprive the society of a philosophical rationale for dealing with persons who are left out of the world of work.

Job Allocation: Women, Minorities, and the Handicapped vs. the Elderly

The American economy has steadily increased opportunities for employment, but not fast enough to accommodate all who want to work. In 1960 only 66 million people aged sixteen years or older were employed; in 1970, 79 million; in 1977, 91 million. But during the past decade the rate of unemployment has also increased. It was only 3.8 percent in 1967, but had increased to 7.0 percent in 1977.[50]

To compound the problem, opportunities to break into the high-skill, high-paying, technical, managerial, or professional jobs to which women, minorities, and the handicapped aspire are becoming scarce. One factor that prevents more of these jobs from opening up is that highly technical industries, such as oil refinery, found it possible to increase production without increasing manpower. Another factor that keeps the number of such jobs at a standstill is the pressure of union power and professional monopoly—a pressure that is strong enough to prevent union members and professional persons from losing their jobs or having their wages, salaries, and purchasing power cut in more than a minor degree, if at all, during economic recession.[51] Employers, unable to reduce these major labor costs, look to other ways of decreasing costs of manpower. They may lay off all those they can (usually persons at the bottom of the employment ladder), may cease to hire any new employees at either a low-skill or a high-skill level, or may mechanize further, so that some jobs go out of existence. All these forces tend to keep the select few in their stable, choice jobs—and to create barriers against the persons who are trying to break into these ranks.[52]

Given these constraints, how should society endeavor to allocate decent jobs to various groups of individuals? Should it strive to open up opportunities for women, minorities, and the handicapped—or to the elderly?

Since the depression of the 1930s, social policy in regard to the elderly has been firmly established to discourage their working. This can be seen in social security provisions, which allow people to retire at sixty-two years of age and impose a high tax rate on the earnings of those who work after retirement. It is also evident in the failure to provide incentives for the elderly to postpone retirement.[53] The basic argument supporting these provisions has been that retirement of the elderly would open up job opportunities to younger workers. But now, because of the financial crisis of social security, the projected imbalance between the working and the retired populations in the twenty-first century, and the political arguments of the elderly regarding their right to work, Congress swiftly passed the 1978 Amendments to the Age Discrimination in Employment Act.

Does this mean that opportunities for women, minorities, and the handicapped to enter or be promoted to high-paying ranks and positions have been partially blocked? Another related question is this: Among which groups of employees should skills be upgraded by investing industrial resources?

Policymakers can answer these questions only by making value judgments. However, a benefit-cost analysis can be a useful tool for decision-making. The current model of benefit-cost analysis seems to indicate that investment is more beneficial for the training of younger workers than of older ones. Unfavorable benefit-cost ratios in training older workers result from the following factors: (1) the relatively short time they will remain in the labor force will lessen the return on investment; (2) investments at an older age are more costly, because earnings forgone will be larger as a result of earlier investment; and (3) the decline with age in ability to learn may bring about a decline in the rate of return on investments.[54]

Policymakers should weigh, against such a benefit-cost analysis, the intangible adverse effects of disfavoring the elderly. When society treats its members badly toward the end of their lives, the desire to live into old age tends to diminish for those who are younger. Old age then is perceived as a dark age that nobody likes to contemplate. This may create unnecessary restlessness among persons of all ages. If one is destined to finish in a dark age, and going into it is sanctioned by society, what is the purpose of living well when younger? Thus in the long run, the mental health as well as the economic productivity of the nation as a whole may be adversely affected.

Is there any way out of the dilemma of setting women, minorities, and the handicapped against the elderly? One way might be to reverse the recent trend toward concentrating the worklife within the middle years. A study shows that the average male spent 62.3 percent of his life in the labor force in 1960 and that this decreased to 59.7 percent in 1970 and is expected to decline to even lower projected percentages in the 1980s and the 1990s, with more years spent for education when young and more years for retirement when old. Another way might be for the government to develop incentives such as tax concessions, which would allow employers to institute educational leaves and sabbaticals at certain intervals, so that jobs could be more fairly shared by women, minorities, the handicapped, and the elderly.[55]

It is also important to recognize that opening up opportunities for employment to women, minorities, and the handicapped is not a zero-sum game. That is, when persons in these categories acquire jobs, they are not necessarily taking jobs away from others. If employers implement nondiscriminatory practices in hiring employees, the best-qualified persons should be hired. Such hiring practices should increase productivity per man hour and bring about higher output without inflation; this in turn should generate greater economic activity and more opportunities for employment for all.[56]

Guaranteeing job security to a greater number of workers than now is the case at present in the United States would not necessarily reduce industrial productivity per man hour either, if industires would change their perspectives on personnel management. Japanese employment practices might be instructive here. In Japan, reorganizing and retraining employees is a constant, integral part of management practices designed to enable industries to meet economic fluctuations without cutting back the number of employees or reducing industrial productivity.

Indeed, enactment of the Full Employment and Balanced Growth Act of 1978, popularly called the Humphrey-Hawkins Bill, reiterates the merit of full employment as a national goal, which was initiated in the Employment Act of 1946. The Act of 1978 requires that the annual Economic Report of the President must include numerical goals for reducing by 1983 the rate of unemployment to 3 percent among individuals aged twenty and over and 4 percent among individuals aged sixteen and over. As the title of the Act implies, it sets forth various other goals, such as controlling inflation, relying primarily on the private sector for the creation of jobs and the expansion of economic activity, balancing the federal budget, and reducing the foreign trade deficit. Despite its relative weakness in singlehandedly implementing the policy of full employment, the Act attempts to improve and coordinate various federal programs related to manpower training and employment, such as those provided under the Comprehensive Employment and Training Act (CETA), the Job Corps, the Work Incentive (WIN) Program, and the employment programs under the Older Americans Act.

The Full Employment and Balanced Growth Act of 1978 also sets forth objectives regarding fair employment. The federal government is committed to do all that it can to reduce and ultimately eliminate the difference between the overall rate of unemployment and the rates among various disadvantaged groups within the labor force, when these differences are caused by improper factors. The groups specifically mentioned are these: youth, women, minorities, the handicapped, veterans, and middle-aged and older persons.[57]

Role of Women at Home and at Work

It is difficult to establish a cause-effect relationship between, on the one hand, the increasing rate at which women participate in the labor force and, on the other, the decreasing portion of their lives that they spend on bearing and rearing children. However, it is important to observe that these two phenomena are taking place simultaneously. This means that working women wish to establish their self-identities not only through what they do at home but also through what they do in the world of work.[58] In a society that seems to value individual achievement above the work required at home to preserve and enhance the family, it is natural for women to seek self-esteem by testing their capabilities in the labor market.[59] Nevertheless, even a society that values individual commitment to work as much as does the United States must make sure that a healthful family environment is maintained, in order to assure upcoming generations of healthy workers. How can such a society reconcile these often conflicting interests: women's quest for joining the mainstream of the world of work and society's objective of maintaining a healthful family environment?

This does not mean that women's work out of the home is always detrimental to the healthy growth of children. As experiences in Britain during World War II indicate, the well-being of children is not necessarily undermined by their mothers' working, if work schedules and other working conditions are flexible enough to meet individual families' needs.[60] However, conditions of employment in the United States have not reached such a stage, so that tension often arises from the maladjusted interface between work and family.

One way to solve this problem is to neutralize women's inclination to prefer paid work outside the home to housework. That is, society might compensate women for being homemakers. Providing income for homemaking might be a powerful inducement for women to stay at home, since a great majority of them work for economic reasons. In 1975, 84 percent of working women either had never married; were widowed, separated, or divorced; or were living with a husband earning less than $15,000 a year.[61]

What kind of a scheme can be devised for paying women to be homemakers? There seem to be two options. Providing children's allowances is one. This approach can be effective in many ways. First, allowances can be concentrated on families who not only need financial assistance but also need the mother to stay at home. Second, providing children's allowances can be considered as wise investments for assuring future personal well-being and future economic growth. However, despite all its positive features, a program of children's allowances has an important drawback. It still cannot uphold the value of women as workers, although it may reward them as mothers.

The other option is to decide that the work women do at home should be paid for and reward them accordingly. The worth of women's housework may be measured in either of two ways. One way is to evaluate the market cost of the housework if it had to be done by a paid worker; the other, to evaluate the earnings forgone by the homemaker—that is, what she could have earned if she had gone out and worked. A study by the Social Security Administration indicates that in 1972 the average market cost of the work done by a homemaker was $4,705.[62] In 1973, the forgone median earnings of a homemaker were $6,450.[63] The difference between the two approaches is that evaluating the market cost of housework would provide larger rewards to women with a larger number of dependents and a larger house to take care of and would give smaller rewards to women with lesser responsibilities; evaluating forgone earnings would reward well-educated women more than it would reward less-educated women. The first approach reflects a social welfare ideology; the second, a market-force ideology. If maintaining and enhancing a healthful family environment for coming generations is the objective, the first approach would seem to be more effective and economically efficient. Paying women to be homemakers, under either approach, could lead toward enabling homemakers to receive social security benefits on their own accounts. However, if the first approach were taken, the level of benefits would not be in proportion to the amount that the women might have been able to earn, but rather would be related to the amount of work that the family needed to have done at home. Social security as currently administered relates benefits to previous earnings.[64] Thus the first approach might invite criticism from all sides.

How can society help women who want to be both workers ouside the home and homemakers? Examples of what other nations have done may offer pertinent suggestions. Sweden allows either spouse to stay home and take care of sick children by providing 90 percent of the wages of the spouse who does this. Sweden also provides unemployment insurance to women who re-enter the labor force, with the aim of helping them upgrade their skills.[65] Many employers in Britain since World War II have developed a flexible working schedule, to enable women with children to work.[66] As these experiences abroad illustrate, and as mentioned earlier, work as an economic activity is rapidly converging with the concerns of social welfare. Sweden and other industrialized countries are searching for and implementing ways to lessen the strains that arise when the economic concerns of work meet and clash with the concerns of social welfare.

Will the United States follow the Swedish approach? The answer seems to lie in understanding *why* Sweden launched such a comprehensive scheme to help women. The Swedes simply made a rational decision to mobilize and upgrade their own female labor force to meet labor shortages, instead of inviting foreign workers to their country.[67] Thus, since the United States has no labor shortage, it is unlikely that this country will follow Sweden's pattern of helping women, at least in the short run.

However, the story of accommodating employment practices to women's needs may be quite different in the long run. Over time, society may clearly see that the well-being of each individual and family, on the one hand, and, the societal interest in keeping the family both physically and mentally healthy, on the other, are actually interdependent. Then the taxpayers throughout the country and the policymakers in Washington may find it advantageous to use public resources to develop programs for female workers, in order to help them combine housework and work outside the home more effectively for the greater well-being of all.

Job vs. Income Support: A Case of the Severely Disabled

The federal government firmly established, through the Vocational Rehabilitation Act of 1973, a public policy that requires employers to hire qualified handicapped individuals without discrimination. How does this policy really work? Can it work equally well for all disabled persons regardless of the severity of their handicaps? The Social Security Administration puts the disabled into three categories. The first category includes the severely disabled, who are unable to engage in any substantial gainful activity because they have a physical or mental impairment that can be medically determined and can be expected to last for a continuous period of not less than twelve months. Severely disabled workers may be eligible for disability benefits under social security. In the second category are the "occupationally disabled," who must change their occupations in order to continue to work. Workers in the third category are called "disabled with secondary limitations"; they can do the same jobs as before, but are restricted as to the amount of work. Given limited resources, how should society treat the disabled of varying severity?

Empirical research findings seem to show that the United States and various European countries are treating the disabled differently, according to their capabilities for earning. The severely disabled, with little capability for earning, are increasingly placed on income maintenance rolls rather than being rehabilitated to the world of work. Worse yet, individuals who are not so severely disabled, but have marginal capabilities for earning, are increasingly called severely disabled and placed on income maintenance rolls.[68] Economists tend to offer two lines of explanation. One is that economic recessions tend to push out of the labor market workers who are the most marginal economically; this often means the severely disabled, since they are likely to be at the bottom of the employment ladder. In addition, the existence of various income maintenance programs makes it relatively easy to shift a disabled person from the employed status to the status of an income maintenance recipient. The other explanation is that government agencies dealing with the disabled are behaving rationally from a benefit-cost perspective. That is, the cost of rehabilitating the severely disabled who have slight potential for earning outweighs the projected payoffs that might be obtained from their increased earnings. But the question remains: Can society treat the various categories of the disabled differently, according to the severity of their handicaps? Don't the severely disabled also have a right to join the world of work in an appropriate capacity?

American society seems to be torn between its stance of equal opportunity for employment and the economic determinants that favor one category of the disabled over others. According to Boulding, this conflict illustrates the difference between justice based on the equality of individuals before the law and justice based on the concept of deserts—or differential claims on society, based on one's contributions to society.[69]

Notwithstanding American idealism about equality before the law, empirical findings seem to indicate that the disabled are treated differently on the basis of the justice of deserts. Nobel justifies this differential treatment on the grounds that the less severely disabled can contribute more to the national output and thus can generate more taxes to support the severely disabled through income maintenance programs, with a proviso that society maintains a positive ideology for providing for the unfortunate.[70]

The foregoing arguments that favor economic efficiency need to be weighed against the intangible adverse effects on the severely disabled, who may not be able to find satisfaction in life and who may feel less accepted by others in the community when they are not permitted to work. Is society willing to spend public resources for noneconomic gains, even though such expenditures will not be economically efficient?

The answer to the question should be a positive one. As already indicated, the idea of work in America is more than an economic proposition: It is a political proposition as well. Without the positive ideology of work and the fair implementation of it to satisfy all who have marketable skills and want to work, the foundation of American society as a community of individuals committed to work will be undermined. Thus, there should be a broad concept of work that considers its political implications as well as its economic efficiency.

The challenges facing this society are clear. First, the society is challenged to create an environment in which the industrial talents and skills of all who seek work—even the severely disabled—can be identified and utilized to their maximum capacity in the mainstream of the labor market. Second, the society is challenged to explore ways in which the severely disabled can be employed, even when such employment is not economically viable to the employer. This may call for tax incentives and direct wage subsidies. To keep the American economy competitive in relation to that of other industrialized countries, the rest of the labor force needs to share the costs of subsidized employment of the disabled. Such mutual adjustment seems imperative to sustain the healthy ideology of work in America.

Welfare Programs for Individuals and Families Outside the World of Work

Just as the labor market is stratified, social welfare programs in the United States have developed three layers. At the top are various private employee benefit programs. In the middle are social insurance programs for all those who participate in the world of work. At the bottom are various welfare programs with cash and in-kind payments, primarily designed to benefit individuals and families who have slight attachment to the labor force. In going down the hierarchy of social welfare programs, the levels of benefits and the degree of social legitimacy attached to the programs decline.

An issue of social policy here is this: Why does society have to stigmatize the recipients of welfare programs? What are the functions of such stigma? One function is to uphold the basic tenet of American society regarding the value of work. A society having an economic system that depends on the voluntary choice of work over nonwork somehow has to stigmatize or make illegitimate the welfare programs for individuals and families without work records. Society then lets those who are stigmatized play deviant roles, thus controlling the nondeviants who are not permitted to cross the line to join the ranks of the deviants.[71] In the process, those in the world of work find there a reason-to-be, and they bask in self-contentment and pride. At the same time, they excuse those outside for not being inside: The outsiders, they say, can do no better. Cursing and pitying are two sides of the same coin. In the final analysis, the deviants are blamed for being deviants. That is, the poor are blamed for being poor.

But a more crucial question is this: If opportunities for employment are unlimited, being out of the labor force can sometimes be considered a voluntary choice. If it is, then the blaming of welfare recipients, which this society tends to do, may be reasonable. However, when a high unemployment rate is part of a deliberate national economic policy, being unemployed or out of the labor force in many cases is involuntary. When it is, twisting the cause-effect relationship of economic dependence from structural to individual faults seems unfair.[72]

Why does this society tend to blame the victims of economic imperfection for their economic plight? One answer may be that in a highly industrialized society, in which the great majority benefit from economic growth, personal faults are attributed to individuals and families who cannot make it to the mainstream, no matter what the cause.[73] But there seems to be more than this involved in America. Is blaming the victims part of the reward-and-punishment system that society has created to prevent the choice between work and nonwork from becoming neutral, and to make sure that work will be always preferred over nonwork? If so, the rite of blaming the victims resembles the ancient rite of sacrificing a few individuals to the forces of the supernatural so that the rest of the society may prevail. Such a comparison is not farfetched in a society which is so committed to work that people have to *work* even to collect donations for charitable causes.

Indeed stigma seems to have functions to play in society. But what about the effects of stigma on welfare families? The public's stereotyped attitudes toward welfare in general and welfare recipients in particular help indoctrinate the recipients themselves, so that their self-images become more negative and their senses of self-worth diminishes. Briar's study of welfare recipients' views shows that a majority of the recipients interviewed believed that a quarter of those receiving welfare cheated the Welfare Department.[74] Briar speculated that such self-denigration might lead to the recipients' willingness to give up their rights to the privacy ordinarily enjoyed by nonrecipients. Sixty-six percent of those surveyed conceded that the Welfare Department had a right to know how recipients spent their money; sixty-three percent believed that the department should make check-up visits at night. A subsequent study by Handler and Hollingsworth reported a similar finding: Approximately half the AFDC mothers in the Milwaukee area did not object to unannounced visits by caseworkers.[75]

The adverse socialization that takes place through blaming welfare recipients for their own economic plight may have profound effects on the children growing up in such an afflicted family environment. They may develop negative self-images and never find an opportunity to grow to their potential. Is this society including these children among the sacrificial individuals and families that it is willing to discount and discard? Whether society intends to reproach and condemn welfare children or not, they are bound to be victims also when their parents are stigmatized for nonwork—and nonwork is damned in order to assure perpetual allegiance to the high value of work. Put another way, nonwork has been damned to glorify work to a point of cultural hysteria. It is a challenge for American society to find a balance between *yin* and *yang* (the feminine passive principle and the masculine active principle, which together made up being, according to Chinese cosmology), so that nonwork can be justified in some circumstances, and, at the same time, work can continue to be valued and appreciated.

How can American society develop the *yin* and *yang* relationship between work and nonwork, so that families unwillingly disfranchised from the world of work can find a legitimate place in society and be cared for through legitimate programs?

To find an answer, we need to know why the adverse relationship between work and nonwork developed in America to start with. Has the value attached to work been overemphasized in developing social policy? Does this society need to search for other values, around which social policy might be developed? Could one of these be the value attached to family? If social policy could be developed around this value, various publicly supported programs could be devised, which would have nothing to do with the employment status of the head of the family. Then such programs as children's allowances and maternity benefits might be more readily accepted in America. If they were introduced, female heads of one-parent families would not be needlessly pushed into the labor force, contrary to their desires; their economic needs could be met through unstigmatized, legitimate programs. Social policy developed around the value of family might also lead to employment practices—such as flexible work schedules and the provision of day care—that would make working conditions better suited to family needs.

Would the development of social policy around the value of family deter economic growth and the building of the American nation? At this stage of the post-industrial era, this does not seem likely. Rather, such development would seem complementary to social policy developed around the value of work. In the early days of industrialization and nation building, this country may have had to rely on the value of work alone to channel the energy of millions of people of all backgrounds into the production of goods and services. But today the United States is in a different, advanced stage of industrialization and nation building. To develop further as a nation, preserving and developing human resources seems just as important as utilizing man hours efficiently. This means, first of all, that the capabilities of every child—regardless of how his family participates in the world of work—need to be cultivated to their fullest. Such a new direction in nation building might lead to a new burst of economic growth as well.

Developing social policy based on the value of family is not an easy thing to do in America, however. Upholding publicly the value of family may conflict with other values, such as individualism, feminism, and privacy, all of which are tied to the value of work.[76] But the American public will have to be led to face the conflict in the American value system that is straining so many families. Facing the conflict and making a rational trade-off may enable the public to deal with the value of work more effectively and realistically.

Conclusions

A steady rise in the living standards of the people in this country has been made possible by the dynamic energy generated in individual Americans. That energy sprang largely from the common belief that work contributed to the building of the nation and that it would bring opportunities for cultivating individual faculties. It is a fine and democratic game that, in principle, applies to all, regardless of race, sex, and national origin. The reality, however, has been far from the ideal; despite the gap, Americans' commitment to work has been remarkably stable and high.

Notwithstanding the widespread complacency about the world of work, policymakers need to be constantly aware of a need to improve employment practices. If the American people should become convinced that these practices are grossly unfair, their disillusionment might well loosen the basic bond that links them together—a bond built by their common belief in the fair game in the world of work. In the absence of other bonds—religion, culture, political ideology—a sudden discovery of gross injustice in the world of work might make them feel aimless, let down, hopeless, and alienated from each other. The nation might lose direction and collective energy, and diminish in character. Constant attempts by policymakers to improve employment practices seem necessary to keep the nation moving forward.

Developing and implementing social policy to widen the door to decent jobs for formerly disadvantaged groups of individuals are not easy tasks. Eonomic limitations, trade-offs among various values involved in policy options, spill-over effects, and long-range effects need to be studied and debated before we can launch new policies.

Although the value of work has been indispensable in the building of this nation, the American people have adhered to it so extremely that it has almost blocked them from finding a positive way to provide for individuals and families disfranchised from the world of work. As this nation enters the third century of its growth and seeks to shift the emphasis from quantity to quality in living, is it not imperative to find a breakthrough and to develop a positive philosophical rationale for providing for the unfortunate few?

It is vital now to determine clearly the values on which the nation's future social policy will be based. These are among the questions that policymakers need to ask themselves:

- Should social policy continue to revolve around the value of work alone? Or should it involve other values as well—such as the value of the family?
- In dealing with the disadvantaged and handicapped workers, should the value of work be applied to all, even the severely disabled? Should getting the disabled into the mainstream of the world of work be attempted, even though it is not economically efficient?
- In dealing with families having no participation in the world of work, should efforts be made to remove or reduce the stigma from nonwork? What can be done to protect the children of nonworkers from this stigma, which constrains and represses and may deaden the will?

This nation is at the crossroads. A new direction in its building—one that makes the most of the capabilities of *all* its people in the home as well as in the world of work—could well lead to a new rise in industrial productivity, a new burst of economic growth, an upsurge of morale, and the development of a more humane community.

Notes

[1] U.S. Bureau of the Census, *Statistical Abstracts of the United States, 1978* (Washington, D.C.: U.S. Government Printing Office, 1978), Table 685, p. 423; and Paul O. Flaim and Nicholas I. Peters, "Usual Weekly Earnings of American Workers," *Monthly Labor Review*, 95, no. 3 (March 1972), Table 2, 30.

[2] *Statistical Abstracts 1978*, Table 685, p. 423.

[3] Wendy C. Wolf and Neil D. Fligstein, "Sex and Authority in the Work Place: The Case of Sex and Inequality," Institute for Research on Poverty Discussion Paper No. 506-78, University of Wisconsin Institute for Research on Poverty, 1978.

[4] For discussion on the human capital theory, see Gary S. Becker, *Human Capital* (New York: National Bureau of Economic Research, 1964); Yoram Ben-Porath, "The Production of Human Capital and the Life Cycle of Earnings," *Journal of Political Economy*, 75, no. 4 (August 1967), 352-365; and Jacob Mincer, "Distribution of Labor Income: A Survey," *Journal of Economic Literature* 8 (March 1973), 1-26.

[5] Aage B. Sørenson, "Growth in Occupational Achievement: Social Mobility or Investment in Human Capital," in Kenneth C. Land and Seymour Spilerman, eds., *Social Indicator Models* (New York: Russell Sage Foundation, 1975), p. 339.

[6] Edward Kalachek and Fredric Raines, "The Structure of Wage Differences among Mature Male Workers," *Journal of Human Resources* 11 (Summer 1976), 484–506.

[7] Charles N. Halaby, "Sexual Inequality in the Workplace: An Employer-Specific Analysis of Pay Differences," Institute for Research on Poverty Discussion Paper No. 502-78, University of Wisconsin Institute for Research on Poverty, 1978.

[8] Wolf and Fligstein, "Sex and Authority in the Work Place."

[9] Duane E. Leigh, "Job Experience and Earnings among Middle-Aged Men," *Industrial Relations* 15 (May 1976), 144.

[10] For detailed discussion on the theory of the segmented labor market, see Seymour Spilerman, "Careers, Labor Market Structure, and Social Achievement," *American Journal of Sociology* 83, no. 3 (November 1977), 551–93.

[11] See Glen G. Cain, "The Challenge of Segmented Labor Market Theories to Orthodox Theory," *Journal of Economic Literature* 12, no. 4, (December 1976), 1215–57.

[12] *Employment and Training Report of the President, 1978* (Washington, D.C.: U.S. Government Printing Office, 1978), Tables A-1 and A-4, pp. 179, 186–88.

[13] Ibid., Table B-4, p. 238.

[14] Paul Glick and Arthur Norton, "Perspectives on the Recent Upturn in Divorce and Remarriage," *Demography* 10 (August 1973), 303.

[15] *Employment and Training Report of the President, 1978*, Table B-1, pp. 233–34.

[16] U.S. Department of Commerce, Bureau of the Census, *U.S. Census of Population: 1970, Subject Reports,* PC(2)-4A (Washington, D.C.: U.S. Government Printing Office, 1973), Table 5, p. 23 and U.S. Department of Commerce, Bureau of the Census, *Current Population Reports,* Series P-20, No. 326, "Household and Family Characteristics, March 1977" (Washington, D.C.: U.S. Government Printing Office, 1978), Tables 1 and 4, pp. 10, 33.

[17] Wendy C. Wolf and Maurice MacDonald, "The Earnings of Males and Marital Disruption," Institute for Research on Poverty Discussion Paper No. 504-78, University of Wisconsin Institute for Research on Poverty, 1978, p. 3.

[18] Lee Rainwater, "Work, Well-Being, and Family Life," in James O'Toole, ed., *Work and the Quality of Life: Resource Papers for Work in America* (Cambridge, Mass.: MIT Press, 1974), pp. 366–67 and Alan Sheldon, J. M. Peters, and Carol Ryser, *Retirement: Patterns and Predictions* (Washington, D.C.: U.S. Government Printing Office, 1975), p. 15.

[19] Robert Blauner, *Alienation and Freedom: The Factory Worker and His Industry* (Chicago: University of Chicago Press, 1964), p. 19.

[20] Barry Bluestone, "Low-Wage Industries and the Working Poor," *Poverty and Human Resources Abstract* 3, no. 3 (May–June 1968) Supplement, p. 9.

[21] Robert S. Eckley, "Company Action to Stabilize Employment," *Harvard Business Review,* XLIV, no. 4 (1966), 52.

[22] Bluestone, "Low-Wage Industries," p. 11.

[23] A. H. Maslow, *Motivation and Personality* (New York: Harper & Co., 1954).

[24] Gary A. Yukland and Kenneth N. Wexley, *Readings in Organizational and Industrial Psychology* (Chicago: University of Chicago Press, 1964), p. 153.

[25] Daniel Yankelovich, "The Meaning of Work," in Jerome M. Rosow, ed., *The Worker and the Job* (Englewood Cliffs, N.J.: Prentice-Hall, 1974), p. 35.

[26] Blauner, *Alienation and Freedom,* p. 22.

[27] Michael J. Piore, "Upward Mobility, Job Monotony, and Labor Market Structure," in O'Toole, ed., *Work and the Quality of Life,* p. 81.

[28] *Work in America,* Report of a Special Task Force to the Secretary of Health, Education, and Welfare (Cambridge, Mass.: MIT Press, 1973), p. 12.

[29] Ibid , p. 82.

[30] Richard E. Walton, "Alienation and Innovation in the Workplace," in O'Toole, ed., *Work and the Quality of Life*, pp. 229-30.

[31] Harold Wool, "What's Wrong with Work in America: A Review Essay," *Monthly Labor Review* 96, no. 3 (March 1973), 41.

[32] Albert Rees, "The Labor-Supply Results of the Experiment: A Summary," in Harold W. Watts and Albert Rees, eds., *The New Jersey Income-Maintenance Experiment, Volume II: Labor Supply Responses* (New York: Academic Press, 1977), pp. 5-32.

[33] Robert L. Kahn, "The Meaning of Work: Interpretation and Proposals for Measurement," in Angus Campbell and Philip E. Converse, eds., *The Human Meaning of Social Change* (New York: Russell Sage Foundation, 1972), pp. 173-74.

[34] For detailed discussion, Martha N. Ozawa, "Social Insurance and Redistribution," in Alvin L. Schorr, ed., *Jubilee for Our Times* (New York: Columbia University Press, 1977), pp. 144-49.

[35] Donna Allen, *Fringe Benefits: Wages or Social Obligation?* (Ithaca, N.Y.: Cornell University Press, 1964), p. 27.

[36] Jack Barbash, "The Structure and Evolution of Union Interests in Pensions," in *Old Age Assurance*, Part IV, U.S. Congress, Subcommittee on Fiscal Policy of the Joint Economic Committee, 90th Congress, 1st session (Washington, D.C.: U.S. Government Printing Office, 1967), pp. 63-64.

[37] Allen, *Fringe Benefits*, p. 40.

[38] Alfred M. Skolnik, "Twenty-Five Years of Employee-Benefit Plans, 1950-74," *Social Security Bulletin* 39. no. 9 (September 1976). 8; and Martha Remy Yohalem, "Employee Benefit Plans, 1975," *Social Security Bulletin* 40, no. 11 (November 1977), 19-28.

[39] Skolnik, "Twenty-Five Years," p. 4.

[40] Walter W. Kolodrubetz, "Earnings Replacement from Private Pensions and Social Security," *Reaching Retirement Age: Findings from a Survey of Newly Entitled Workers, 1968-70,* Social Security Administration, Office of Research and Statistics, Research Report No. 47 (Washington, D.C.: U.S. Government Printing Office, 1976), Tables 13.9 and 13.14, pp. 194, 198.

[41] Charles S. Wilder, "Time Loss for Work among the Currently Employed Population," *Vital and Health Statistics,* Series 10:71, National Center for Health Statistics (Washington, D.C.: U.S. Government Printing Office, 1972).

[42] Walter W. Kolodrubetz, "Characteristics of Workers with Pension Coverage on the Longest Job," *Reaching Retirement Age: Findings from a Survey of Newly Entitled Workers, 1968-70,* pp. 151-85.

[43] Skolnik, "Twenty-Five Years."

[44] Charles A. Reich, "The New Property," *Public Interest*, no. 3 (Spring 1966), 57-89.

[45] 42 U.S.C. § 2000e et seq.

[46] 41 C.F.R. chap. 60.

[47] 29 U.S.C. § 793(a).

[48] 29 U.S.C. § 794.

[49] Public Law 95-256, 95th Congress.

[50] *Employment and Training Report of the President, 1978*, Tables A-14 and A-18, pp. 202, 210.

[51] For discussion of this kind of "ratchet effect," see William H. Branson and James M. Litvack, *Macro Economics* (New York: Harper and Row, 1976), p. 207.

[52] Arnold R. Weber, "The Rich and the Poor: Employment in an Age of Automation," *Social Service Review* 27, no. 3 (1964), 254.

[53] For a detailed discussion, see Martha N. Ozawa, "The Earnings Test in Social Security," *The Social Welfare Forum, 1978* (New York: Columbia University Press, 1979), pp. 152-66.

[54] Sørenson, "Growth in Occupational Achievement," p. 341.

[55] Fred Best and Barry Stern, "Education, Work, and Leisure: Must They Come in That Order?" *Monthly Labor Review* 100, no. 7 (July 1977), 3–10.

[56] Isabel V. Sawhill, "Perspectives on Women and Work in America," in O'Toole, ed., *Work and the Quality of Life*, pp. 99–102.

[57] *Congressional Record–Senate*, October 13, 1978.

[58] Karl E. Taeuber and James A. Sweet, "Family and Work: The Social Life Cycle of Women," in Juanita M. Kreps, ed., *Women and the American Economy: A Look to the 1980s* (Englewood Cliffs, N.J.: Prentice-Hall, 1976), pp. 49–50.

[59] See Martha N. Ozawa, "Women and Work," *Social Work* 21, no. 6 (November 1976), 455; and Alvin L. Schorr, "Family Values and Public Policy: A Venture in Prediction and Prescription," *Journal of Social Policy* 1, Pt. 1 (January 1972), 33–43.

[60] Pearl Jephcott, *Married Women Working* (London: George Allen & Unwin, 1962).

[61] Anne Draper, "Why Women Work," *AFL-CIO American Federationist* 84, no. 5 (May 1977), 22–23.

[62] Wendyce H. Brody, "Economic Value of a Housewife," *Research and Statistics*, Note No. 9–1975 (Washington, D.C.: Social Security Administration, Office of Research and Statistics, 1975).

[63] Thomas F. Bradshaw and John F. Stinson, "Trends in Weekly Earnings: An Analysis," *Monthly Labor Review* 98, no. 8 (August 1975), 26.

[64] Currently, wives who have no earnings record are provided with dependent allowances equivalent to 50 percent of the worker's benefit.

[65] Alice H. Cook, *The Working Mother: A Survey of Problems and Programs in Nine Countries* (Ithaca, N.Y.: Cornell University School of Industrial and Labor Reltions, 1975), pp. 14, 44.

[66] Jephcott, *Married Women Working*.

[67] Cook, *The Working Mother*, p. 58.

[68] Sar A. Levitan and Robert Taggart, *Jobs for the Disabled* (Baltimore: Johns Hopkins University Press, 1977); and John N. Noble, "Rehabilitating the Severely Disabled: The Foreign Experience," a paper delivered at a seminar on current policy issues regarding disability, sponsored by the Disability and Health Economics Research Section, Rutgers University, February 28, 1978.

[69] Kenneth E. Boulding, *Beyond Economics: Essays on Society, Religion, and Ethics* (Ann Arbor: University of Michigan Press, 1968), pp. 49–50.

[70] Noble, "Rehabilitating," p. 17.

[71] Erving Goffman, *Stigma: Notes on the Management of Spoiled Identity* (Englewood Cliffs, N.J.: Prentice-Hall, 1963).

[72] William Ryan, *Blaming the Victim* (New York: Vintage Books, 1971).

[73] Harold L. Wilensky, "Class, Class Consciousness, and American Workers," in William Haber, ed., *Labor in a Changing America* (New York: Basic Books, 1966), p. 39.

[74] Scott Briar, "Welfare from Below: Recipients' View of the Public Welfare System," *California Law Review*, 54 (May 1966), 370–85.

[75] Joel F. Handler and Ellen Jane Hollingsworth, "Stigma, Privacy, and Other Attitudes of Welfare Recipients," *Stanford Law Review* 22 (November 1969), 4.

[76] For a detailed discussion, see Sheila B. Kamerman and Alfred J. Kahn, "Exploration in Family Policy," *Social Work* 21, no. 3 (May 1976), 181–86; and Shirley Zimmerman, "The Family and its Relevance for Social Policy," *Social Casework* 57, no. 9 (November 1976), 547–54.

4

Work, Personal Change, and Human Development

Leon W. Chestang, Ph.D.
Wayne State University

This chapter is one of the first attempts in the social work literature to include and emphasize a "work focus" in teaching human growth, developmental phases, and the social environment. It asserts the significance of work in its own terms and does so in a manner consonant with the author's commitment to work and the ideas of Freud, Erikson, and Maslow.

The main argument is that in order to teach the subject of social work, we must include the element of work. To fail to do so is to attend to only a part of the developmental and maturational process. Chestang suggests that we have tended to pay more attention to love, eros, and intimacy than to work, creativity, and performance. If we are to reach a synthesis in which neither love nor work dominates our explanations, they must merge as complementary.

Love (or its quest) and work (or its pursuit) are separate life events only for didactic or analytical purposes. In life (or, as Bertha Reynolds would say, "in social living") the two merge and become interdependent, each, however, having the potential for a reciprocal impact upon the other. The implications for teaching and for practice readily follow. Work (like love) becomes a microcosm of life. Clients' styles of coping with work may provide models for coping in familial and social situations. Hence, in any setting in which we practice, Chestang would ask us to reflect on how much we know when we know about a client's work for a differential assessment about his social functioning and the nature of his problem(s). While work frequently may represent a relatively "conflict-free sphere" (in Heinz Hartman's sense) and not predict social functioning in other spheres, functioning in both arenas may essentially be the same. Work may in fact be the easier realm for the client in the initial phase of the helping process. The important point, however, is that either similarity or difference in functioning in these two areas represents a significant consideration.

Students must be taught to help clients talk about their work (or lack of it) as well as their family lives, social networks, and early experiences. To do otherwise is to explore only partially, and would constitute an error of omission. It may send the message to the client that work is not important, or, worse still, that the social worker simply does not understand the range of what is significant in his or her life. Thus, "tell me about your work" is as important as "tell me about your life, your family, your friends."

The dual reality of love and work (or job and family) may be most apparent, as one Wingspread conferee noted, for the more than one million working women who will become pregnant this year. How they deal (or do not deal) with the often conflicting life demands of work, career, and intellectual generativity, on the one hand, and love, family, and parenthood on the other, are compelling issues stated, unspoken, or implied.

Another Wingspread attendee observed that work is a major theme—if not the central theme—in clinical social work practice, in general, and in family treatment in particular. She noted, therefore, that industrial social workers cannot practice well without a focus on the family; and, similarly, that family therapists in typical mental health settings usually are most productive when they focus with family members on the complementarity and counterpoint of their social functioning in the world of work.*

In a somewhat Eriksonian sense, and with acknowledgments to Perlman and Mahler, Chestang takes a close look at life's transitions and the evolutionary adaptations that take place in the life cycle with particular attention to love and work. He illustrates the inherent reciprocity between the two as they mutually condition one another. Much as Alfred Adler might argue, people have a need to make a contribution, to make their marks, even to reach for a bit of immortality, and one's work, along with one's children, may represent such an effort even for those in what might appear to us to be humble occupations.

Clearly, work is not always fulfilling or a matter of choice—fostering growth of the mind, the body, and the human spirit. Frequently it is routine, unsatisfying or stressful—a means toward the end of economic survival. Sometimes it is physically hazardous and toxic or emotionally exhausting and unrewarding. Such are the exchanges inherent in workforce participation, particularly, as the author notes, for racial minorities, for women, and for the disabled. We are already familiar with these exchanges and paradoxes in the demands and rewards in family-centered

---

*We are grateful to our colleague, Professor Florence Vigilante, for calling this interrelationship to our attention.

roles of maturation, separation, marriage, parenthood, and passing; now we need a consciousness-raising to their parallel relevance in the domain of work.

Finally, Chestang notes that it was not the purpose of this chapter—nor the larger goal of this book—to add on another dimension called "work" to our teaching function. Rather, the explicit goal is our need to integrate the concept of work into what we teach and already have mastered, so that our message will reflect the reality of life as much for our clients as for ourselves.

Work has been the subject of many venerable adages: "Man shall live by the sweat of his brow." "Work is not only a way of making a living; it is a way of making a life." These adages, intended to inspire and motivate, first were given voice by authorities and moral leaders. In recent years, however, these external sources of inspiration and motivation have given way to more personal and private reflections on the meaning and function of work in the life of each person. In the wake of the technological explosion, the civil rights movement, and, more recently, the women's movement, work and working have become more than the scourge of man or a moral imperative. They have become the subject of serious political and philosophical discussion, the aim of which is to understand the meaning of work and how to actualize its potential for a person's growth and development.

This new attitude toward work and the searches that it has inspired grows out of the recognition that work is an activity central to survival, personal change, and human development. Moreover, work has come to be accepted as an integral aspect of personal identity, with the potential for fostering a person's sense of social contribution and validating the meaningfulness of one's life. Therefore, the ability and the opportunity to work—vital during adolescence and young adulthood—have significant ramifications throughout the entire life cycle.

The aim of this paper is to outline and discuss some of the important considerations, including theory, research, issues, and problems related to work as a factor in human development. This will be done in the context of highlighting significant human behavior content, which will heighten the awareness of social work students to this vital aspect of life and enhance their effectiveness in dealing with individuals, families, and groups where work is a central element of social functioning.

Personal and Social Meanings of Work

The point is deceptively simple: What one does, how well one does it, and the feedback one gets from others all contribute to the development of a sense of who one is. Not only does work contribute to the sense of who one is, it also gives stability and continuity to that sense once it has been established. Work, then, is a central element in achieving and maintaining a sense of personal identity.[1]

The much-quoted formula attributed to Freud that the ability to love and to work is the keystone of mental health points to the fundamental nature of work as an internal organizer. This assumption merits elaboration. If love and loving imply relating the self to another with warmth and caring, abandoning narcissistic, selfish interests, then work and working imply investing the self in meaningful, valued activity for the purpose of concretizing experience and validating one's place in the social system. Robert White has shown that pleasure in activity—even when it is not purposive—aids the development of ego capacities in infants.[2] In a similar vein, Perlman has discussed the role of work in requiring the "steady maintenance of certain disciplined modes of self—and task—management. Impulsive and irrelevant motivations must be held in leash."[3] The formulations of White and Perlman suggest that the play-activity of the child, like the regularized, purposive activity of the adult, serve at these different stages of life to organize the person's inner world and to help him subdue the disorganizing influences of unrestrained drives and motivations.

The paradox of work is that it is both private and public in its meaning for the person. These two dimensions of work have been examined, though not always emphasized, in social work literature. Studs Terkel's popular volume on the subject addresses some of the personal meanings of work in our time. His book, he says,

> . . . is about a search . . . for daily meaning as well as cash, for astonishment rather than torpor; in short for a sort of life rather than a Monday through Friday sort of dying. Perhaps immortality, too, is part of the quest. To be remembered was the wish, spoken and unspoken, of the heroes and heroines of my book.[4]

These are the private meanings of work. We will include more about this later, as our subject is examined at different stages of life.

The other side of the paradox—work's public ramifications—is equally important to an understanding of how this activity affects human development and social functioning. These ramifications have been summarized in another context by Perlman:

> Work, at its least, then, offers a man or woman these rewards: a social identity and linkage with other persons of his age, sex, and status; a socially recognized function.[5]

The public ramifications of work are all the more pertinent to this discussion, for in our age of equalitarianism, it has become fashionable to avoid discussions of one's line of work. Many younger persons hold that to talk about one's occupation is to assume a false identity through one's job. Those who agree with this view believe that a person's real self should somehow emerge through person-to-person interaction around some undefined topic. Their belief, firmly held, is that a person is more than what he or she works at. There is, of course, more than a small truth to this position, but the problem is how to make observable and how to activate what that something-more-than-one's-job is.

The problem with this line of reasoning is that it fails to distinguish exaggerated efforts to gain status or bolster the self from legitimate and appropriate identification with and pride in one's work. Further, this line of thought fails to appreciate the interrelationship between the public and the private significance of work. That interrelationship is this: Most fundamentally, the world of work provides the person with a sense of having an impact on his environment. This, in turn, contributes to one's sense of competence and self-esteem. At the same time, these private meanings of work have social significance. Through work, the person is linked to a social network of other persons of similar age, sex, and education. In addition, work serves to integrate the person in his culture, for in the exercise of one's job functions, each person becomes a practitioner of those trades and crafts, arts and sciences, professions and business enterprises, and—yes—drudgeries and "dirty work" that are esteemed or at least essential to the perpetuation of the culture. In this way, bearing the burdens of one's work becomes public testimony that one is a bearer of one's culture. In their turn, comrades and contemporaries, by their judgments and praise, their criticism and commendation, contribute to the person's private estimate of his worth and inner sense of satisfaction, both with the self and the products of his efforts.

The concrete and material rewards that working brings are no less important than the emotional and psychological implications discussed above. Let me state the obvious—through work a man or a woman is able to secure his or her most basic needs for food, clothing, and shelter. Through the independent pursuit of these, a person conforms to the physical requirements for survival. That this is done signifies that one adheres to the cultural expectation that the mature person should provide for himself or herself and for those for whom he or she is responsible.

The relationship between material rewards and cultural expectations has further implications. If the fact of working is testimony to adhering to cultural expectations, then the ability to acquire the symbols of success—such as homes and cars and television sets—or to buy books, attend concerts, and travel is evidence that work yields those things valued in the culture or at least in one's immediate society. This, in turn, gives status to the person, both because of what he possesses and because he acquired this through his own efforts.

The social status flowing from work goes further still. The particular type of work one does, that is one's specific occupation, how well one does it, and the estimate of its value by the society all contribute to the status a person enjoys on account of working. Before saying more, it should be pointed out that the term "status" as used here does not imply self-centered attempts to diminish others by flaunting one's attainments. It refers instead to the recognition *granted by others* as a token of their appreciation and esteem of the person and his products. In this light, the practitioner of medicine and the machinist, the lawyer and the laborer, each can potentially derive status from his or her work.

"Meaning," that much overused word in our time, sounds almost too weighty to be used in this context. Yet it remains relevant and true to say that work is a way of finding meaning in one's life. This assertion can be made in very practical terms: A person, at some point during his working life, usually at middle age and beyond, comes to question what his life has been about. Beyond personal identity, material benefits, and social status, this question addresses the issues of the essence of life and the role of the individual in it. And beyond procreation and the preservation of the species, the meaning of life for the individual human being is intricately and significantly tied to work.[6] In clarification of this point, it must be said that work is the arena in which the person experiences vitality in the exercise of his competencies and skills, in which he tests his abilities, in which he pushes himself, sometimes to the limit, in the effort to do the better job. Work is also the arena in which the person experiences the satisfaction of a job well done.

Work as a way of finding meaning in one's life brings together the personal and social dimensions of our subject. One's fellows on the job by their comaraderies, by their support and commendation, are making an evaluation which in combination with one's own assessment, gives a greater substance to one's efforts and at the same time relates one to a social world. When one's work is valued and has significance within some group or societal context, an important aspect of the meaningfulness of life is experienced firsthand.

From the above outline, then, work can be said to be related to human development in at least four ways: (1) as an internal organizer (2) as social learning (3) as a source of social recognition and status, and (4) as a way of finding meaning in one's life. These are familiar themes to the student of human behavior, but the role of work in facilitating or blocking the attainment of these human needs has not been a focus in the theoretical and practical instruction of students entering the profession. Some theoretical perspectives and concepts, which have the potential for illuminating understanding of this dimension of life, are discussed in the sections below.

Some Useful Theoretical Perspectives and Concepts

Freud's famous dictum about the ability to love and to work established the contribution of work to human development. A number of other perspectives also are relevant, either because they specifically address work as a factor in human development or because they address issues related to prework skills or issues related to particular stages of life.

Work as an Internal Organizer

From earliest infancy, the human organism engages in activity, which, according to Robert White, gives pleasure in itself but which also promotes the evolution of ego potentials and personality organization. These activities are reflected in the infant's focusing attention on people, reaching and grasping for objects, and learning to wait and to delay gratification. Behaviors such as these are important, White says, because they foster a *sense of effectance*. Further, as the infant accumulates experience and gratification through these activities, the *sense of competence* is enhanced. Thus, White proposes, these activities become ends in themselves, leading the infant to be motivated by effectance (the desire to have an effect on the environment) and competence (the pleasurable experience derived from having had an effect).

Ego psychologist Margaret Mahler has also discussed the internal organizing functions of interactions between mother and child during the first years of life. The mother's holding, feeding, touching, and talking are essential to the development of the sense of self and awareness of the environment. This process occurs, however, in a symbiotic union between mother and child. This idea emphasizes the mutual and reciprocal nature of these interactions, calling attention to the importance of the child's response as his contribution to the process.[7] These early transactions between mother and child and between the child and objects in the environment aid internal organization by awakening ego potentials and by enhancing the child's awareness of self, space, time, and objects. These acquisitions have broad implications for personality development, but they also are relevant to a discussion of work, because these behaviors and acquisitions can be viewed as crucial prework attainments, fundamental to the person's later ability to engage in formal, structured work. For example, the inability to focus attention on a task or to delay the pleasures of the moment (surrendering to the least distraction) may originate in the early experiences and socialization of the person.

The infant's early activity is fundamental to the later ability to work, but it is not work itself. These early activities are precursors to work, and the internal organization they foster is a stage-appropriate step in a continuing process, to be taken over by other steps appropriate to each subsequent stage of life. The play-work of the preschool child is another of these steps. Taking care of dolls, "working" in and around the home "like Mommy and Daddy," or going off to work like parents is a stage appropriate way for children of this age to acquire a sense of routine and the regularity of chores and to further consolidate the growing sense of effectance and competence. The sense of one's place in a particular family, including roles and expectations, gives coherence to one's sense of self. Thus, the child's play-work and the parent's real expectations that she will put the toys back in their place when she is finished with them; that she will respect the property and feelings of others in the family; and that she will become increasingly autonomous all contribute important elements to the child's perception of herself as a member of her particular family and as a person with unique competencies.

As the child matures into latency, she usually is assigned more specific and structured tasks. These, of course, may be related to home, but for many children, actual paid work experiences begin. Whether putting out the garbage at home, doing errands for family and neighbors, baby-sitting, selling newspapers, mowing lawns, or any of a myriad of other jobs done by latency-age children, this work, in addition to any monetary reward it carries, brings also a stronger connection that "I can." Thus, Erikson's industry and White's effectance and competence are made concrete and operational in the latency-age child's growing (sometimes exaggerated) belief in herself and in her abilities. For our purpose, it is important to remember that this connection was earned through the child's own work.

Work in adolescence is an arena for experimenting and testing, contemplating the future, and planning—albeit the adolescent's plans may be revised many times. The spurt of physical growth and the bodily changes that accompany it, the emergence of more complex intellectual operations, combined with the novelty and profundity of introspection lead the adolescent to imagine untold horizons at one moment and to experience confusion, if not despair, the next. Work during this period of life can serve the dual functions of providing adolescents with a real experience against which to test their abilities and to begin the process of choosing a career, and of harmonizing the seemingly discordant strains of changing physique, strange emotions, and recurring questions about the future. The working activity accomplishes this by being a vehicle for the expenditure of excess energy arising from impulses and by answering in concrete ways the adolescent's questions as to: Who am I? Where am I going? And what will I do when I get there?

The function of work as a regularized activity comes into the foreground in young adulthood and beyond. The human need for order is well established, and work offers order and consistency to one's days. Most individuals accustomed to going to work each day become frustrated and irritable (if not anxious) if the opportunity to work is removed for an extended period of time. This response is seen as frequently among persons working in their own homes as it is among those employed outside of the home. Witness the many women who seek "something to do" when their children achieve the independence of going to high school and college. This response is also seen with regularity among persons with adequate financial means, and even when financial need is not present, we still hear workers commenting on their satisfaction in having something to do. Work organizes one's time, with its established hours for beginning and ending the work day. The knowledge that one is expected on the job is an impetus to struggle against inclinations toward lethargy or indolence. As such, a sense of responsibility and commitment to tasks is strengthened, contributing to the coherence of personality and identity.

In later life, what one has worked at can become a source of solace, as one looks back at jobs well done. In this way, ego integrity, which is the sense that what one has done is acceptable to the self, provides an abiding feeling that death does not signal the end of one's meaning. The life review for the older person should include a large measure of work history, for all that has been said to this point suggests that an imprint of one's mark in the world is made by the force of one's work. It must be added that the organizing function of work does not end with advancing years. The continuing contributions of older persons who work as volunteers on many fronts or who continue to work at jobs on reduced schedules serve to keep intact their senses of identity and self-esteem through the work itself and the independence giving self-esteem that it makes possible.

With the above in mind, the statement (indifferently made by some uninvested workers) that their jobs are merely "a place to go" and the prescription, often medically given, that a person "needs something to do" take on a deeper meaning.

They suggest very simply that without this "place to go" or this "something to do" one's life would be threatened by the absence of a way to use one's time, rendering the individual vulnerable to a lack of purpose and order, increasing the potential for the upsurge and expression of personally and socially injurious actions.

Work as Social Learning

Many human behaviors are acquired by watching another person, that is by observation of a model. This idea applies to people of all ages, but it is especially relevant to an understanding of the manner in which children acquire attitudes, preferences, and skills related to work. Several principles cited by Kagan and others and drawn from experiments by Bandura can be stated as follows:

1. The acquisition of imitative responses is affected by whether or not the model is rewarded or punished by his acts.
2. Learning is more likely to occur when the organism wants or needs to obtain a certain goal.
3. Subjects are more likely to imitate the behavior of prestigeful than non-prestigeful models.
4. Models who are similar to the subjects themselves have a greater effect on behavior than dissimilar models.[8]

The implications of these principles for children's acquisition of attitudes toward work and work habits are clear, but a brief comment on each of them will further demonstrate their implications for persons of other ages as well.

Repeating behaviors modeled by parents is a part of every child's repertoire. Parental reinforcement of these imitative responses increases the likelihood that the child eventually will learn (adopt as his or her own) the desired response. This pattern of imitation-reinforcement-adoption is, of course, the way much of childhood learning occurs. Through repetition of parental verbalizations and of parental behaviors during feedings, and through imitating parental behaviors in numerous other situations, children acquire the desired responses. In like manner, children acquire attitudes, orientations, and skills related to work. Observing parents doing household tasks in the home introduces the child to the idea that someone must prepare the meals, clean the house, mow the lawn, make needed repairs, and do a host of other jobs if the family is to function. Moreover, the child may observe the parents jointly participating in these tasks, or the child may witness a division of labor. In the course of performing these duties, the parents convey important attitudinal orientations toward work. These orientations suggest how the parents feel about work, the quality of their acceptance of the necessity of work, and their perspectives on certain work as being sex-typed. What the child is learning can readily be observed in his or her imitative behavior, that is, the desire to cook like Mommy, if that is the pattern in the home, or fix or build like Daddy, if the traditional pattern is followed by the family. Whatever the family's pattern, however, the child's observations of the parents' activities and attitudes become essential ingredients of his or her own perspective on work.

The relationship between investment in work and obtaining a certain goal is the point of Bandura's second principle. This idea is applicable to early childhood as well as to other stages of life. The young child picks up his toys at the end of a play session in order to please the parents; teacher reinforcement and parental rewards motivate the child to invest in school work; a vacation, a new car, or a promotion gives impetus to the adult's willingness to extend himself or herself in work. These and many other goals that have meaning for an individual lighten the burden, spark the motivation, and heighten interest in working.

The status, relationship, and skill of the model also are important motivators, because a person is more likely to emulate prestigeful than non-prestigeful models. The social and personal value placed on prestige makes such models desirable to the person and suggests to the learner that he or she can hope to attain a similar position. Small wonder, then, that commercials and other forms of advertising rely on professional athletes, actors, and, more recently, respected political figures to convey their messages. The success of advertising campaigns can be accounted for in part by the public's trust in such persons, but it is also explained by the public's desire to emulate these prestigeful models. When the learner's relationship with the model is characterized by warmth, respect, and emotional support, the relationship becomes the foundation on which all other learning, technical and attitudinal, occurs. Through a positive relationship with the learner, models convey their focused interest in and concern for the welfare of the learner, thereby opening the learner to accept the model and the message. The writer's research suggests that this factor was a vital element in the willingness of a group of black youths to accept the teaching of models, regardless of the models' race.[9]

The fourth principle set forth by Bandura suggests that a model who is similar to the learners themselves has a greater effect on behavior than a dissimilar model. Again, the advertising industry has capitalized on this principle by using children to promote products designed for children, and so on. That a larger number of blacks and Hispanic Americans are seen in advertising reflects a response to affirmative action, but it also shows the advertisers' awareness of the greater impact of an ethnic model on ethnic consumers.

In addition to the broad social implications of the concept outlined above, the ramifications of this idea for smaller units, such as the family, are perhaps of greater importance. The critical position of parents and other relatives to serve as models for children with regard to work are highlighted. Parents who themselves are employed, who are invested in their work, and who reap benefits from their employment are conveying messages to their children about the importance of the child's patterning his own behavior after them. The other side of the coin, however, also merits comment. When parents are unable to work because of job shortages, lack of skills, or discrimination, children may learn not to expect employment or to doubt their ability to succeed at working. In like manner, if parents are uninvested in what they do, or if by their work habits they convey indifference, lack of responsibility, or low esteem for working, these attitudes and behaviors also are being modeled, and their children are likely to take these attitudes into their own work lives.

Social Recognition and Status

Perlman has made the point that people work for social recognition.[10] Whether one is a writer cloistered in a room or a welder standing in full view of foreman and colleagues on the assembly line, one is pushed and sustained in work, at least in part, by the knowledge that others whose judgment one values will, when work is done, make some approving response. Such approval assures a person's link with other people and gratifies one's own sense of self-love, which is fundamental to self-esteem.

Erikson has suggested that during the stage where generativity vs. stagnation is the main crisis, work is related to the adult's responsibility to "Care for the Creatures of this World." "Generativity," he says "is primarily the concern in establishing and guiding the next generation. . . ." Insofar as work is a primary vehicle of generativity, this concept is another way of talking about a person's tie to others through work. But if work is a way of caring *for* others, it also is a way of being cared *about* by others. Erikson acknowledges this in his comment that if he had been writing about adulthood in his *Childhood and Society,* "it would be indispensable and profitable . . . to compare economic and psychological theories . . . and to proceed to a discussion of man's relationship to his production as well as his progeny."[11]

The emphasis in the present discussion, although it cannot be detailed in all of the relevant facets, is on the relationship of a person to production and society. The theme is that this relationship is one by which a person gains social recognition and status. A child fulfills these needs as a leader on the playground; the adolescent meets them through his emerging abilities and skills, both intellectual and athletic, and through his facility with his peers. The main road to fulfilling these needs for the adult, however, is work. A familiar piece of social banter comes to mind: "He does not hold a job there, he holds a position." The conversation has left the realm of specific job tasks. It is now about one's place in the hierarchy. The conversation is about status, about a person's value and importance as a member of a group or organization. Status, then, is socially ascribed and relates to the positive estimate of a person's competence by valued others. It also reflects the esteem in which one is held by others in consequence of one's performance. The effect of this for the person is on enhancement of self-esteem and an increased feeling of being accepted by the group.

Social recognition and status through work are not easily acquired or equally available to all workers. This is particularly true for members of minority groups and for women in American society. Unemployment among blacks in general and black youths in particular is more than double that of the population at large. Racial discrimination and prejudice greatly limit their access to the more desirable and prestigious jobs. In addition, black persons often find themselves in a double bind when they lack either the experience or the skills for desirable jobs, and these deficits are caused by past or current discrimination. Racial consideration (because the person often is unable to do anything about it) bears heavily upon the person when he enters upon the tasks to which he is assigned. The effect of discrimination bears all the more heavily when the individual is both highly capable and motivated. A young black man, a part-time business administration student at a respected university, describes his frustration:

> I get pretty peeved off lots of times, because I know I can do other work. They have their quota of blacks and they have just enough so you can't say they're prejudiced. I'm trying to graduate from college and I'd like to go into industry where the money is. I have all sorts of qualifications for the kind of work I want, but none has been offered to me. In 1969 they ran an ad in the paper for a junior accountant. I have a minor in accounting, so I applied. They wanted a person with good aptitude in mathematics and a high school graduate. I had an associate arts degree from junior college and two years of accounting. They took me to the head of the department. He asked, "What makes you want this type of work?" (Laughs)[12]

Status and social recognition are denied many people because of their race or sex, but within the inner circle of the plant or the office, the nature of one's job may be the culprit. A twenty-four-year-old white female, a college graduate with a major in English literature, tells of her experience working as a receptionist.

> I changed my opinion of receptionists because now I'm one. It wasn't the dumb broad at the front desk who took telephone messages. She had to be something else because I thought I was something else. I was fine until there was a press party. We were having a fairly intelligent conversation. They they asked me what I did. When I told them, they turned around to find other people with name tags. I wasn't worth bothering with. I wasn't being rejected because of what I had said or the way I talked, but simply because of my function. After that, I tried to make up other names for what I did—communications control, servomechanism. (Laughs)[13]

The two persons speaking above are representative of hundreds of others in similar circumstances for whom the consequences may be apathy, indifference, and anger, or, for others, the expenditure of inordinate amounts of emotional energy adapting and coping. In either case, job satisfaction is lacking, and job performance suffers.

The symbolic interactionist perspective of George Herbert Mead, however, provides a systematic way of thinking about interaction with significant others. Several concepts from Mead's theory are especially relevant. They are Mead's concepts of the self, the generalized other, and self-consciousness. According to Mead, the self is unique to man and "develops in each individual through the process of social experience and social communication, and it continues developing throughout our life."[14] The self consists of the *I* and the *me.* The *me* is the social self, reflecting the way we see ourselves and the way others see us. The *me* comes about through taking the attitude of others toward us. These others are referred to as *generalized others*. This process of taking the attitude of generalized others is accomplished by imagining how others see us or interpret our meanings. A person may take the attitude of a particular other when he is interacting with him, or a person may take the attitude of others in general by imagining how others feel about his leaving a job or getting a divorce.

The *I*, on the other hand, is the subjective aspect of the self. It is momentary and fleeting, and it cannot be observed or objectified. The *I* is our responding and experiencing in this present moment. When the response of others does not call up the same responses in oneself, a person may become *self-conscious*. Through this process, an adult may be moved to change his behavior in order to achieve consistency or harmony between his experience of his self and that reflected by others. Similarly, a person may be demoralized by the conflict between the response of generalized others and his own response to self. The implications of these concepts for the social meanings of work and a person's transactions with generalized others, on and off the job, are numerous. These concepts help to clarify the role of support and censure in regard to a job, and they illuminate the negative impact of race and sex discrimination in connection with work. They also have implications for therapeutic activities aimed at helping workers to change attitudes and job performance.

Work as Meaning in Life

Taking care of future generations is what Erikson said "generativity" is all about. The concept includes *productivity* and *creativity*, too, but Erikson cautions that these terms can never replace the main thrust of generativity, which is establishing and guiding the next generation. Sheehy called these same issues the "mid-life passage" in her tracing of the dangers and opportunities faced in middle age. The dangers Sheehy points out are regression, stagnation, and personal "inauthenticity." They are based on efforts to return to or to recapture the past at a time when physical powers are declining and minor changes are occuring; they are based on holding onto a hard-won status quo, fearing that any change will tear one's world apart; they are based, too, on denying or avoiding personal change by engaging in excessive activity on irrelevant projects, all of which cause one to miss the moment and cover oneself in superficiality.[15]

In contrast, however, the declaration that "I did that," when made in connection with a work task, is a statement about having affected materials or human relations in such a way that a new or unique product emerges. The declaration contains a not-so-subtle boast, but it can be forgiven if one understands and accepts the individual's pleasure and pride in having influenced the outcome of factors in the environment. White's description of the infant's pleasure in activity is no less true of older children and even adults who become excited and enthusiastic when grappling with a difficult problem or some complex task. Indeed, it is the challenge (not necessarily the solution) that holds the person's interest and keeps him tied to a job. (We are aware, of course, that many people persevere at unpleasurable tasks for goals that are far removed from their jobs. It must be remembered, however, that for them pleasure in activity may be secured through some other route and that their work is not necessarily defined by their jobs.)

The satisfaction of a job well done is the end result of competence, but competence has both personal and social aspects. A person can stand back and look at a finished product; it can be held in his hands; or it can be simply appreciated by its creator. All the while, the individual passes on his or her own judgment as to its quality, and if the work is approved by the self, one's sense of competence is enhanced. The sense of satisfaction flowing from this merges with the sense of competence to produce self-esteem. That these processes precede any social confirmation of one's work emphasizes the personal meaning that work has for the individual's sense of competence and effectance.

Work as personal fulfillment is closely related to the above processes, but in addition it is related but not restricted to what Maslow referred to as self-actualization.[16] Through work, a people can realize their potential, exercising to the fullest their physical, intellectual, social, and creative abilities. Lest this appear to be an overidealized or unrealistic picture of the opportunities available to many workers in their jobs, it must be clarified that self-fulfillment is a subjective sense that can be experienced by those who have done the best that they can and as much as they can, given their situation. Moreover, personal fulfillment may be a function of attaining personal goals associated with personally meaningful values. In this light, barriers—human and environmental—to self-fulfillment limit but do not prevent the attainment of personal fulfillment. With the above in mind, it can be said that through work valued aspirations and objectives may be striven for and obtained. Thus, becoming foreman or supervisor may be as fulfilling for a given person as becoming company president or board chairman; while developing and implementing a social program for the elderly may be as fulfilling as devising a strategy for national health care. What is important is that the individual derives through work a sense of satisfaction based on the exercise of the best of his or her abilities in a task that is personally meaningful and socially useful.

Social confirmation is essential, because it gives meaning to one's work beyond the self. The acknowledgment of others links the individual and her work to a social context, which in the last analysis defines both its value and its meaning. This is why all workers, whether they are on assembly lines, in kitchens, in artists' studios, or the hideaways of writers—all of whom may have judged their own work satisfactory—await with anticipation and anxiety the judgments of their foremen, spouses, contemporaries, and critics.

It is not only judgment that binds workers to their society or gives substance to their work. The sense of social contribution growing out of the usefulness of one's products to others gives the sense of being purposeful and needed—both vital to a person's self-esteem. The press of financial circumstances and the need to get ahead can outweigh the social orientation in some younger workers, but as one matures into middle age and beyond, this orientation may change. Consider the statement of a union official on this point.

The almighty dollar is not the only thing in my estimation . . . I can concentrate on the social aspects, my rights. And I feel good all around when I'm able to stand up and speak up for another guy's rights. That's how I got involved in this whole stinkin' mess. Fighting every day of my life. And I enjoy it.[17]

This life stage, therefore, is full of opportunities. Both Erikson's and Sheehy's studies suggest that work can be a vital part of seizing this potential. If a person's work is to aid in meeting the challenge of this period—finding meaning in life—work must be understood in a different context and must be approached with a new attitude. Working now must be understood as a means of establishing and guiding the next generation. Teaching younger workers, one's children, yes, but also the progeny of others; passing on what one has learned must be in the foreground. Serving as a mentor to younger persons, opening doors for their development and contribution, may be emphasized above one's own needs and personal interests.

This is the new attitude that one brings to work: "I will give all that I have to promoting the welfare of the next generation. These young people will be in the forefront of life's activities, and it is my responsibility and my joy to contribute what life and experience has taught me."

The payoff of this different understanding and new approach is that it allows one to develop a new autonomy and greater authenticity. While increasing material satisfactions, securing a coveted promotion, and acquiring status among one's contemporaries may have been the goals of other times, now the goal of work is building the future, making a valued contribution and leaving one's mark. Through these processes one grapples with old motivations, revalues old goals, and emerges revitalized and renewed.

Work and the Life Cycle

We turn now to a discussion of the relationship between major developmental tasks and crises and the personal and social prerequisites for effective working at each stage of the life cycle. Our aim will be to show the process by which attitudes toward and the capacity for work are acquired and maintained and to highlight concepts that may be useful to social work students and practitioners in understanding persons where work-related issues are concerned.

Preschool Years

We have already alluded to the important part played by the young child's early developmental attainments and interactions with parents in preparing the child for the world of work. Our task now is to describe briefly how mastery of major developmental tasks related to work is achieved.

A major developmental task of early childhood is forming meaningful attachments to the mother and later to other family members. The child's attachment to the mother, of course, develops through repeated nurturing sequences. The mother's feeding, comforting, talking, and playing with her young child, in combination with the growth of more complex biological functioning, results in bonding between them. This early attachment and the trust that grows from it are vital precursors to an ability to invest the self in a person and in a task. The failure of adequate mothering or premature and traumatic separation from the mother can greatly inhibit the child's capacity for caring about either people or life events. Similarly, the child's move toward autonomy during the second year of life can greatly influence the quality of his later orientation toward work. The child's recalcitrant responses of "No" to adult requests and the awkward but determined efforts to button his own buttons or to tie his own shoes reflect the emergence of independence of thought and action. With appropriate parental support and direction, these developments become key elements in the child's learning initiative as an attitude and an orientation.

Early efforts at mastery also are critical precursors to the attitudes and skills that are necessary to work. Fraiberg's description of a small boy named Tony who handled his fear of the strange, the unfamiliar, and the unknown by seeking to discover how the object of his fear worked is a case in point.[18] With a screwdriver, young Tony (to the frustration of his parents) would unhinge cupboard doors, remove casters from chairs, or "find the noise" in the vacuum cleaner. These investigations were Tony's way of controlling dreaded objects in his environment. From knowing how a thing worked, Tony gained control of it and thereby erased his fear. Fraiberg points out further that children show a preference for particular styles of mastery. The same fear of vacuum cleaners might be handled by another child through play action—by becoming a vacuum cleaner himself. Clearly, if you can *be* the feared contraption and then, at will, return to being yourself, what is there to fear?

Children's preferences for different styles of coping are to be accepted as efforts at mastery, which may later serve purposes far removed from their original aims. In Tony's case, for example, by the time he reached the age of four, his interest in exploring, taking apart, and fixing had become a pleasure in itself. Whether his mechanical interest persisted into adulthood is not the main concern. What is important is that he acquired an orientation toward investigation, a learning he was likely to use in problem-solving, regardless of his adult occupational choice.

Children are often observed simulating work—patterning their "work" activities and attitudes after parents and significant others in their life spaces. The familiar simulation of parental tasks around the home will call to the reader's mind many ready illustrations. The mother's and the father's occupations, including the manner in which they dress for work, their attitudes—including the rushed breakfasts in order to be on time and their frustration at intractable tasks—also are observed and imitated by the young child. True, this is child's play, but if, as Erikson has said, "play is the work of children," then what children observe, imitate, and act upon reflects important learning and socialization. Moreover, when children's simulation of work activities and attitudes modeled by parents is understood in this context, the conception of play as meaningless becomes invalid, and the nature of models and their behavior becomes an issue deserving thoughtful consideration.

Childhood

During the middle years of childhood (seven to twelve), the child still is highly involved with his nuclear family, but, at the same time, he is increasing his involvement with persons beyond the family. The school and playground now are major centers of learning. Teachers and peers grow in importance as influential mentors. Examining the contributions of these institutions and individuals will shed light on their impact on the child's learning about work.

The school as an institution with an identifiable culture provides a helpful point of departure. Among the first observations (lessons?) the child learns upon entering school is that his place as the center of his parents' attention, love, and interest must now be shared with as many as thirty-five others. Moreover, the child is confronted with an additional lesson: His productions at home aroused parental pride and were displayed on the kitchen bulletin board or the living room wall for all to see. His work was good, simply because he did it. At school, however, his work will be judged on the basis of its merit, and the standard will be apart from factors related specifically to his personality and background. There is still more: Mother and Father loved him because he was flesh of their flesh; his teachers' affections will be increased only if he performs. This is a demanding curriculum, and it is quite apart from the formal study of reading, writing, and numbers. For teachers, this "hidden curriculum," one researcher found, is the important one.[19] A few more of its lessons need describing.

The child soon finds that the culture of school is a culture of structure. School "takes-in" and "lets-out" at designated times. You are censured for being late to school, or for not getting work in on time, or for doing work poorly. In contrast to the relaxed, unstructured atmosphere of home, you must now get permission to talk or to use the toilet, and you must wait your turn even to contribute to the subject being discussed. On the playground, you must learn to accept group choices of games to be played and your own part in the game, even when these are at odds with your personal preference. In a word, the child learns to compromise. These are but a few of the lessons that he learns in the hidden curriculum, but enough has been said to make the point that the culture of school and the requirements of the playground have much in common with the culture of the workplace. Leaving behind past hopes and wishes, his imagination, once wild and free, must become civilized and trained so that this person, "psychologically already a rudimentary parent, can . . . begin to be a worker and potential provider."[20] Thus, the child confronts the crisis of industry vs. inferiority. No longer able to rely on his personality and his parents' love to assure his future, he now learns to gain respect and social recognition through his own productions and creations.

If the child learns to doubt his abilities or to question his skills, or, if because of physical handicaps, sexism, or racial discrimination, his opportunities to be industrious are restricted, he may limit his ambitions and restrain his hopes for success in the work world. The danger of the period, then, is in developing a sense of inadequacy and insecurity, which, if carried into formal work roles, could lead to job failure or robotlike performance of tasks, leaving the person with a sense of emptiness in working.

Adolescence

The struggle for identity is the crucial developmental task of adolescence. Establishing who one is and where one is going is a complex task, involving much social experimentation and personal introspection. The optimal outcome of these activities is for the person to acquire a sense of "personal sameness and historical continuity," which is to say that she feels a certain coherence about her past, present, and future. This means that each of these periods is reciprocally linked to the others. Personal introspection, however, must be concretized, and social experimentation must be actualized in real interpersonal relationships and through observable attainments and achievements.

The real interpersonal relationships of adolescence take on a new quality, which reflect at once the minimal autonomy of the maturing youth and her continuing need for guidance and support. They also show a need for independence from parents and a heightened sense of attachment to peers. These dualities pose complex adaptive tasks for the adolescent. No longer a child but not quite ready for the adult world, almost mature physically but not yet psychologically, the adolescent feels a nagging uncertainty about the present and future. Of one thing she is certain (at least some of the time): Adults, especially parents, cannot undo these uncertainties. Her peers, who have lived through or who share similar feelings and achievements (won through intellectual and physical ability), promise solace and hope. The adolescent turns, then, to her peers and her skill in a grand quest. The experiment concerns testing her mettle against the requirements of life; the quest is about discovering her identity.

The world of work provides a suitable laboratory for this experiment. Here, as is appropriate to their stage, they can be both learner and doer. In the laboratory of work they can examine the myriad of available occupational possibilities, selecting those most appealing for trial. They can compare their abilities and their desires with actual experiences and judge whether they are suited for a particular career. They also can learn here that work can be both personally and materially rewarding.

The adolescent's doing, his actual work, can be instructive, too. Through working at a job, the adolescent affirms or changes self-perceptions about what he or she can or cannot do. He can also learn that persevering at a task can lead him to transcend personal limitations. If the experiment is favorable, he can validate his abilities and discover promising directions for his future. These activities and the psychological processes that accompany them have been involved not only in finding a job but also in finding an identity. Thus, work and achievement during this period can help the adolescent to solidify his sense of self and free him to approach the future with confidence. The adolescent's confidence, however, can be eroded and destroyed if available adult models exhibit only the least desirable job possibilities, if his exposure has been limited to a circumscribed sphere of work, or if in his experience antisocial activities, such as gambling, pushing drugs, and other forms of hustling, are more rewarding than socially useful work. Clearly, adult role models are vital during this period, in spite of the adolescent's struggle to reject them.

Achievement, accomplishing that which is personally satisfying and socially useful, gives substance to identity. The sense of who one is and where one is going is insufficient to maintain this feeling or to convey it to others. A person's achievement gives him something to point to (and others something to see) as evidence of the meaningfulness of his existence. Because they are the product of personal investment, achievements become important ingredients in an adolescent's growing sense of identity and living monuments by which he can be identified by others.

Mechanistic and unimportant work, depreciating and boring work, will continue to be done by many for the sake of survival. Insofar as food, clothing, and shelter are the only motivations for work, self-esteem through work may be threatened. Insofar as achievement resulting in personal satisfaction and a feeling of social contribution are linked to work, self-esteem will be enhanced. In a society where self-esteem is jeopardized for many youths due to institutional practices of discrimination and a general cultural devaluation of their personhood, technical skill and achievement through work may be the only viable course to a healthy sense of personal identity.[21]

Adulthood

If the central developmental crisis of adulthood concerns entering into a meaningful intimacy in lieu of sinking into lonely isolation, investments beyond the self are vital to resolving this crisis. It is in adulthood that Freud's formula about what a normal person should be able to do well takes on significance. "To love and to work"—it is an elegant statement, because it is both simple and profound. It is a statement of maturity, a maturity expressed in emotional commitments and genital love and in a "general work-productiveness," free of obstructive childhood aims and wishes. To put the matter simply, it is about a maturity so free of childhood interferences that the person is free to invest his energies in a loved person *and* a loved activity, deriving pleasure and satisfaction from both.

Investing one's energies in a manner such as described above carries a great challenge, made greater by the additional demands and adult coping imposed by complex personal and family responsibilities characteristic of adulthood. If one is to meet this challenge, one must develop a means of resolving conflict and realize the gratifications and opportunities inherent in the transactions between work and love. The great psychological threat of young adulthood is isolation;

in the middle years, it is the sense of stagnation; and in old age, despair threatens social functioning and self-esteem. Whether one succumbs to these threats depends in large measure on the extent to which one masters the peculiar tasks of work and love occasioned in each of these stages.

As the years progress, child-caring and child-rearing, combined with increasing financial responsibilities, become focal concerns. The responsibilities and obligations inherent in the marital relationship and relationships with friends are equally demanding on the middle-aged person. All of this may be occurring at a time when the individual is striving for occupational success and is focused on future goals and personal security. In the midst of these conflicting demands, some individuals may seek to escape the stress of personal obligations by an obsessive involvement in work or try to release tension through sexual liaisons unencumbered by commitment and caring. Still others abandon all personal and social responsibilites and "drop out," or they may search for solace in excessive recreation, alcohol, or drugs.

The failure of these attempts may be attributed to the absence of what Karl Menninger has called the "vital balance" in the work and love transactions of the individual.[22] The presence of such a balance implies a recognition of the reciprocal relationship between maturation and mastery, such that the sense of competence and self-confidence accrued through a person's life and work both equip and free him to accept and cope with his personal life. In like manner, buttressed by the support, comfort, and sustaining qualities gained through loving and being loved, the person is able to invest his or her energies in an activity (work), as well as in a person to which he or she is committed. In this way, the person's potential for creativity and personal stability are strengthened.

If, on the other hand, the person's work is stifling and frustrating, or if it deprives him of dignity, creativity, and self-esteem, the fallout of these frustrations may be felt in his or her personal relationships, leading to conflict, depression, and impaired social functioning. Problems of a personal nature (whether they are marital issues, conflicts with children, or difficulties with parents) can deplete a person's energies, inhibit creativity, and hinder effectiveness on the job.

Maturity and mastery in work and love, then, are mutually advanced through work, yet work and the workplace are not without their own requirements and hazards as the individual seeks to escape isolation. Whether one enters the work world as a high school dropout or a college graduate, the questions are the same: What kind of work shall I look for? What jobs are available to a person of my abilities?

In answering these questions, a person approaches the critical intersection between work and the life cycle. The internal push of biological and psychological growth and the external pull of social expectations urge the person to seek through work some clearer definition of the self, some firmer hold on reality. This is the process of truly becoming an adult. Levinson has detailed this process for young men in a study which attempts to understand the progression of their lives over the adult years. From the study of the lives of forty men between the ages of thirty-five and forty-five, Levinson and his colleagues discovered that a man's course in this period depends heavily on how he masters the tasks of the previous "novice period," that is the period between the ages of seventeen and thirty-three. Four main tasks confront the young man at this time: "(1) to define his dream of adult accomplishment; (2) to find a mentor to guide him; (3) to develop a vocation; and, (4) to open himself to new intimate relationships." For many young men, the process of completing these tasks is fraught with conflicts (often related to their relationships with parents and/or mentors), indecision (related to their career choices), and frustration (often connected with their impatience with the pace of progress toward their goals). These problems, according to Levinson, are not to be construed as delayed adolescence. Facing and mastering them are necessary parts of becoming an adult.[23]

In connection with this discussion, it may be relevant to emphasize that this whole process revolves around work and to point out that as work aids in concretizing one's identity, it also serves to mark the transition from adolescence to adulthood.

While no parallel data are currently available on how young women move into adulthood, it can be assumed that the existing cultural pattern of assigning a more limited sphere of vocational choices and opportunities to women has placed severe restrictions on their options in the process of becoming adults. As women continue to challenge this pattern, however, it is likely that we will see a different model of their transition to adulthood, and that homemaking, child care, clerical occupations, and the like will represent only a few of the many courses women will be able to follow in pursuit of adulthood.

It is appropriate, then, to examine some of the factors affecting occupational choice and socialization to the job. Although it might appear contradictory in a democratic society, it remains true that social class plays an important role in occupational choice. There is a reciprocal relationship between a person's preferences and his socialization to the job. Job choice begins in the training requirements or preparation, but, because of the costs involved, the training that one has access to and the amount of training that one can afford often are determined by one's social class. Moreover, a person's interest in a particular career is highly affected by his exposure to others in a particular profession, and persons of middle- or upper-middle-class backgrounds are more likely to have encountered role models who will help to shape and sponsor entry into particular vocations.

Restrictions on occupational choice imposed by background factors such as social class, ethnic origin, intelligence, sex, and race serve to limit the range of occupations to which an individual may aspire in complex and often illegal ways. Some victims of such discrimination nevertheless find means to gain entry into an occupation and be less bound by these factors than their peers. Yet, a "simple survey of occupations indicates that some are disproportionately Jewish, white, male, black, or poor." Kimmel has suggested that these factors restrict occupational choice in the same way that they restrict choice of a marital partner: They set the boundaries within which a person searches for his occupation (or his mate).[24]

Role models play vital parts in one's choice of an occupation. The writer studied the lives of twenty successful black Americans, seeking to learn how they achieved success and maintained their self-esteem. The subjects came from both poor and middle-class families. An examination of critical incidents in the lives of these persons revealed that role models (parents, relatives, and interested persons—both black and white) played major parts in the subjects' career interests, regardless of their economic statuses. What was noteworthy about the two groups was the different way in which the role models exerted their influence on the subjects. Among the middle class, role models served to reinforce and stimulate an exciting value orientation and career aspiration. For the poorer subjects, the role models became active intervenors—guiding, challenging, and pushing the subjects to a heightened awareness of their abilities and potentials. Among the poor subjects, identification with a person not of their own background can be a prime motivator to move into careers heretofore closed to them.[25] Similar findings are reported by Scanzoni, in his study of blacks above poverty level.[26]

Finding a "fit" between one's self and a job is another factor affecting occupational choice. People tend to seek the types of work that correspond with their self-perceptions, personal inclinations, and attributes. A person entering the field of law, for example, may feel committed to justice or enjoy helping people solve legal problems; persons who enter the field of psychotherapy (whether as psychiatrists, psychologists, or social workers) may see themselves as helpers, as problem solvers, or just as being interested in human welfare. Such personal inclinations are complex, but the people who usually feel at home in their work are those whose internal orientations "click" with their occupational selections.[27]

Not only is it true that congruence between one's work and one's inclinations makes for harmony in the personality but recent research and theory also suggest that the kind of work that a person does can have important consequences for personal change and development during the adult years. George Herbert Mead's analysis of the *self* and the role of the *generalized other* offers a useful framework for understanding personal change in adulthood. By responding to how others perceive us, we adjust our attitudes and feelings about ourselves. This is especially true when there is incongruence between our self-perception and that of others. In the work setting, this phenomenon is often observed when a person moves from line or staff to a supervisory or executive position. As people assume responsibilities requiring decision-making or directing the work of others, they begin the process of changing their attitudes about themselves. In time, these new behaviors and the attitudes that accompany them become integrated, and the people feel themselves to be (and are experienced by others as being) changed.

Because it occurs in a social context, the kind of work that a person does can have an impact on personality change, and this can be negative as well as positive. An example of the former is seen in a situation where the job one does is not challenging or is blatantly depreciating from the worker's perspective. If significant others in the person's environment agree with this assessment, the person may feel inadequate, incompetent, and a failure. Such an attitude toward the self may be taken by a person who, up until now, had held quite a different view of himself. Unless the person who is caught in such circumstances can rationalize the necessity to remain in this work on the basis of meeting survival needs or family responsibilites, or unless he is emotionally supported by generalized others from another sphere of his life, his work can serve to erode his sense of personal worth, which will soon be reflected in his personality and in other areas of his social functioning.

For women, traditions and stereotypes relating to their sex are a powerful force, unfavorably influencing not only their occupational choices but also their incomes and their ability to move up the career ladder. In spite of this influence, the number of women in the paid labor force has been steadily increasing since 1900.[28] In that year, 20 percent of women over fourteen were in the labor force. By 1973, the percentage of women in the labor force had reached 44.7 percent. The pattern of female participation in the labor force from 1900 to 1940 was primarily one of younger women. A major shift in this pattern was reflected in the 1950 census, which showed an impressive rise in the participation of middle-aged women in the labor force. In 1970, 50 percent of married women between the ages of forty-five and fifty-four were working. The trends described above are generally true for all women, but the increase has been greater among white women than for nonwhite women. Black women (the largest group of nonwhite women) historically have been forced by necessity to work, so that the greater increase among white women means that whites are now beginning to catch up with black women.

Why do women work? For most women, the decision to obtain work outside the home is made for economic reasons. They work because their families need the money they earn, or they work to raise their family's standard of living. The rising costs of food, children's education, and medical care stimulate still other women to seek employment. "Few women," according to one observer, "have the option of working solely for personal fulfillment."[29]

A number of other social and economic factors also are involved in women's decisions to work, such as rising divorce rates, greater life expectancy, and decreasing real family income. These factors make work for many women a necessity. Thomas' analysis of the data on this point is relevant. In the two-year period from 1975 to 1977, female-headed households increased from 12 percent to 14 percent. When it is noted that only 29 percent of all female-headed families receive some form of public assistance, it is reasonable to conclude that the large majority of these women must work. The trend toward working among women becomes even more apparent when marital status is considered by race. A greater proportion of minority wives (54.9 percent) than minority single women (48.5) or those widowed, divorced, or separated (45.7) were likely to be in the labor force. There are some differences among white women. The white working wife was not as likely to be in the labor force (44 percent) as the single white woman (61.2 percent), but she was more likely to be working than her counterpart who was divorced, widowed, or separated (39.8 percent). Thus, Thomas concludes, "no matter how it is considered, financial need remains among the strongest factors that cause women to enter the labor force."[30] The restriction of women to sex-typed occupations and the inequitable practices such as unequal pay for similar work are not likely to prevail, due to affirmative action regulations and the strength of the women's movement. Therefore, as women become more assertive—insisting on equality in the labor force—and as equal opportunity laws are enforced, it is expected that the occupational choices made by women will increasingly reflect the same factors that influence men: competence, role models, experience, interests, and personality.

The Occupational Cycle

Having set forth the crucial factors influencing vocational choice, it is now appropriate to discuss some of the critical points in the occupational cycle and to relate these to personal change and progression in the life cycle. These *turning points* or *crisis points* in the occupational cycle correspond to the developmental crises with which each person must cope, and they have important implications for social functioning both on and off the job.[31]

Entry into the occupation. The first of these turning points, occurring at the conclusion of the process of occupational selection, is entry into the occupation. Having been oriented toward the job during the period of anticipatory socialization, the person now enters the job for the first time. A major task of this period concerns confronting the *real* demands, the *real* expectations, and the *real* rewards. Usually these factors differ from what one had expected and may result in some conflict for the individual. This point is well illustrated by the experiences of a new social work student entering his field placement for the first time. Filled with exuberance and social commitment, the student may find that the demands of his clients' problems are beyond his knowledge and skill, or that he cannot solve *all* of the problems that he sees around him. Moreover, the agency's requirements for forms to be filled out and reports to be made may not be to the student's liking. Further, the expectations of the supervisor may be experienced as more (or less) than the student can handle.

A young black woman known to the writer faced a similar set of circumstances upon entering her first job as a power machine operator in the garment industry. Trained as a fashion designer, she found her task of sewing on only the bibs of caps used by the military to be monotonous and uncreative. Needing the job to help support her husband through graduate school, she worked hard to earn extra money by going beyond her quota. This reward sustained her on the job, but as soon as it became available, she accepted a lesser-paying job, sewing in a small boutique that offered high-fashion dresses to women of means.

In both instances, these persons had to confront the conflicts between their prework expectations and the real requirements of their jobs. In the first case, the social work student had to become socialized. The seamstress, unable to concord her expectations with the real requirements of the job, elected to leave a higher-paying but unsatisfying position for one that was in greater accord with her self-perception. The symbolic interactionists would say that each of these persons had to develop a new *me* during the period of job socialization and that the seamstress, because she was *self-conscious* in the factory job, moved to a different work situation in order to allay the uncomfortable feeling brought on by the conflict between her *I* and her *me* when she worked in the factory.

The middle years of the occupation. The second major crisis period in the work cycle occurs during middle age and poses additional and complex hurdles for the individual. Like the previous crisis, this one, too, involves readjusting goals and hopes and bringing them in line with the possible. Consider the person who had hoped to be regional sales manager by age forty or the plant worker who had hoped to be foreman by middle age; both of these persons must now face the fact that if they are to reach their goals, they must get busy. On the other hand, factors over which a person has no control may operate to prevent the attainment of such goals. In this case, one may have to settle for what he has and find satisfaction in his present work. This middle-years crisis is influenced by what may be called the career clock, an internal sense that one is "on time" or "behind time" in career development.[32] It is typical during the middle years (approximately forty to fifty-five) for a person to become highly aware of the amount of time he has left before retirement and of the rate of his progress toward his occupational goals. The person who is "late" or who perceives his goals as increasingly unrealistic may begin to change to goals more consistent with what is likely and possible; or the person may decide to change jobs "before time runs out."

The two main dangers of this period are (1) of developing a sense of stagnation if one is not moving forward in one's work or (2) of developing feelings of frustration at being locked into a job because of being "priced out of the market" or because leaving a job may jeopardize a pension or because one's age precludes finding another suitable job. Diminished self-esteem may result from these work-related issues, leading to depression and despair. On the other hand, satisfaction and hope may be derived from working in a cared-about job where one has made steady progress and felt a sense of social contribution. This outcome (and its opposite) heavily influence the nature of a person's feelings and outlook toward the next occupational crisis—retirement.

Retirement. There are at least three dimensions to retirement: It is an *event*, a *status*, and a *process*.[33] Each of these dimensions relates to and impacts upon the developmental crisis of this stage of life. Erikson has identified this crisis as integrity vs. despair. The symbolic interactionists' perspective suggests that retirement necessitates still another shift in one's *me*, or social self.

As an event, retirement marks a transition point. The Social Security Legislation of the 1930s has been primarily responsible for placing retirement at age sixty-five. In some fields, however, retirement may occur as early as the completion of thirty years of continuous service, resulting in retirement for some individuals as young as age fifty. Still other occupations (such as the professions and political office) have not established an age for work termination, so that some individuals continue to work into their seventies and eighties. Many persons, when they do retire, seek other full- or part-time jobs. With rising life expectancy in the United States, an increasing number of individuals are reaching retirement age. Retirement may be celebrated as a transition point, and the individual may be given some recognition for his service at a banquet or a company ceremony. In other instances, retirement may be noted in the organization's journal or the local newspaper. The more common experience, however, is for this event to receive little or no attention, except from those closest to the individual. Thus, most individuals move into retirement unceremoniously and with little or no recognition. Retirement, then, is a social event without much social meaning.

Whether it is announced with fanfare or allowed to occur unnoticed, retirement carries profound meaning for the individual. These meanings embody challenges and opportunities, but they also represent major losses. One loss, reported by most retired persons (and feared by those still employed) is *money!* In a study cited by Kalish, nearly half of those retired said that money was the most serious retirement-related loss.[34] Income for many retired persons may drop by 60 to 80 percent, reducing many older persons to a life in or near poverty. Even if an older person does not live in poverty, finances can be a serious problem. Inflationary conditions make living on a fixed income a severe economic handicap. Housing and medical costs have risen steadily. The cost of health care for older persons is three and one-half times what it is for younger people, and all the public programs combined pay only two-thirds of the bill.[35] Thus the common assumption that the overriding impact of retirement has to do with the loss of meaning, of job-related status, and of the social relationships that work provides is not accurate. Money remains (and perhaps even gains) a priority for most elderly persons.

Retirement is also a status. The individual now belongs to a group that is distinguished by the fact that its members have ceased regular, formal work. For some older persons, this status is liberating, freeing them to take up long-delayed activities, such as hobbies or travel. Investing their energies in projects that they could not undertake earlier may lead to stimulation, as these retirees devote themselves to civic and community endeavors or contribute their knowledge and experience to younger persons in their fields of work. For these individuals, the crisis of retirement is eased. Where financial resources and opportunities are available, the challenges and opportunities of retirement can make of this event an adventure undertaken with eagerness and vitality.

The above methods of dealing with retirement are more characteristic of middle-income and professional persons, but some persons of lower economic status may also reflect this pattern. Such a happy outcome, however, is not characteristic of the experience of most retirees, as factors in addition to the loss of income complicate their adjustments to retirement.

Disengaging from work, accepting the event, and adjusting to the status—

including finding a satisfactory means by which to continue one's growth and development—are all aspects of retirement as a process. The quality and character of this process for a given indivdual are influenced by the interaction of biological, sociocultural, and psychological factors. Thus, the state of a person's health, for example, especially if it was poor health that precipitated retirement, can evoke conflicts about disengagement from the job and hinder the capacity to enter into a meaningful retirement through part-time activities or to gain pleasure from travel or leisure.

Sociocultural factors, insofar as society provides no meaningful role for the retired person, add further potentials for a poor adjustment to retirement. If the retirement was forced, in contrast to voluntary, the person may feel rejected and pushed out. Forced retirement is often the first of a growing list of choices to be removed from the individual. Indeed, social agency programs designed specifically for the elderly are so structured that even recreational and leisure activities are decided for the person. Persons of higher income may be able to anticipate a different set of circumstances upon retirement. A study done at Cornell University, for example, suggested that these persons tend to work longer because they are freer to choose between retirement and continued employment, due to the nature of their occupations.[36] Moreover, their higher incomes often make it possible for them to independently determine how their leisure time is spent.

The impact of psychological factors on retirement relates to the person's evaluation of the meaning of his contribution during the working years and the extent to which he harbors lingering doubts about his own value. A person's preretirement adjustment heavily determines how successful he will be in managing the psychological tasks of retirement. If an individual has been isolated during his young adult years or has developed a sense of stagnation during his middle years, retirement may deal a devastating blow to his sense of ego integrity. Studies of retired persons suggest that the "well adjusted" tended to be "mature," relatively free of neurotic conflict, and able to accept realistically the decline in roles, physical disabilities, and even death. The poorly adjusted tend to be those "angry men" (and, one imagines, "angry women") whose feelings have been tainted by real or imagined failure to achieve their goals. Characteristically, persons in the latter group handle the problems of old age by blaming themselves or others for past failures. For such persons, retirement, the last years of life, may become tortured experiences.

Research on personality traits and characteristics suggests that a person's style of coping remains relatively stable over time, and that retirement may have different meaning for individuals of different personality types. These studies conclude that retired persons differ from one another at least as much as younger persons differ from their age mates.[37] In our efforts to understand and to help older persons deal with the crises of retirement, we would do well to keep in mind that among retired persons (as with younger people), those who function best do so when their social environments permit them to grow to their fullest potentials.

Conclusion

This paper has stressed the importance of work throughout the life cycle. It has been suggested that work can serve as an internal organizer, enhancing the structure and coherence of the personality; as a vehicle for social learning, providing opportunities for work rehearsal and the acquisition of attitudes and interpersonal skills required in the world of work; as an avenue to social recognition and status, offering opportunities to fulfill personal goals and social expectations; and, ultimately, as a source of meaning in one's life, giving substance to one's past and concretizing one's values and hopes for the future.

We have shown that even in the earliest years of childhood, the person is being oriented toward the requirements of the work world and socialized toward the attitudes and behaviors that will prepare him for formal work roles when he matures. The developmental crises of each stage of life have been discussed and related to the role of work in facilitating (or blocking) mastery of the challenges of each life stage. For many individuals, race, sex, ethnicity, or disability intrude into the relationship between work and human development, compounding the difficulties. For these persons, social provisions through laws, public policies, and social opportunities that open doors previously closed to them will be necessary. For all persons, however, regardless of background factors, work may provide the most realistic and available means to achieving self-esteem and the most viable course in the quest for meaning in their lives.

Notes

[1] Erik H. Erikson, *Childhood and Society* (New York: W.W. Norton, 1950), pp. 261-62.

[2] Robert White, *Ego and Reality in Psychoanalytic Theory* (New York: International Universities Press, 1963), pp. 33-37.

[3] Helen Harris Perlman, *Persona: Social Role and Personality* (Chicago: University of Chicago Press, 1968), p. 73.

[4] Studs Terkel, *Working* (New York: Avon Books, 1972), p. xiii.

[5] Perlman, *Persona*, p. 81.

[6] Ibid., p. 59.

[7] Margaret Mahler, *On Human Symbiosis and the Vicissitudes of Individuation* (New York: International Universities Press, 1968).

[8] A more complete discussion of Bandura's research may be found in Paul Henry Mussen, John J. Conger, and Jerome Kagan, *Child Development and Personality*, 5th ed. (New York: Harper and Row, 1979), pp. 31-34.

[9] Leon W. Chestang, *Achievement and Self-Esteem Among Black Americans: A Study of Twenty Lives*, unpublished Ph.D. dissertation, University of Chicago, School of Social Service Administration, June 1977.

[10] Perlman, *Persona*, p. 79.

[11] Erikson, *Childhood and Society*, pp. 267-68.

[12] Terkel, *Working*, pp. 229-30.

[13] Ibid., p. 57.

[14] George Herbert Mead, *Mind, Self, and Society* (Chicago: University of Chicago Press, 1962), pp. 173–78.

[15] Gail Sheehy, *Passages: Predictable Crises of Adult Life* (New York: Bantam, 1976).

[16] Abraham H. Maslow, *The Farther Researches of Human Nature* (New York: Viking Press, 1971), chapter 3, "Self-Actualization and Beyond."

[17] Terkel, *Working,* pp. 259–60.

[18] Selma H. Fraiberg, *The Magic Years* (New York: Charles Scribner's Sons, 1959).

[19] For elaboration of this idea, see Phillip Wesley Jackson, *Life in Classrooms* (New York: Holt, Rinehart, and Winston, 1968).

[20] Erikson, *Childhood and Society,* pp. 258–59.

[21] Erik H. Erikson, *Identity, Youth, and Crisis* (New York: W.W. Norton, 1968), p. 316. See also Chestang, *Achievement and Self-Esteem Among Black Americans.*

[22] Karl Menninger, *The Vital Balance* (New York: Viking Press, 1963), p. 295.

[23] Daniel J. Levinson, "Growing Up with the Dream," *Psychology Today,* 11, no. 8 (January 1978), 30–31, 89.

[24] Douglas C. Kimmel, *Adulthood and Aging* (New York: Wiley, 1974), pp. 246–47.

[25] Chestang, *Achievement and Self-Esteem Among Black Americans.*

[26] John Scanzoni, *The Black Family in Modern America* (Boston: Allyn and Bacon, 1971).

[27] Kimmel, *Adulthood and Aging,* pp. 248–49.

[28] Irene H. Frieze, *Women and Sex Roles: Social Psychological Perspective* (New York: W.W. Norton, 1978), p. 151.

[29] Veronica G. Thomas, "Women in a Changing Society," in *The Social Welfare Forum* (New York: Columbia University Press, 1978), p. 197.

[30] Ibid.

[31] Kimmel, *Adulthood and Aging,* pp. 251–52.

[32] Ibid., p. 254.

[33] Ibid., pp. 255–56.

[34] Richard A. Kalish, *Late Adulthood: Perspectives on Human Development* (Monterey, Calif.: Brooks/Cole Publishing Company, 1975), p. 108.

[35] Shura Saul, *Aging: An Album of People Growing Old* (New York: Wiley, 1974), pp. 14–15.

[36] Kimmel, *Adulthood and Aging,* p. 259.

[37] Ibid., pp. 262–63.

5

The Client as Worker:
A Look at an Overlooked Role

Helen Harris Perlman, D. Litt.
University of Chicago

Often we pay little attention to the obvious, taking it very much for granted until we have an "a-ha experience" (one in which the proximate but long ignored is recognized and identified). This appears to be the situation with the work of our clients and the environment at the workplace. Helen Harris Perlman identifies, with a sense of awe and surprise, the omission, in the casework literature, of attention to the "objective conditions and the subjective meanings of work." The author acknowledges the illogic of the situation, viewing work as an unseen but often dynamic contributing factor in the lives and problems that clients bring to the social worker. The remainder of the chapter, therefore, is a beginning effort to remediate this omission.

This limited engagement of social work with the world of work or the work of our clients has many possible explanations. Perlman suggests a few, ranging from the historic fact that workers were usually men—at work all day and inaccessible to social agencies that were open only during working hours— to the more unconscious bias resulting from the fact that social workers ignored and mistrusted the work system because they felt impotent to enter or influence it and, therefore, regarded understanding of it as relatively useless knowledge. The author calls attention to changing conditions, including the entry of our traditional client populations into that world (in the great ingress of married women and mothers) and the new awareness within the work setting of the interconnections between work and family, between job producitvity and personal well-being. These realities, she suggests, make it essential that social workers re-examine and redress the gaps in knowledge and interaction.

The chapter proceeds to a well-informed and extensive discussion of work and its role not only as an economic but also as a social and psychological support system. The author notes the ambivalence and inconsistency with which American soceity, social workers, and clients may regard work. Although complaints of the meaninglessness of work are common, and we as professionals empathize with a definition of work, especially of manual labor, as boring drudgery, we all also struggle for the rights of the disabled to find work and of the aging to remain at work. We avow the need for women to enter the workforce to achieve fulfillment, while we question, and rightly so, the policy that forces single, unskilled, welfare mothers to make some contribution to the family's economic support by accepting employment, no matter how marginal. Perlman reminds us that these inconsistencies, teetering as they are between the positive and the negative, represent dilemmas of values, practice, and policy, which the social work profession has all but ignored.

The impact of work is many-faceted. The author suggests that work can cause mental health problems by making people feel like robots, by forcing workers to deal with boring activity or authoritarian settings, by questioning their worthiness, or by exhausting their energy. It can also cause unfulfilled expectations or can be encountered as a debilitating experience by the ill-prepared applicant. All this is acknowledged by the author, who, nonetheless, gives work high marks for the gratification it can provide to many. She quotes Conrad's Charlie Marlow: "I don't like work . . . no man does— but I like what is in the work—the chance to find yourself."

For the social worker who would help the client find herself, work and what is in it become of primary importance. Thus, Perlman comes to the rationale for her chapter—the mandate that we understand our clients as workers, their environment as the workplace—so that we can use this knowledge in the helping function. She points out the differential significance of this understanding for different problems, different occupational groupings, persons in different roles. Case vignettes support the notion that regardless of individual differences, however, this understanding is instrumental to "helping people cope with problems in their psychosocial functioning."

Consistent with the theme of the diversity of people and jobs, she notes, for example, the specific issues involved in the developmental process of preparing youths for employment. She decries the lack of professional specialization that can provide appropriate social work supports for bridging this transition in institutional settings like schools and family service agencies. It is the application of knowledge to specific dimensions of professional practice with individual clients that the author sees as the payoff for considering the overlooked role of the worker as client.

Perlman makes a strong case for the connection between the troubles people have in work and the troubles people bring to social work. She concludes that what is special about social work is that it deals with the individual in the situation and the situation as it affects the individual. Work and the work environment, she notes, may be part of the relevant environment for some clients, the only relevant environment for others, or it may be that accomplishments at work constitute the only reaffirmation of worth available to a client who is self-riddled with nonwork connected difficulties. "What is in the work" for each man and woman—". . . it is incumbent upon the helper to know and understand its objective realities as well as the client's subjective sense of it. "

It is an interesting omission when you stop to think about it. The omission, that is, of our attention to the objective conditions and the subjective meanings of work in the lives of the people who become the clients of social workers. The problems people bring may fester in their self-to-other relationships; in their self-to-tasks involvements; in their self-to-circumstantial difficulties; in their internal malaise and dissatisfactions; and in combinations of these. Whatever the identified problem, the person who suffers it is simultaneously carrying and trying to cope with a complex of other role relationships and tasks and their behavioral requirements. Among them is work, the involvement in some chosen or imposed job for a major part of each day.

"To be able to love and to work" is held to be the mark of adult psychological maturity. Attributed to Freud, it is a criterion generally agreed upon by both clinical and casual observers of human personality and behavior. "To love" has been central in the interests and the therapeutic focus of all the psycho-dynamically oriented professions, social work among them. The forms in which problems in loving manifest themselves are manifold: in friendship, colleague, marriage, and parent-child difficulties. They range from open hatred and abuse to excess investment and protectiveness, from cold rejection to passionate possessiveness. They include self-hatred acted out in acts of self-destruction; overromanticized and underrealized expectations; incongruities between love capacity and love hunger; these and other variations in caring, in concern, affection, empathy, possessiveness, sex, reciprocity, passion—all the faces of love—are limitless. They have been explored and explained as subjects of study and clinical help for many decades in social work's effort to understand better and to enhance personally satisfying and socially constructive human relationships.

But the many faces of work have had limited attention. Of course, attention has been given and appropriate, if limited, actions have been taken in situations of *no* work, or unemployment, enforced or voluntary, and in situations of underemployment. No work or insufficient work and the complications that result have been the subject of social work's concern as a social problem, symptomatic of socioeconomic dysfunction, and in their effects upon individual families and persons who suffer the sequelae. However, the need for work, the wish for it, and the loss of it have been seen by caseworkers largely in economic terms. This aspect is basic, and cannot be underestimated in either its practical or its psychological imports.

What has been less recognized and thought about (if social workers' publications and clinical accounts are accurate reflections of their practice) is the place and effect of work in the everyday life of those who do work, of the men and women who hold jobs, who go to their workplaces five days a week, who regularly invest at least one-third of their time, unmeasured amounts of energy, and often intense emotion in the performance of tasks for which they receive money compensation. What they do, how they do, what they feel about it, what work does to or for them—of this we know very little. Working tends to be taken for granted. If the "bread winner" works and "earns a living"—all to the good. Attention by the social worker is, appropriately, focused upon whatever other problems are brought for help: the unhappy marriage; the children's behavior; the aged parent who needs care; the family member with mental or physical illness—these and all the other person-to-person, person-to-situation transactions that may go wrong in the course of living. None of them is necessarily a work-created or job-induced problem. Yet, *any of them may be significantly affected by the work life of one of the adult participants in the problem. In turn, it may spin off to affect job performance.* This is the concern of this paper.

Work has been central in human life since "Adam delved and Eve span." From the time of leaving school (at whatever educational level) to the time of retirement (chosen or mandated), most men and a rapidly increasing proportion of women are employed in paid work. A major portion of their waking time, and energies, and of their conscious effort and attention is invested or absorbed by what we still (all but archaically) call "making a living." The forms that making a living—work—take are multiple and varied. The conditions it sets, the demands it makes, the rewards or punishments it metes out, the drudgeries and stresses it imposes, or the stimulation and nourishments it offers—all these are reacted to and coped with more or less satisfyingly by the worker. His or her feelings, attitudes and ideas—about self, about Life (thus, with a capital L), about today and tomorrow, and behavior, both on the job and in after hours, are likely to be significantly influenced by daily experiences at work.

This is because, as we have long averred, the live human being is an integrated, complex "system" in continuous active interpenetration with the other persons and circumstances that we call his "eco-system," his dynamic environment. What he feels, thinks, does in any salient segment of his daily life may, in great or small degree and in benign or noxious ways, permeate the other segments of his life. When what he experiences is emotionally charged—when it "grabs him where he lives," and "gets under his skin," it reverberates into the inner recesses of his being. It may take permanent residence there, or it may make a glancing impact, but it will color and shape a person's mood, views, attitudes, and behaviors, all of which are likely to affect his other relationships and circumstances.

Thus, work may enter the marriage bed. The man who feels physically and psychically exhausted by his day's work may have sexual dysfunctions that are only secondarily related to love or "techniques"; the woman, resentful at having worked all day and then having had to pick up the kids and the groceries and having slapped together some dinner and fed and bedded the children, may be quite unresponsive to her husband's sexual overtures. Work may enter parent-child relationships. The father, bridling under his foreman's watchfulness and criticisms, may take on the tyrant role himself at home and yell at his children for their trivial offenses. (There is an old folk saying: "The slap to your child is meant for your mother-in-law.") Or he lashes out at his adolescent son who is not trying to "better" himself. Work may be so taxing, with so few and meager rewards that the family—wife, children, old parents—is blamed for it. They are the slave-lash—"I do it for them." Or, in reverse, work may be so totally engrossing that it all but obliterates interest and emotional investments in other persons who need or reach out for attention and caring. Recent stories out of Washington recount the resentment of wives and children whose husbands/fathers are involved in the too-absorbing work of politics; and the absorption of professional workers and business executives in their work lives is an old plaint in their families. Interestingly, the person himself—you, I, our client—may not even be conscious of the interplay between work life and other vital daily involvements.

Because this daily experience of working may affect and permeate many other aspects of the worker's life, as well as the lives of those who are in association with him, it behooves social workers to take a more careful look at work and at the particular client's experience of it.

What we do not lift into conscious awareness is not consciously manageable. So it is relevant to ask ourselves why it is that work and working has had such scant notice and analysis in our years of exploring and dealing with the gamut of cause-effect influences in the individual's daily social living. The reasons that leap to mind are varied and of unequal significance. A few of them are set down here simply as starter-stimuli to further reflection on how it is we have taken our client's work world so little into account.

Until recent years a "worker" was usually a man. In family casework agencies, he was usually the unseen but often complained about husband and father. In child guidance clinics, in school social work offices, in children's hospital wards, he was seen only rarely. He was the father of the child, but his work role seemed to have precedence over his parental role. In relief-giving organizations, it was the husband and father who lost his job and looked for work, but it was the wife and mother (in casework's early days) who applied for "the welfare."* In marital, debt, illness, and child-behavior problems, it was almost always the woman who came as applicant for help. She had the time. More important, women's "right" to dependency, to complain, to ask for help was taken for granted. For men to ask for help—especially from a woman—was a disgrace. Their wives went to the social

---

*I can remember in the middle '30s how radical—and right—it seemed when someone suddenly suggested that the man, the family's normal source of support, should be the applicant for financial aid, not his wife.

agency, while they sought work or the company of other men who shared the misery of unemployment. Thus, the "worker," the man in the family, was rarely at the center of the caseworker's attention.

There were and are many kinds of problems for which help is sought that are unrelated to economic needs. The working man was able to keep his distance from them in two ways: (1) he actually could not take time off from the job to come to the agency or clinic; and (2) work—as is often still the case—offered him an escape, a defensible defense against being responsible or involved in problems of child-rearing, household management, or the many other difficulties of marriage, parenting, and homemaking that were (and, in certain sectors of the population still are) held to be "woman's business." So, social workers rarely saw the family member who worked.

Recent years have brought many changes in practice that are responsive to changes in the views of men's and women's roles and relationships and, of course, to the accelerating involvement of women in paid work outside the home. Many social agencies have accommodated their time schedules to clients' work schedules. And the solution of family problems are today held to require the participation of any or all of the persons involved in the difficulty. Yet work, and its possible reverberations into the problem area for which help is being sought, has yet to be attended to.

Another major reason for our scant attention suggests itself. Caseworkers feel—not without reason—that they have little entree into and little power in the world of industry or business. This is particularly true when the world of work is so megapolitan, bureaucratized, rigidly structured—when the individual employee is so remote from his employer—that the work place appears alien and forbidding to the social worker. It is often not even understandable, much less navigable. Our occasional interventions with employers in the client's behalf (when this has been agreed upon with the client) have occurred when businesses were small and the employer and employee knew one another. This is more rare today. The fact is, however, that there are a growing number of possible intermediaries representing the employer or the union—personnel officers, foremen, supervisors, shop stewards, psychologists and social workers in counseling positions—who, if and when necessary, can be approached in behalf of a client who is an employee. Yet, quite aside from whether such intervention would be wanted or needed, the caseworker often feels uncomfortable in this unfamiliar territory. (Did he not choose his own profession, indeed, in part because he rejected these many aspects of big business—its mechanization, competition, depersonalization, and motivation for personal profit?) So the client's world of work remains for the most part a terra incognita.

Add to "unknown" the possibility that business and industry are distrusted. Social work is in the liberal, humanistic tradition. Business and industry have traditionally—and traditions die hard—been viewed as exploiters of workers, as adversaries in the contest between what is profitable for the employer and what is profitable for the worker. The ramifications of this view deserve a full and honest examination, for which there is not enough space here. Such a view can only be pointed to here as a past, and perhaps to a lesser degree, present barrier to the social worker's venturing into the world of his client's work.

Another major reason for our uneven perspectives and insights into people's experience of work lies in the jumble of paradoxical and ambivalent social attitudes that have arisen about work within the past several decades. Like all other members of their society, social workers are culture carriers, subject to the shibboleths and spirit of the times. So they are often unsure of what they think or believe or even know about the uses of work in the lives of most human beings.

Several decades ago, the worker's reactions to work became a central interest of a number of sociopsychological researchers, resulting in many published studies. One is aware, as one examines these, of a range of contradictory findings, of questions unasked or unanswered, and of sometimes hidden (unconscious) values held by the researchers that might have colored the responses.

Contradictory findings must, of course, be expectable, since "work" is so infinitely varied in its purposes, its conditons, its demands, and its rewards. Add to this the infinite variations in workers themselves, and there are further complexities. One study of workers in industry, for example, found that work was not a "central life interest" for three out of four men.[1] (What was? Nobody asked.) A study of professional nurses, on the other hand, indicated that four out of five considered work and the workplace as their central life interest.[2] The difference in findings are, of course, explainable by a number of variables. However, what a study "shows" may be picked up because it supports a personal conviction and may be cited and widely publicized as though it were definitive, often far beyond what the researcher would have claimed.

As for unconscious bias: Is it possible, for instance, that routine or automated jobs disturb the researcher to some greater extent than the worker—and that such aversion is conveyed in the attitudes and queries of the interviewer? Is it possible, further, that questions about gratifications or frustrations on the job have been insufficiently separated out from all those other sources of gratification or frustration that human beings carry? That, for instance, unhappiness at home or about life in general may be projected into the job, with some expectation that work will—or ought to—make up for other felt love-status-reward deficits? Or that for the person who reports dissatisfaction with work there needs to be considered its fantasied and actual alternative? In short—the existent research on work raises as many questions as it answers, and offers support for almost any position taken in regard to work's meaning in present day life.

In the 1960s, on the tide of new views and versions of the human condition and existence, there rose to prominence the concept that work must be "meaningful." "Meaningful" has rarely been explicated for its meaning. "Creative" is another frequently used desideratum, but this, too, has its ambiguity. It poses any number of practical questions, among which would be what prevalence of creative capacity is assumed to exist in the population and how many opportunities exist or can be "created" in the world of work for the original and idiosyncratic inputs that creativity implies?

In the introduction to his popular and much-cited collection of interviews with workers, Studs Terkel says that their search was "for astonishment rather than torpor."[3] That is hardly surprising. (Or should one say "astonishing"?) Which of us, at work or elsewhere, does not hope for that leap of mind and heart at discovering the unusual or experiencing mastery? But realistically, how often can peak experiences—those of astonishment and wonder—occur? There is no question but that certain kinds of work (working with people, for instance) provides far more instances of surprise and unexpectedness than work with things that are routinized, mechanized, completely predictable. Indeed, this is probably one of the conditions that makes social work and other "human service" professions engaging. But the fact to be faced is that for many essential jobs in today's work (and in yesteryear's, too), there are only small rewards in the execution of the task itself. The saving remnant may lie in the presence of other sources of "payoff" or satisfaction that attach to the work. These sources will be touched on later. Here we note only that we tend to deplore situations that fall short of an ideal, and that run-of-the-mill work is among them.

Before we sweep aside most work done by most people as "meaningless" (except for the money it provides), it behooves us to ascertain what its meaning actually is for this or that individual client, and to ponder further on what the notion of "meaningful" means. Perhaps "meaningfulness" does not inhere in materials, conditions, or activities. Perhaps it is in part the product of a person's investment of expectations and interest in work that is recognized in gratifying ways by one or more significant others—such as co-workers, husband, boss, or friend. And perhaps what is held to be "meaningful" or "good" or "intolerable" to one man or woman is seen and felt differently by another. Have stereotypes dulled our perceptions?

There is, furthermore, a prevalence of certain obvious inconsistencies in our thinking about work: for example, at the same time that work is deplored as "dehumanizing," "alienating," or "exploitative," there is a great hue and cry against early retirement of workers. Some of the concern about mandatory retirement is due to the financial difficulties the retiree may encounter. But most of it seems to be related to its deleterious psychological effects upon the worker—the loss of role, loss of association with fellow workers, loss of purpose and place. Suddenly, it seems, at the point of retirement, certain vital "meanings" in work make themselves manifest.

A like inconsistency is revealed in the push by and upon women to enter the labor force. Side by side with studies and opinion pieces on the tedium and depersonalization of most work, there stand the persuasions and demands that women be given open access to it. Homemaking and child-rearing are held to be less "meaningful," less "creative" than—what? Selling notions? Being part of a typing pool? The fact is that the roseate promise held out to women about the work world is largely a promise to middle-class, college-educated, "liberated" women. Most women who go to work go into nonastonishing jobs. So do men. Are these meaningless? Actually, no one is yet certain.

Realities of the World of Work

Aware now of some of the factors and notions that have shaped our neglect of the place and point of work in the lives of our clients, we may turn to look with some greater interest at a few of the realities—good and bad—that characterize the world of work today. We venture into this in the open recognition that there will be many exceptions, many ifs, ands, and buts to the generalizations that follow. What will be noted are those common, usual conditions encountered by most workers in today's urbanized, multispecialized world of work, and those frequently articulated attitudes and feelings with which work is permeated.

In rough sketch: work is a human being's "activity that produces something of value to other people."[4] Needed or wanted by others, it serves a social purpose. Thus it is rewarded by some form of payment—most often by money, sometimes by social recognition, at best by a combination of both.

To work is to carry on certain tasks under certain stipulated conditions. The means and conditons by which such tasks are to be dispatched are provided by the employer, as is the compensation for the time, energy, and expertise provided by the worker. The bigger the employing organization, the more likely it is that this contract of reciprocal rights and responsibilities is explicit, standardized, guarded, and negotiated by the workers' organization—the labor union.

Today's worker enters into highly structured systems. Quantity and quality of goods and/or services must be produced or distributed within a specified time, by specified methods, subject to overview and evaluation by the employer or his representatives. Since most work tasks are interdependent with those done by other workers, timing output, quantity and quality, interpersonal relations, and job-appropriate behavior are continuously subject to requirements, appraisals, and approvals. These characteristic conditions of work in the modern world, often a source of difficulties and dissatisfactions among workers, have been extensively described and documented.[5] Here a few problems are set forth briefly, noted because of the frequency with which they are articulated in present-day complaints about work.

"Work Makes a Person into a Robot."

The classic reference to being a robot is, of course, to the worker on a "belt-line" job, but clerical workers in large insurance companies, banks, or computer-operation companies may be just as automated and faceless. There is often in the worker a sense of being little more than a replaceable part of a machine. Relationships are chiefly to papers and/or machines, and the import of the data they carry may be a mystery or a matter of small interest to the worker. There is scarce allowance for individual preferences, style, tempo, "bright ideas," or complaints. Minimal attention is paid to the individual in such jobs, except as his production markedly exceeds standards or (more often perhaps) falls below them. In short, many jobs today are not person-enhancing, relationship-need fulfilling.

"Work Is Boring."

When tasks are repetitive, routinized, fragmented parts of the whole, when no variety of pacing, materials, or process is present, when the job requires less of capacity and skill than the worker has on tap (or feels he has) then such work is, indeed, a bore. And Satan may find mischief not only for idle hands but for bored ones, too. The complaint of work being boring also ties in with depersonalization.

Bored workers raise some troubling questions. One is whether many people in today's world have lost—or never had—the capacity to be interested, to see into and beyond the obvious. In order to be "astonished" (to use Terkel's work ideal) or to find "meaning" in what one does, it is necessary to have the openness to experience and the push to make meaning (rational or emotional) of it. All of us know people who are chronically "bored," not just with their work but with other aspects of their lives as well. They may restlessly seek excitements of sex, alcohol, or drugs, or they may become the passive receivers of images of excitement via television or spectator sports. Empty of inner resources, they try endlessly to take in stimulation from the outside, yet find it wanting or evanescent. They were often "bored" youngsters at school, unable or unhelped to find the connection between themselves and the potentially interesting subject matters to which they were being exposed. The exact nature of the widespread present-day psychological "disease" of boredom cannot be dealt with here, but surely plays some part in work boredom. Aldous Huxley offered a cynical solution to the problem of such boredom with his "Brave New World," in which the social planners conditioned numbers of new-born babies to be so insensitive and unperceptive that they would willingly take on the menial and boring jobs essential to the society.

This does not for a moment deny the emptiness that inheres in such work as requires minimal input from the person and, in turn, gives minimal feedback. It does, however, suggest that in the individual case, when the complaints include "boredom" (whether on a paid job, or in parenting, or at school—all of which involve "work"), it behooves a caseworker to examine, together with the client, both the subjective-personal and objective-reality facts of this unhappy state. Recent experiments in a number of work places to heighten and maintain worker interest are quite encouraging.[6]

"I Don't Like Being Bossed."

The bigger the operation, the greater the necessity for the systematic regulation of its parts. Thus the workplace today is often a bureaucracy—which is to say that roles and tasks are clearly defined, as are the rules and expectations that govern them, and that of necessity there is a hierarchical structure of authority and responsibility. While for production and distribution purposes such organization is both effective and efficient, for the individual worker it may hold a number of frustrations and dissatisfactions. There exists a great divide between the workers and the "top men" or sources of power with whom they might wish to communicate, either with complaints or constructive suggestions. Each worker must go through "channels" of lower-echelon management persons, who may block rather than facilitate such passage.

Expectations and regulations are set forth and enforced by someone with delegated authority—the foreman, the supervisor, the manager. When that person tends to act in an authoritarian manner ("as if he is the boss"), or even when he validly invokes his right and responsibility to give directions or criticisms, he may rouse hostility in the worker. This is particularly likely to occur in persons who enter the work world already smoldering with anger at those "in charge," those who have wielded power over them, whose criticisms or requirements have seemed to be directed not at their performance but at them as persons. As at least one study revealed, and as informal comments frequently show, the dream of the American worker is to "be my own boss."[7]

Social workers not infrequently encounter family problems where harsh authoritarianism on the part of the husband and father plays an important part in the conflict. The defensive need to "be the boss" when one has felt "bossed" is often seen in these instances; or there may operate an "identification with the aggressor," a knuckling-under to authority with the subsequent need to vent the felt aggression elsewhere.

"Time Waits for No Man"—or Woman Either.

Among the most common irritants to workers and to employers are the rules that govern time. Not only is a certain quantity of production or service expected within stipulated time units but the worker is expected to be at the job "on time" and not to leave before a specified time. (And the worker who leaves *after* such time may also be criticized—not by the employer, but by peers.) Most people in our culture are time- and clock-ruled well before they enter the world of work. There are, however, subcultures for whom time is either more fluid or held less important than is usual in our American society. Members of such groups may have difficulty adjusting to the constricting time-demands of organized work.

Furthermore, the present-day work place is rarely near home. Travel to and from work extends the work day, and whether in one's own car or on public transportation there are tensions created by traffic jams and vehicle failures. When geographical distance from work eats time it adds to the strains of the work day.

Time schedules are being given a fresh look, however, by some industries and businesses. The idea of "flexitime" has entered their vocabularies and planning. Rearrangements such as shorter hours, later or earlier work shifts, and part-time employment are under consideration and experiment. Such flexibilities hold special import for women workers, many of whom still carry their mothering and homemaking roles along with their paid employment.

"Work Takes Too Much, Gives Too Little."

It cannot be ignored. There are (and have been, since time immemorial) many jobs, often essential to the general welfare, that are underpaid, underrecognized, or even denigrated socially. They are "dirty" or back-breaking or "sometime" jobs, to be done by what is called "casual labor." They require more brawn than brain. Little education or skill is involved. This kind of physically demanding but socially demeaning work (once, it must be remembered, the most usual occupations of the "working class") has been a persistent concern for social planners and utopian dreamers over centuries.

"Who collects the garbage in Utopia?" This is a question amusing on the face of it, that has been seriously considered by every responsible social planner, because in any model society work is supposed to enhance each man's (or woman's) self-respect and self-actualization as well as contributing to the general communal welfare. Thomas More, in his 16th-century *Utopia* rotates his population through various kinds of work, so that everyone does some dirty work. Bellamy, in *Looking Backward* (late 19th century) mobilizes an "industrial army" in which the young adults entering the world of work are conscripted to carry the menial jobs for several years before they are free to enter occupations of their choice. Skinner, in his 20th-century *Walden II*, arranges that the more trying and unattractive the job the more "work credit" is given the laborer, which buys him more leisure time and other privileges. Actual communal experiments, especially in the second half of the twentieth century, have often foundered on this very problem—the unwillingness or unreadiness of commune members to do the necessary but unskilled and "hard" or "dirty" kinds of work.

Jobs such as these often go begging for takers, spurned by even the long-unemployed. And they pose a practical and philosophical dilemma for those who, along with social workers, wrestle with the issue of whether an able-bodied individual "ought" to work as a moral obligation, to free his fellowmen of the costs of his maintenance, or whether he is entitled to choose what he will or will not do and have his economic needs met simply because he is a human being.

We have also mentioned the "casual laborer." (Who, one wonders, is "casual"— the worker or his hirer?) The underemployment, the lack of financial security plus the generally poor pay, the being "used" as an "animate tool" (Aristotle's definition of a slave) and then cast off, cannot but add to any worker's already entrenched sense of discouragement and worthlessness.

In recent years and in some places there has been an upgrading of some socially demeaning jobs—by union organization of the workers, by payment of adequate-to-good wages, and by the enhancement of status by changes of job title, such as "sanitation worker" in place of "scavenger" or "garbage man." Nevertheless, for the person who has been thrust into such work for lack of past or present opportunities, or for the person who feels he or she has potential for "better things," such jobs may be a continuous and valid source of discontent.

"Work Falls Short of (Unrealistic) Expectations."

Several subtle and insufficiently recognized social conditions today may account for the frequent sense of disillusionment and restiveness that is found in people at all job levels.

A large number of young adults simply fall into the job market. They have given little thought to work or to what it may require of them. Nor have they had any preparation by which they can anticipate either its demands or its values. They have seen work as a way of escaping from school and/or of earning money to buy clothes, recreation, or freedom from control, but they have never perceived work itself in any but its disagreeable aspects.

In some homes, there may have been no work model. In the street life of the slums, the people who earn good money are often in illegal, trickster occupations. In intact families of the working class, the father may return from work "dead beat," disgruntled with his day, his pay, while the mother, out of financial necessity, may be squeezing unsatisfying work into an already-overburdened schedule. For both, the small conflicts and petty demands that they encounter when they return home are irritants that occur in all families at times, but there is no escaping them when there are crowded quarters and pinched pocketbooks. Moving from blue to white collar, the "hard day at the office" replaces the "hard day at the factory," but both may present to impressionable children a picture of work as an activity that is chiefly burdensome. At the top of the heap are those parents who so "love their work" that they are almost totally immersed in it, not only at the work place but at home, too. Only narrow margins of their time or attention are spared for the family. Work then may be rejected by the children, felt to be the robber of the love and attention that are longed for.

Outside the family, there have been of late many social "promises" made to young people that have resulted in their overblown expectations. A longer time spent in school is held forth as a guarantee of satisfying employment. But the work that must be done in that extended school time is neither clarified nor emphasized. Add to this the frequent promise (via public programs) of a "job for everyone." It becomes a shibboleth. It holds forth a one-sided commitment to—what? What sort of job, for instance? Requiring what sort of input by the would-be employee? Requiring what kinds of preparation, and offering what rewards? The street-corner man or teenager knows only that no job has come to him, or that he doesn't relish what is available. In schools, in social work, in popular articles, there is little probing or discussion with the young about realistic choices in work, what they require of the worker, or even about alternatives to work. Without work—what would a person do? "Have leisure" or "develop my interests" are common answers. Rarely is it recognized (as Shakespeare said three hundred years ago) that "If all the year were playing holidays, to sport would be as tedious as to work." Nor is it recognized that leisure, if it is to be more than temporary release, if it is indeed to "develop" interests and capacities, also requires work, in the sense of an investment of time, energy, abilities, and disciplined activity.

Perhaps the foregoing is too dark a picture of the problems that seem to be frequently encountered in the work world today. The rationale for dwelling upon them is twofold. Negative attitudes about work persist in our present-day culture, reluctant as we are to relinquish dreams of limitless freedom from constraints. More relevant, however, is the fact that social workers deal with people who are experiencing temporary or chronic problems in coping with some aspect of their daily living—and work difficulties are among them. Any effective exploration of what a person's work problems consist of requires intelligence of what work problems are commonly made up of.

The Gratification Offered by Work

How is it that most workers, most of the time, grumbling and griping as they go, seem to want to be employed? All everyday evidence supports that conclusion—with, of course, the probability that most workers would welcome a better paying job, a more interesting and less demanding one. Recent studies report that the great majority of present-day workers are "satisfied with" or actually "like" their work.[8] This item, like "dog bites man," does not make interesting newspaper copy or television script, so it has gone all but unnoticed. But it deserves thoughtful consideration, especially by social workers whose concern with work-related problems involves knowing what personal gratifications and life-enhancing values work may offer to a given client.[9]

The most obvious gratification that work provides is money. Beyond essentials for physical survival, it buys many other things, too. Today's wages and salaries purchase many luxury items—television sets, cars, washing machines. (One is immediately aware of how swiftly yesterday's "luxury" becomes today's "necessity.") It buys commodities that ease drudgery, facilitate tasks, or add variety to the day's living, and it buys release from work's humdrum by providing vacations, social contacts, and leisure-time occupations.

Other benefits, present and future, are bought by working. Old age and health insurance and unemployment compensation are public provisions; corporations and large private organizations offer pensions and health insurance supplements; and for the unionized worker, there are legal and credit aids, health and housing services, educational and recreational opportunities. Beyond these tangible economic benefits are more subtle psychological ones. "Money talks." It says, among other things: "What you do is valued." While this may be a source of disgruntlement when a worker feels he or she is financially *undervalued*, it is in general a social affirmation of "value received." It has often been noted that among volunteer workers, whose major gratifications come from the rewards of interpersonal recognitions and their inner sense of contribution to the well-being of others, there often crops up some expression of resentment that their work is not truly "valued," because it is not paid for in "hard cash."

Beyond money, work holds a number of further incentives and satisfactions. One is reminded of what Conrad put so trenchantly into the mouth of his Charlie Marlowe: "I don't like work . . . no man does—but I like what is *in* the work—the chance to find yourself. Your own reality . . ."[10]

"What is *in* the work" is the gist of what follows.

In work, said Freud, a person is "securely attached to a part of reality, the human community".[11] This same idea is expressed by a present-day social scientist, following his study of over fifteen hundred employed men: ". . . work still remains a necessary condition for drawing the individual into the mainstream of social life . . ."[12]

Basic to every individual's sense of personal security, of having a place and a purpose in the social system, is the experience of "belonging," of being connected with others in a regularized, reliable, established way. Work offers this sense of social bonding, both to tasks that are held to be socially valuable and to other persons with whom, interdependently, those tasks are performed. There are many facets to this phenomenon.

Companionship with fellow workers is one. As at least one study found, the daily social intercourse with fellow workers was the "most missed" aspect of work by men who had been retired.[13] Even though such on-the-job companionship may be maintained at a fairly superficial level of comraderie, it meets in part the need to be connected with others—whether to share jokes, to vent and share gripes, to counteract loneliness, or, at best, to provide a variety of relationships and a sense of support.

The development of unions and the increase of their power heightens the worker's sense of bonding with a group that is recognized as a force to be dealt with. It is possible that each worker takes into himself some sense of the strength that is provided by union with one's peers.

Away from the job, there are other kinds of social recognition and affirmation in a steady job. Like it or not, an adult in our society is "placed" and establishes some primary identity by what he or she works at. "What do you do?" "What's your work—your field?" These are questions, abrasive or courteous, that we all encounter early in an acquaintanceship. They are asked in an attempt to establish where a person stands in the social system and are based on the assumption that every adult "works at" something. And the man or woman who does not work (for pay, as volunteer, or self-employment) feels awkward and "out of it." Many a woman still speaks self-deprecatingly of being "just a wife and a mother."

Students of personality development seem to be giving increasing recognition to the growth of the sense of selfhood and of identity security as a consequence of the active engagement of the person with other persons or tasks when what is made to happen is held to be "good," or desirable. The knowledge of the self as a producer, a maker, a provider or facilitator, an agent of some change, gives added dimension to the person when there is some evidence that what is done is needed or approved of by significant others. "I *am* because I *do*" is Lois Barclay's formulation of the little child's self-awareness and confidence via the effects he creates and the things he is able to master, and this is especially true when the people close to him mirror and confirm his competence. By adulthood, of course, this is both a diluted and a ramified experience. Nevertheless the sense of self as producing or as enacting functions that are socially valued accrues to one's self-measurement and self-regard.

Work gives form and purpose to the day. It regularizes and stabilizes a significant segment of each day; it mobilizes and channels each person's intentions and activities. Often the time, place, and purpose constrictions that work imposes seem irksome. Yet, as attested to by retirees and persons laid off from work for extended periods, it is common with the loss of work to experience a restlessness, an unsettled, unanchored feeling. The employed worker feels an intensified pleasure in his free time; the person who does no work (study and avocational interests which are goal-oriented must here be included as work) finds himself "killing time," uneasy about its drag or flight, annoyed to find that his freedom places upon him the burden of choices and decisions about what to do with himself. If work is not too stressful or consuming, it constitutes a reliable back-bone in the day of many persons—supporting, as it were, the body of their other, less-regularized activities.

Sometimes for good, sometimes for ill, work serves as an escape, a kind of defense against many of life's vicissitudes. By its very objective requirements, its regularity, or by the undemanding or underpinning relationships with fellow workers, it may serve to bind anxieties.[14] It may dilute the impact of other problems or help to suppress acute awareness of them. This has been suggested as one reason for the difficulty that social caseworkers have had in involving the working man in family problems. Aside from the reality that his work hours do not always fit those of the social agency, and aside from his sense that by his hard work and family support he earns the "right" not to be bothered with domestic affairs, he may also feel the fact that work and the diversions it offers protect him from the impact and import of family difficulties.

In quick sum: For the workers who constitute the four-fifths who report themselves mostly "satisfied," work holds rewards and gratifications beyond (but in no way discounting) money—interpersonal relationships, social status, and personal-identity-supports, the stabilization of daily life, the provision of tangible benefits, and some psychological privileges. Polls and single-answer questionnaires do not provide insights into what "satisfaction" may exist beyond these rewards, which among them seem to take prior place, or what combinations of work experiences and off-the-job experiences create a "happy" or "unhappy" worker. Just as we know less about good health than about sickness, so we know less about the satisfied than about the dissatisfied or unsatisfied worker. We do, however, seem to have enough evidence of the worth and use of work in the lives of adults to be tempted to paraphrase Voltaire's irreverent dictum about God: If there were no work, it would be necessary to invent it.

Understanding Clients as Workers

In any profession, the acquisition of knowledge and understanding is for use. Its purpose is to inform and affect what the professional person sees, infers, and does. So the foregoing glimpses into work in the lives of people who become clients of social workers must be followed by considerations of their practical use in helping people cope with problems in their psychosocial functioning. The following discussion is confined to the major segment of social work that is concerned with direct service to individuals, families, and sometimes small groups purposely formed to deal with a common problem. The "case," the individualized instance of a problem and help sought by a single person, a family unit or a small group, is the unit of service.

Paramount in some problems, contributory in others, work penetrates and/or is penetrated by many of the personal-familial difficulties with which social workers typically deal in many kinds of agencies and organizations. Roughly categorized, these are the most common:

1. Problems of interpersonal relationships—marital, parent-child, self-to-others, and self-to-circumstances wherein the wage earner's work is an unseen but often dynamic contributory factor.
2. Problems in work performance—where off-the-job circumstances may be cause or contributor, and/or where conditions in the workplace itself may be creating difficulties.
3. Conflicts and stresses in carrying two roles, particularly common for women, whose wife-and-mother tasks and outside employment impose multiple demands.
4. Unpreparedness for entry into the work-role—adolescents, disabled adults, and others.

The first of these problems may be seen in two brief case examples:

Mrs. M. came to a family agency for help, she said, in "saving my marriage." Young, attractive, the mother of one child and pregnant with her second, she felt there was "nothing left" of the marriage. Her husband had nothing to say to her, he showed only perfunctory interest in her when he came home each evening; she felt cut off, abandoned.

Mr. M. did not respond to an invitation to talk things over. He felt marriage counseling was "unnecessary," even absurd. However, in a telephone call, he was persuaded by the caseworker to "take a chance" on one interview, and he reluctantly agreed. He was a well-put-together junior executive in a large business organization. After the caseworker's introductory sharing of the problem as his wife saw it, Mr. M. still shrugged the problem off.

MR. M: To me it seems trivial . . . silly. . . .
CW: Well, for instance—how about doing a sound-movie picture for me of one of your evenings at home?

MR. M: Okay. When I come home in the evening she wants somebody to talk to, she wants companionship. And the job I have is not taxing physically. But it is taxing mentally, and especially for me, because I am trying as hard as I can to do the best that I can, so that I can get ahead as fast as I possibly can. . . .

CW: Mm—go on. . . .

MR. M: And when I come home in the evening, I'm *tired*. Whereas she's been alone and quiet. I want an evening *alone*. I have been carrying on quite a bit of conversation all day long, and by this time I'm—well, sort of "sometimey." At work I am forced—not forced—but I mean . . . .

CW: It's in the nature of the job.

MR. M: Right! I have to, you know, I have to be congenial, naturally, to the people around me. I meet customers and I have to talk to them. And you have to be on your Ps and Qs, and as I say, it's a *strain*.

CW: Um—hm . . .

MR. M: *Always*. Because I'm trying to do as good a job as I can. At any rate when I come home in the evening I'd like to relax and I'm tired out. . . .

CW: You want to be left alone.

MR. M: I want to be left alone. And this, of course, is the opposite of what she wants. . . .

CW: I guess you didn't even think of this when you got married.

MR. M: Well, no, I sure didn't.

CW: What do you do? What job do you do?

MR. M: I'm with X Corporation.

CW: I mean, exactly what do you do there?

MR. M: I'm in training right now. [He goes on to describe in some detail his various responsibilities for the supervision and accounting for the sales and service personnel who deal with the company's customers.] At times it's a strain.

CW: You have to deal with other men all day long?

MR. M: Right! Men and women both.

CW: You try to increase—or check—their production? Or . . . ?

MR. M: I try to guide them—along general lines—I try to keep them on a straight course if possible. And I deal with customers, too.

CW: Do you think your wife gets the picture of the kind of situation you operate in during the daytime?

MR. M: [Looks thoughtful.]

CW: I mean, have you shared with her what goes on, so she gets some idea of the strain you're under?

MR. M: She has a general idea . . . but I don't think we've ever sat down and talked it over. . . . I never thought about it until now—to tell you the truth. . . .

Just this far, and the point of this illustration is clear. This couple's affectional, companionate, and even sexual relationship have been significantly affected by the husband's work life. It would be simplistic to assume that Mr. M's work requirements and ambitions were the single cause of the marriage rift. (But, it must be said, this is no more simplistic than the "sexual dysfunction" or "lack of communication" that is at times latched onto as *the* cause of a marital breakdown.) What is obvious is that for this man work is both a demanding and a consuming interest. It is a potent influencer of his attitudes and behavior. It is scarcely understood by his wife. It might, however, become a shared understanding between them, subject to their mutual exploration, perhaps conciliation, perhaps modifications of expectations and behavior on both sides.

A second brief example:

> Mrs. G., married eight years, mother of two children, came to talk about leaving her husband. Increasingly she was finding him "repulsive" sexually, dull, uncompanionable.
>
> Uneducated and unskilled, he worked in a junk yard. He worked "hard" and steadily. He was a "nice" and conscientious man. His earnings were regular, though marginal. Nothing in the course of his work day offered him interest or stimulation; his only contact with other people was when they came to sell or buy the tires, bottles, metal which he sorted and roughly inventoried. He came home every evening exhausted, filthy, depressed, and sullen. Even after bathing, his hands remained cracked with dirt, his nails black and broken. They had nothing to talk about. They saw nothing better ahead. She could no longer bear the physical stigmata of his job nor the deadening effect it had had on his personality.

It is scarcely conceivable that this marriage, or indeed the life of the family, could be saved without full consideration of the work of this husband-father-wage earner, its noxious effects, his possible alternative work opportunities—and so on. Here again, work and its impacts may not have been the basic problem in this marriage. But "basic problems," we remind ourselves, are rarely accessible to ready change. Derivative problems, alive and potent in the present, such as daily work involvements, are far more open and reachable for modification. Thus "what's *in* the work" for each man and woman and its repercussions into other life roles cannot be ignored.

Work's repercussions are often seen and felt in parent-child problems. The man whose work day is too full of noise and disorder may demand *"Quiet!"* as he enters his doorway and is greeted by quarreling or even happily noisy kids. The woman who has "put in a hard day," even if it has had its compensations, finds herself furious that her adolescent children have neglected their assigned tasks; or she is too pressed to sit down with the youngster whose teacher has sent a note indicating that he is in trouble, and instead scolds: "I'll whip the daylights out of you if I get another note like this!"

Actually, we social workers need look no further than into our own daily work lives to recognize the often vital effects—sometimes benign sometimes noxious—that work has upon off-the-job relationships and transactions. It bears repetition: Any role, the work role included, that excites feeling, that is charged with emotion either chronically or at crisis-points, will have its resonating effects into other aspects of a person's daily living. Thus, when one of the participants in a problem is involved in regular employment, some attention must be given to its bearing upon the problem brought for help.

There is, of course, the turnabout. Just as a person's work life may permeate other parts of his daily experience, so his troubles on the outside may be brought to the job. Worries and angers about relationships, debts and unmet needs, illness, about the care and safety of the children—these and other concerns may so trouble the worker that job performance is seriously affected.

It is this concern that is probably the motivator for the growing interest by business and industry in utilizing social workers to deal with such problems. Whether such motivation is less "pure altruism" (if such indeed exists) and more enlightened self-interest is not the issue. Primary is the plain fact that an unhappy, discontented, malfunctioning worker-on-the-job is likely to be an unhappy, discontented, malfunctioning *person*, and this is the concern of the social worker.

How much and in what ways is this work dysfunction due to the actual job realities—to the lack of fit, say, between the worker and his occupational tasks, to poor working conditions, to conflicts with supervisors or work-mates, and so on? How much and in what ways is the work dysfunction created or exacerbated by off-the-job circumstances? These are among the questions that the social worker must ask and answer to assess the work problem and plan for dealing with it, whether within the workplace itself or on the outside.

A major concern to industry today is the high incidence of alcoholism. Whether this incidence is indeed an increase over what it was in the past is a matter for speculation, since facts are not available. What is known is the frequency with which "drink" as the "curse of the working class" has appeared in literature, reformist tracts, and historical accounts over the past few centuries. In any case, modern complex machines and high standards of work efficiency make drunkenness or its aftermath a greater hazard than before. Absences, irregularities, and accidents on the job are the offshoots of alcoholism. Not too long ago, it was assumed that job monotony and stress drove men to drink. Recently, addiction has been attributed to an individual's high levels of biochemical sensitivity to even a moderate intake of alcohol. Almost lost sight of today, however, is the old-fashioned and yet not altogether disposable possibility that problems in family life may play a potent part in the worker's seeking the escape that drinking proffers.

A major concern for social workers today are those workers whose jobs may be most often invaded by problems from the outside. They are the most recent entrants into the labor force: women who are mothers of young, care-needing children. They fall into three categories: (1) mothers who seek the gratifications of work, yet are continuously hampered and harassed by home problems; (2) those who feel they must work to supplement the family income and meet needs; and (3) those who are being pressed to work by others, chiefly because they and their children are financial burdens upon the community.

Despite the advances in recent years toward work equality for women, there remains a persistent inequality between a father-worker and a mother-worker. They may carry equal jobs or positions and earn equal wages or salary. But, with exceptions that are more rare than they are usual, the home- and child-care arrangements and tasks tend to remain for the woman to take over on her return home from work. They are the traditional responsibilities carried by women: grocery- and meal-planning, clothing and household goods shopping; attendance on the sick or otherwise attention-needing child; arranging for dentist, doctor, dancing lesson, birthday party appointments; reciprocal aids and hospitalities and active participation in events or crises or even celebrations in the circle of family and friends. Such trivia can, by their pile-up, constitute a tensional burden that the worker-mother carries to her daily job.

Furthermore, unless there is some surplus of money, adequate home- and child-care services cannot often be bought. To work or not to work may become a nagging dilemma. Mothers who take on paid employment because they actually need the money carry, then, a double burden. The child-care arrangements they make are usually in the homes of other women or in organized child-care centers. Either of these may be at some distance from home or the workplace. The time, energy, and strategies involved in covering these distances is not inconsiderable. The occasional crisis in the care-agent's household, a child's illness, a transportation breakdown—such difficulties cause absence or tardiness that creates tensions in the employer and employee both.

What gains or losses accrue to the children have only been guessed at. The "latch-key child" may run the streets until his mother returns home; the child who attends a well-run nursery or after-school center may be having an enriched learning and companionship experience. But dependable and adequate child-care facilities remain in short supply. At her paid work, the mother's home- and child-management difficulties may fester uneasily under the surface, sometimes causing her to make mistakes, to be irritable to customers or fellow-workers. After work hours, the accumulated stress may play out in family relationships.

Perhaps most problematic to large numbers of social workers is the usually spouseless mother "on welfare." Should she be pressed to work so as to earn some part of her maintenance, if not to get off the relief rolls? Recurrent waves of public opinion push for this, and the social worker is not immune to this pressure. But public opinion, even official social policy, delivers a double message. It says in one breath that child-rearing is a mother's priority task. (It was only a few years ago that a presidential veto wiped out a projected development of child-care centers on the basis that their use would undermine parental responsibility.) At the same time, little attention or social approval is given to the work of rearing children, or to the handicaps of single parenthood accompanied by strictured funds, inadequate housing and household equipment, paucity of educational and recreational outlets, and all the other handicaps to adequate family living that inhere in chronic hand-to-mouth poverty. Further—if mothering is indeed held to be vital to children's well-being, are there articulated, generally accepted criteria for, say, its minimum requirements? Or "crediting" for the efforts—the work—that must go into their achievement? Is there public policy and general recognition that goes beyond mere sentiment for the resources that must exist to bolster otherwise economically and psychologically impoverished family life? And what are the payoffs, the incentives for the "welfare mother" who is urged to take an outside job? She will encounter all the problems of other working mothers. What will her compensations be? Minimal reward creates minimal motivation.

The recurrent issues involved in work for mothers on relief are complicated and of a magnitude that calls for large-scale policy reconsiderations and rearrangements. However, in the individual instances that caseworkers encounter, that need here-and-now help, these (and further) questions call for individualized discussion with each mother of the pros and cons, sacrifices and gains, wishes and realities. Essential in such discussion is the social worker's awareness and control of his or her own biases and inclinations about working mothers and an informed, down-to-earth grasp of the specifics of what work life may offer and what gains and losses may ensue for the individual woman, whether she yearns for or feels forced to take on work outside her home.

Yet one further group of work-related problems that is well known to social workers remains to be touched on. The persons who bear them are youngsters and adults at all economic levels. Their common difficulty is that paid work for them is blocked by some personal incapacity or circumstantial obstacles. Unemployed, some of them want to work, some do not, and some are uneasily ambivalent. Their inability to get or hold a job may be due to emotional-mental instability, to mental or physical disabilities, to personality or characterological problems that include no sense of the self as "able." They may lack language or interpersonal skills to communicate effectively for even a job application; they may never have known work satisfactions in school or at home; or, if there has been some recent physical or mental breakdown, they may be fearful of re-entry into new or unfamiliar employment.

A heartening number of programs have been developed across the country for the retraining, rehabilitation, and vocational guidance of physically and mentally handicapped would-be workers. Many of these programs utilize social workers as counselors, as "influencers" of the family attitudes and behaviors that affect those of the prospective worker, and as resource persons for necessary services and aids beyond those that are directly work-related. But before the handicapped would-be worker can make use of guidance or training he must want to do so, he must have some motivation toward or confidence in the value and rewards he may expect if he engages himself in work training.

In hospitals, clinics, schools, and family agencies, social caseworkers frequently encounter patients, students, and drifters whose motivation to work is ambivalent and shot through with self-doubt and fears of others—people who are uncertain about work possibilities or about their own goals. They need several different kinds of help: to examine and come to know their own potential capacities and limitations; to become informed about the existing opportunities that will prepare them for work; to weigh and consider the realistic tasks, the behavioral demands, and the potential rewards in the work world. If preparation for work is chosen, they may also need the social worker's active help to link up with the resource.

Preparation for entry into the world of work ought not be confined to handicapped or unskilled adults. Many young people could also benefit from it. Especially for those youngsters who have spent their school days fruitlessly, "fooling around," "getting by," "serving time," to become a worker is a major role transition. Many youngsters have had few worker models to learn from; many want to earn money but have given little thought to what will be expected of them in return or what they themselves are able and willing to invest.

It is yet another indication of how little thought has been given to the role of work that while there has been a flurry of courses offered to high school students in preparation for marriage and for parenthood, few such courses are offered in preparation for work, which usually precedes those other roles. True, students in some schools do get "orientation" and work-training programs on how to behave in a job interview, how to fill out a job application, and other "how-to" guides. Underpinning these, and potentially of more basic value, there ought to be small group discussions on the facts of work life, of the ethos (not the "ethic") of the work world, of worker rights and responsibilities, of work requirements and opportunities.

No discussion of the interpenetration of work life and other daily life experiences can overlook the many instances of positive, supportive, gratifying effects of work in what may otherwise be dreary or disheartening. Consider these examples:

> Mrs. Y, a 55-year-old childless widow, has her ailing, emotionally dependent mother living with her. If it were not for her work (as "secretary" in a large typing pool), she would not be able to pay for the daytime helper who attends to her mother's needs and does the light housework. More important, perhaps, is that without work her daily life would be one of isolation and confinement. As it is, she goes off cheerfully every morning buoyed up by the anticipation, not of the pile-up of the innumerable small and boring tasks she must execute, but of the chit-chat at coffee breaks with "the girls," of the appreciations expressed by this or that user of her services for her speed, her clean copy, or of her new blouse or hair-do, of window-shopping at lunch, of her bowling evening ahead. Work, in brief, brightens her daily life with companionship and variety.
>
> Mr. Z is an insurance adjuster. At home is his mentally retarded little boy and his anxiety-ridden wife. He carries them both in the pit of his stomach, but during his work day he is relatively free of his

dark sorrows. This is because he enters a world where he is regarded by his superiors, whom he respects, as a competent and effective company representative. Moreover, he enjoys the variety of the customers he encounters, especially when what he does seems to be appreciated by them and found helpful. He is liked by his coworkers, several of whom he counts as friends, since they are sympathetic with his family problems and, in turn, often turn to him to talk over theirs. In his work, in short, he finds recognition of his capabilities and an affirmation from his superiors, peers, and customers that he is valued. When he returns home to confront its problems he carries in him some sustaining sense of having a back-up source that supports his spirit and steadies his feelings and behavior.

Why, one must ask, would it be desirable or helpful for the Z family's social worker (operating out of the pediatric neurology clinic to help the Z's deal with their damaged child with less anxiety and tension) to draw Mr. Z out about his work at some point in the course of their talks together? What purpose might such an inquiry serve in any case where the problem presented is manifestly neither a cause nor an effect of work difficulties, or where work is clearly an asset to personal and family stability? It is worth some consideration. We are generally so continuously focused upon our client's failures and troubles that we seldom turn to encourage him to tell (and thus himself to hear and to know more fully) what his past or present areas of satisfaction are—where he has coped successfully, where he feels "good." Such a shared account, received with responsive appreciation by another, gives a person some heightened sense that he is more than just a help-^rs prol   ., So, if it is not flagrantly irrelevant, and if one is in search   ..iace ..i .ne client's life where positives may be affirmed, his work adequacy a..d satisfactions may be worth talking about as a reinforcement of his sense of self as a "coper."

Of course, the rule that governs all good interviewing holds: What one dwells on, when, and what emphasis of time and detail is given to a subject depends upon the problem presented and the solution that is sought. Exploration of the work life oi a client may have only tangential relevance. Yet we cannot know until at least a tentative glance is given to it how potent for good or ill the person's everyday, all-day experience of making a living may be. In the case fragments cited earlier, that of the junior executive consumed with "making good" and that of the junkman sunk in personal as well as marital despair, work and its emotional plus-and-minus meanings could be seen as a core dynamic. Yet it might easily have been overlooked.

Whether the worker-client is helped by some social welfare agency or within the workplace itself, the caseworker's helping process is essentially the same. The clear identification of the client's problem for which he wants or needs help, the caring attention paid to his emotional investments or responses to it, the demonstration and assurance that the helper is *with* and *for* him, the cards-on-the-table coming to understandings ("contract") about what real and accessible means and actions may be utilized—about who does what and why, the consideration of action alternatives and probable consequences, the guided choice of some next steps—all these mutually discussed, reflected upon, considered and reconsidered interchanges between client and caseworker are generic to the problem-solving methods of casework. In no sense are they cut and dried. They are shaped, colored, varied by the individual situation, by the specialness of person, problem, and place.

The specialness of each person needs no discussion here. It has had extensive and intensive exploration in social work's value system and psychological knowledge. The specialness of the workplace and its rules and tasks (as is the case with the specialness of a school or a hospital system) and the particular problem centered upon at a given time—these are the substance of specialty.[15] When the problem involves work or the workplace, it is incumbent upon the helper to know and understand its objective realities as well as the client's subjective sense of it.

Valuable as they are, counseling and guidance services are not always all that the client-as-worker needs. His problem often requires the finding and providing of tangible means. It may require changes or rearrangements of the circumstances or conditions that are inimical to his coping. It is often necessary, then, for the social worker to take an active lead in making the linkage or connection between the client and the resource he needs, and to set the necessary changes in motion.

"Active intervention," "linkage," and "advocacy" slip easily off the tongue or pen, but they are processes that involve time, grasp of realities, and skill. There may be several different realities to be grasped. One is the nature and operations of the system (here let's say a factory, a business corporation, a union) to be dealt with. Another is the aims, views, and motivations of the persons who activate the system, since the fact is that all resources and opportunities are conveyed and controlled by people, who must be worked *with* and *through* if one is to influence what they will do and how they will act toward the client in whose behalf we intervene. Yet a further reality is that the client himself may feel or behave in ways that will hamper rather than further his use of the means he needs.

Thus the social worker's helping service goes beyond individual or small group counseling. He or she must often reach out to the client's "significant others," to those persons who are or who may be involved in the problem, either as contributors to its existence or as potential contributors to its easement or solution. They may need to be engaged both in some sympathetic understanding of the client and his special needs and in some willingness to lend themselves to meeting them.

This influencing of persons who control aids and means in order that they may come into some workable linkage with the client is what is meant by social work's long-honored tradition of "environmental modification." This is, in modern times, an ecological perspective. It recognizes the continuous interpenetration between the individual person and the persons and circumstances with whom he lives and tries to cope. Therefore it demands active efforts to find and to facilitate the client's constructive use of available means for his problem's solution. Those efforts require some substantive knowledge of and respect for the conditions and the resources one reaches out to enlist and affect. And they require considerable skill in overcoming the frequent resistances and heightening the cooperation of the people whose "yea" or "nay" may determine the course and outcome of the client's problem.

It is often the case, then, that social workers in family and child agencies and in a host of other human welfare organizations may need to reach into the workplace both via the client's account of its relation to his problem and in direct negotiations with the employer, his representative, or union personnel. On the other side, the social worker in the union or industry may often need to refer his clients out to such available resources as are appropriate to his problem, and, beyond referral, to enable his client and those resources to successfully connect with one another. At the same time, and often in the same case, he may need to try to influence such persons and conditions in the workplace itself—the work environment, the "system" of peopled roles and arrangements, the "significant others," who, by their authority or attitudes, affect the client as worker.[16]

It is this ecological perspective, this awareness of the continuous input and feed-back between people and the other people and the circumstances we call "environment," and the trained-in readiness and skill to influence the latter as well as the former that may be said to be the distinguishing mark of social work help. Perhaps this is what gives social work its special usefulness in any organization— the world of work included—that seeks to lower the obstacles that block a person's personally satisfying and socially satisfactory functioning.

Conclusions

There remains much more to be delineated and discovered and considered about human beings and their age-old, life-long involvement in work. Within the limits of this chapter, it has been possible to open only a few perspectives on our clients as workers. Mostly its purpose has been to raise the conscious awareness and interest of social case- and group-workers to our own culturally induced biases and disregard of the meanings of work in the lives of most adults; to alert us to some of work's difficulties as well as to some of its satisfactions; to suggest its interlacings with other vital roles in people's lives; and to touch upon the implications of these insights for our continuous efforts to ease people's problems and enhance their everyday living.

One hears the echo of Conrad again. "What is *in* the work" for each man and woman, what chance it offers them to find themselves and their reality. This is what we need to know more fully and truly in every case.

Notes

[1] Robert Dubin, "Industrial Workers' Worlds: A Study of the Central Life Interests of Industrial Workers," *Social Problems,* 3, no. 3 (January 1956), 131–42.

[2] Louis Orzack, "Work as a Central Life Interest of Professionals," *Social Problems,* 7, no. 2 (Fall 1959). The studies in notes 1 and 2 are both reprinted in E.O. Smigel, *Work and Leisure* (New Haven, Conn.: College and University Press, 1963).

[3] Studs Terkel, *Working* (New York: Pantheon, 1974), p. xi.

[4] *Work in America: Report of a Special Task Force to the Secretary of Health, Education, and Welfare* (Cambridge, Mass.: M.I.T. Press, 1973), p. 3. Another definition: "Work is the involvement, investment [of a person] . . . in some actions or processes that aim to produce a planned product or outcome." Helen Harris Perlman, *Persona: Social Role and Personality* (Chicago: University of Chicago Press, 1979), p. 82.

[5] See, for instance, Georges Friedman, *The Anatomy of Work* (Glencoe, Ill.: The Free Press, 1961); "The Characteristics of Work Environments," chapter 5 in Walter Neff, *Work and Human Behavior* (New York: Atherton Press, 1968).

[6] "Case Studies in the Humanization of Work," *Work in America,* pp. 188–202.

[7] Robert H. Guest, "Work Careers and Aspirations of Automobile Workers," *American Sociological Review,* 19, no. 2 (April 1954), 155–63.

[8] In 1973, an "over-all response" to polls that asked about satisfaction or dissatisfaction with the current job revealed that over three-fourths of the workers queried reported themselves to be "satisfied" on the job. See John T. Dunlop, "Past and Future Tendencies in American Labor Organization," *Daedalus* (Winter 1978), p. 89. Similar findings by other studies are reported in Rosabeth Moss Kanter, "Work in a New America," in the same issue of *Daedalus,* p. 54. In a 1965 study of "happiness," nine hundred men averred that "work is of crucial importance" to their happiness. One-third of unemployed men report themselves "not too happy," compared to a little more than one-tenth of employed men. See Norman M. Bradburn and David Caplovitz, *Reports on Happiness,* National Opinion Research Center (Chicago, Aldine Publishing Co., *Monographs in Social Research,* vol. 3, 1965), pp. 14–15.

[9] This section deals only briefly with what is presented in more detail in chapter 3, "Work," in Perlman, *Persona.* See also chapter 4, by Leon W. Chestang, beginning on p. 61 in this book.

[10] Joseph Conrad, *Heart of Darkness.* Marlow has been toiling over his broken-down old steamboat, and his full comment affirms a further often-overlooked truth: "I had expended enough hard work on her to make me love her," he says. He is aware that investment of interest and energy creates an emotional bond between the self and an "object."

[11] Sigmund Freud, *Civilization and Its Discontents,* 1930.

[12] Harold Wilensky, "Varieties of Work Experience," in Harry Borow, ed., *Man in a World of Work* (Boston: Houghton Mifflin, 1964), p. 148.

[13] See Herman Loether, "Meaning of Work and Adjustment to Retirement," in A. Shostak and W. Gomberg, eds., *Blue Collar World* (Englewood Cliffs, N.J.: Prentice-Hall, 1964).

[14] A study of two matched groups of depressed women showed less impairment of overall functioning in those who were employed outside the home. Myra M. Weissman and Eugene S. Paykel, *The Depressed Woman: A Study of Social Relationships* (Chicago: University of Chicago Press, 1974).

[15] The setting within which social work is practiced will heavily determine the possibilities of focus of service. See Helen Harris Perlman's chapter 4, "The Place," in *Social Casework: A Problem-Solving Process* (Chicago: University of Chicago Press, 1957) and "Generic Aspects of Specific Settings," *Social Service Review,* 23, no. 3 (September 1949), 293–301 and in *National Conference of Social Work,* 1949.

[16] For discussion of problems and process in influencing persons whose behavior and decisions affect the client's problem, see "Relating to Significant Others," chapter 8 in Helen Harris Perlman's *Relationship: The Heart of Helping People* (Chicago: University of Chicago Press, 1979).

6

"What Do You Do?" An Inquiry into the Potential of Work-Related Research

Jerome Cohen, Ph.D.
University of California, Los Angeles

Brenda G. McGowan, D. S. W.
Columbia University

The unemployed, alone among those with work-connected problems, have com-manded the attention of social work researchers. As a result, work is almost uni-versally absent as a variable in studies of clients, service needs, delivery systems, or social policy issues. This neglect continues, even though researchers know that work not only binds one to society but determines, in significant ways, the life chances for family members. Cohen and McGowan attribute this gap to multiple causes: acceptance of the myth of the separate worlds of work and family; a long-standing social work view that considers psychosocial needs as manifestations of personal problems, all but obliterating the significance of the environment, including the workplace; and a limited awareness of the contribution of work in psychosocial functioning.

But, the authors imply, these circumstances are changing. The massive entry of women into the workplace has discounted the myth of separate worlds. Re-ports that some work dehumanizes its participants demand that social workers prepare to understand the needs of such clients. Experience among practitioners in the new field of industrial social work documents the importance of work in people's mental health. These new ideas have sparked interest in a work-related research agenda. This chapter identifies the components of such an agenda, de-scribes the preferred methodology, and offers examples of the specific studies that might be undertaken.

Because so little research has been done, the possibilities seem almost infinite. The area of mental health alone includes studies of such topics as: the relationship between work and emotional problems, the contribution of work to recovery for the mentally ill, the impact of work on personal worth and family well-being, and the manpower needs that will stabilize the work lives of those for whom job uncertainty leads to excessive anxiety. The authors believe that our goal should be to study issues that will inform policy debates and practice systems. They offer some guidelines to direct our choices—we need studies that will offer specificity, focus on transactional issues, use nontraditional but relevant data sources, and offer a basis for a dialogue between researchers and practitioners. A good starting point, the authors suggest, would be to examine the meaning that social workers attribute to their own work, to help us understand our own circumstances and to raise our consciousness concerning the importance of the work experiences of others.

Our own self-awareness may be a necessary first step, but the research imperative goes beyond such self-information. Cohen and McGowan outline a series of data needs, which could serve as the basis for a work diagnosis comparable to the information collected presently to achieve a family diagnosis. In raising the issue of how work-related problems place at risk certain populations—for example underemployed persons, retired workers, and women—they make us wonder how we have treated such clients for so long without studying the specific mental health implications of work for specific client groups.

Having identified the variables appropriate to undertake a work diagnosis, the authors suggest the potential value of using work and occupational choice as an outcome variable as well. The universal difficulties encountered in evaluation research on social programs, they suggest, might benefit from the insights of industrial social work. Practice in the world of work views job maintenance often as both a goal and an outcome measure. The application of this variable to the evaluation of social work intervention in community-based settings, they argue, might help overcome the problems encountered by the lack of uniform measures in evaluation research. (Of course, they recognize that such research also faces the need for uniform, defined input—a need that remains, even if the issue of outcome measures is resolved.) They urge research, as well, on the opportunities and problems faced in industrial social work, so that we do not proliferate a field of practice without understanding its contribution to human well-being. Such efforts, if we gathered critical incidents, for example, would offer the additional spin-off of helping to illuminate practice in other settings. It would provide the base for developing theoretical constructs as to how services might or should be structured to meet the different needs of different workers.

In its review of the research enterprise, the chapter is filled with examples of studies that might be done. It can serve as a handbook on the link between methodology and specific research questions. The discussion of the conditon for carrying out research in work settings, furthermore, translates easily into the importance of confidentiality, the privacy of information, and the rights of human subjects in all research activity.

In essence, Cohen and McGowan raise our consciousness to a set of unutilized data concerning work and work settings. These data resources, when incorporated into our research thinking, can lead to improved research concerning what we always do, as in new outcome measures for evaluation research; new questions for our customary efforts, as when we study the relation between work and psychosocial functioning; and previously unexplored horizons for what we might do in the future to understand the responsibilities and opportunities of social work.

The last kind of research thinking is best illustrated by the enumeration of research questions involving the incongruities between family and work roles. How, the authors ponder, do individuals resolve the conflicting life-cycle and career demands they encounter: delayed schooling and the economic responsibility of parenthood, the simultaneous occurrence of the "best" years for child-bearing and career advancement, the attention required by young children overlapping the peak period of attention demanded by career development, the reinforcing emptiness of retirement and child leaving? Understanding these relationships might well offer new policy and practice initiatives, thereby fulfilling the basic function of research in social work.

So prominent is the role we assign to the work that people do in our expectations and judgments of them, that we might well change the familiar American greeting, "How do you do?" to "What do you do?" Relative to that prominence, little attention has been given to this activity in the professional literature on social work practice, programming, or policy development. More attention has been paid to the consequences of the lack of work, but even in this regard, the focus has generally not been on the importance of work itself; instead social work research has concentrated on the economic and social problems that the lack of work creates. For example, a recent review of major social service studies conducted during the 1970s on selected populations-at-risk makes almost no mention of the world of work except in relation to the problems experienced by families with no formal links to the labor force.[1]

Discussion of the critical meaning of work for the effective psychosocial functioning of individuals and the welfare of society at large is more likely to be found in the social and behavioral science literature. Theoreticians of the most diverse persuasions, from Freud to Marx, have drawn attention to the importance of work for healthy emotional maturation, effective development of personal and social identity, and social and economic well-being.[2] Research findings regarding the role of work in the lives of individuals and its implications for social work practice and policy analysis have been summarized in other chapters, so they need not be reviewed here (see chaps. 4, 5, and 3, by Chestang, Perlman, and Ozawa, respectively). It is clear that work constitutes a major indicator of both social status and self-esteem and that its effects are experienced not only by the individual but also in the boundaries of all the social systems within which the individual functions: family, community, and society. Social status and the economic rewards of a particular type of work may determine the neighborhood in which one lives, the school attended by one's children, the friends one has, the activities one can afford, the amount of education one may accumulate, and even the life-style one will adopt after leaving the work force. Work, then, may be characterized as an essential part of life and one that binds each person to society and determines the life chances for all members of a family.

In brief, for direct service practitioners, work can be viewed as a major psychosocial factor, which must be assessed in order to understand the actions, problems, and potentials of their clients. Similarly, for social planners and policy analysts, the world of work provides a range of social indicators by means of which they can assess the needs of different population groups and the adequacy of current social provisions, the community impact of recent demographic shifts, and the effect of various social policies on individual functioning and family life.

Given the centrality of work in relation to personal and social identity, family life-style, and community functioning, as dictated by both the values and the economic resources it helps create, what accounts for the limited quantity of social work research on this topic? The answer is something of a paradox. While social work has been in the forefront of those professions concerned with the identification and resolution of individual and social problems in matters of economic need and the unavailability of work as related to that economic need, it has at the same time tended to ignore the relationship of work to the problems of non-economic psychosocial adjustment or to the distribution of social benefits among different groups of workers.

There would seem to be several reasons for this gap in social work research. First, as Kanter has suggested, all social science research, reflecting the predilections of capitalist institutions in a modern industrial society, has tended to operate on the myth that family and work are separate worlds.

> Separation of the occupational and family sectors of society came to be considered, by modern Parsonian theory as well as conventional wisdom of the post-World War II period, essential to the smooth functioning of each institution and thus to the integration of society as a whole. . . . The work world's interests were served in Parsonian theory by making sure that only one member of a conjugal family unit played a "fully competitive" role in the occupational system and that workplaces were clearly distinct from residences. The family's interests were also served by this separation (and exclusion of married women from careers), for intimacy and solidarity can be retained, the theory held, only if husband, wife, and children do not engage in direct competition for prestige or rate performance by impersonal standards.[3]

Social workers, ignoring their own experience of listening daily to clients discuss the difficulties of reconciling work and family demands, have somehow chosen to accept this myth and to concentrate their practice and research efforts on discovering means of enhancing individual and family functioning.

Second, a desire to achieve professional status and scientific respectability forced direct service practitioners into what has been termed "premature closure" on a model of practice in which psychosocial needs are customarily viewed as manifestations of personal pathology. Adoption of this practice model has blinded practitioners and researchers alike to the importance of work in clients' lives.

> In retrospect, it is easy to see that one of the unplanned outcomes of adopting the medical model to implement the scientific commitment was to direct attention to presumed individual defect, thus obscuring institutional or social inadequacies. The model tended, in use, to obliterate awareness and concern with social systems and social processes.[4]

Finally, among social workers engaged in community organizing and planning, an almost exclusive concern with the sources of poverty and potential solutions to this problem has tended to obscure other psychosocial components of human behavior and the social environment.

It is tempting, but futile, to decry the fact that social work research is so heavily influenced by its political and social context. As Zimbalist's careful analysis of historical trends and landmarks in social welfare research demonstrates:

> . . . Values pervade not only the interpretation of findings, the techniques for obtaining those findings, and the underlying parameters in which they [are] couched but also—and perhaps most significantly— the very perception and choice of the research problem qua problem in the first instance. This value grounding of empirical inquiry is not unique to social work. . . . But perhaps nowhere are science and value more directly and inextricably joined than in social work, at the very nexus of constructive interaction between the individual or group and the surrounding environment.[5]

Therefore, a more realistic approach is to take advantage of changing public and professional perceptions of need in order to obtain the fiscal and institutional support necessary to explore uncharted areas. Fortunately, there are several forces converging at present which highlight the potential benefits of work-related research for social workers, and many of the newer practice models in which social workers entering the field are now being trained support utilization of the findings from such research.

Potential Benefits of Work-Related Research

Perhaps the most significant force emphasizing the importance of work-related research is the dramatic increase in the proportion of mothers of young children entering the labor force. Now that approximately half of all women with children under eighteen are participating in the labor force, it is impossible to cling to the myth of separation of work and family roles.[6] Another factor that contributes to the current interest in work-related research for social workers is the report of widespread alienation among American workers.[7] Certainly a profession which claims that one of its primary missions is to individualize client need and enhance the social environment can no longer ignore a sector of life that many find so dehumanizing.

A third force contributing to the current concern about work roles and opportunities is the growing recognition among federal policymakers that the only way to insure equality for all Americans is to find ways to ease entry into the labor market for groups traditionally excluded from the work force. For example, President Carter announced that his major domestic initiative for 1980 was a $2 billion youth program aimed at finding solutions to the problem of scandalously high unemployment rates among minority youth. The Vocational Rehabilitation Act of 1973 was designed to insure affirmative action for handicapped persons in all worksites receiving any type of federal support. And there are a number of ongoing efforts to provide fuller employment opportunities for women and senior citizens, many of which have involved social workers at various stages of program design and implementation.

Finally, the developing field of industrial social work is beginning to document the importance of work and the workplace in the lives of clients, thereby forcing social work educators to give increased attention to these phenomena. But this documentation is sparse, and frequently it is not provided in a manner that can be integrated into the consciousness of planners and practitioners in other fields of social work practice. Therefore, there would seem to be a clear need to develop a work-related research agenda that involves and has implications for a broader segment of the social work community.

What are the work issues that might attend to this requirement? Social work as a profession has been powerfully influenced by issues of individual and family adjustment within the context of a mental health perspective. The most extensive groundbreaking programs in industrial social work, supported by labor, management, or government funding, have all been in this practice arena. It would seem that this is a reasonable place to begin the inquiry into work-related research questions. A number of practitioners and investigators have been concerned with the relationship of work to emotional problems and symptoms associated with the mental health–illness continuum.[8] It is possible to identify questions central to the understanding of psychosocial functioning as it relates to work. For example, how is the client's work related to personal life satisfaction or dissatisfaction? What relationship does this have to self-esteem? Is this associated with whether the work is clean or dirty? Work of the mind has historically been viewed as a higher calling than physical labor. Do white-collar workers always share higher self-esteem than blue-collar workers? If not, what are the conditions of work that determine adequate self-esteem? Have the counter-culture trends of the 1960s in trying to recapture the worth of crafts filtered down into the larger population of young adult workers, or was this just a romantic escape for children of the middle class? What is the relationship of educational preparation to the work that is actually being done? Women, for example, are notoriously underemployed in relation to their educational attainment. What does this do to their sense of personal worth?

A knowledge of manpower needs and trends may be helpful in forecasting the level of security or anxiety that workers in particular occupations experience. How are individual and family functioning affected by the length and time of the day in which work occurs? When work is primarily physical or mental, do the other unused functions tend to atrophy? Does geographical distance between home and work affect relationships in the separate communities in which work and home living occur? Are there special risks to health that are related to the type of work, and does worry about these risks drain energy that would be more useful for other purposes? Does the manner of pay, either weekly or monthly, determine consumer practices and financial indebtedness? How do the requirements of work for manners, travel, clothing, tools, etc. impact upon individual and family? Is the work perceived as menial, boring, and uninteresting, or is it exciting and fulfilling?

In recent responses to articles and reports concerning "worker blues," there have been a variety of perspectives on whether work ever has been exciting and fulfilling for the majority of workers in America.[9] Therefore, it could be important to know whether the client's work is primarily of intrinsic or of extrinsic value in reward terms. Some work constitutes a way of life that is used as a central focal point for all activities, while other work is associated with the development of the economic benefits that allow individuals to carry out other activities of central concern to them. Many workers dislike the kind of work they do and stay on the job only to pay for their subsistence and leisure. Some work to escape boredom, but find that work is not a solution and therefore change jobs frequently. Others find work creative and stimulating and spend many extra hours to find ways to do their work better. Still others may not find their work intrinsically satisfying, but are so involved with the goals associated with their efforts that they continue nevertheless. And many workers may not dislike their work, even though aspects of it may present specific problems. Such variations need to be identified and considered in relation to specific populations and types of problems.

Each of these issues could provide the basis for significant research efforts. It would take many lifetimes to discover answers to the questions just enumerated. Yet, these questions refer only to the relationship between work and mental health. Many other research problems could be posed regarding the relationship between work and family life, child development, aging, community development, social control, and so forth. Hence, it is clear that there is no shortage of work-related research issues for social workers to explore. The real dilemma is how best to allocate the limited resources available for social work research in order to begin a systematic process of data collection in this relatively uncharted area.

Guidelines for Social Work Research

We would propose four guidelines for future work in this area. First, specificity is essential. For example, while issues of worker satisfaction levels may be debated in terms of general theory about worker satisfaction or alienation, it is more central to social work efforts to assess the extent and composition of such responses in particular workplaces and in particular industries. It is only in this manner that the potentials for professional understanding and for intervention supported by research data may be realized. Eventually, constructs will emerge that will tie various types of work and conditions of work together so that they may be predictive at a higher level of specification, but the groundwork of understanding the particulars cannot be sidestepped.[10]

Second, social work research efforts should focus on the transactional issues that have direct relevance to policy, programming, or practice. The core of social work activity is the effort to enhance transactions between the person and the environment. Therefore, although it might be interesting to explore many basic research questions, such as the impact of different parental working hours on child development, studies of this type can be left to the pure social science disciplines. Given limited resources, a more appropriate focus for social work research would be the effort, for example, to determine what types of social supports are necessary to offset the potentially negative effects of traveling fathers (or mothers) on child development.

Third, greater effort should be made to identify and disseminate work-related research findings from data sources not traditionally used by social workers. Governmental agencies—such as state and local health and environmental protection agencies, the Census Bureau, the Department of Labor, the Social Security Administration, and the Center for Epidemiological Studies of the National Institute of Mental Health—all routinely collect a wealth of aggregate data, which could be readily utilized by social workers attempting, for example, to assess service needs in a given community or among a specific occupational group. In addition, private sources—such as Chambers of Commerce, occupational and commercial associations, unions, and voluntary health plans—often gather data on specific population groups. Wider dissemination of the information available from these sources could do much to sensitize social workers to the work-related needs of different client populations.

Finally, mechanisms should be developed to foster ongoing dialogue between social work researchers and practitioners on work-related issues. The traditional separation between practice and research has long plagued the social work profession. But the very fact that work is such an unexplored issue among social workers provides an opportunity to create new patterns of collaboration. The joint sponsorship of the project that led to the publication of this book provides a good model of the type of collaboration that is needed, as does the work of the Industrial Social Welfare Center at Columbia University. Certainly, practitioners in industrial settings who are already sensitized to the significance of work in the lives of their clients could help social work researchers to formulate the research questions that might have the greatest yield for practitioners in other fields of practice. Similarly, by use of single-case study designs, practitioners in other fields who begin to focus more explicitly on work issues might be able to identify tentative hypotheses about ways to intervene with different types of work-related problems; these could then be tested more systematically through larger-scale research studies.

And research data on the specific strains and satisfactions inherent in different work roles at different times in the life cycle could well be used to inform current policy debates regarding various welfare and employment strategies.

Agenda for Work-Related Research

With these guidelines or caveats in mind, we would like to propose an agenda for work-related research which could be used to enhance social work practice and policy analysis in various fields of practice. Although many other issues could be explored, we have attempted to identify what we view as current research priorities. This agenda highlights four major areas in which social work research is needed: (1) special aspects of direct practice with workers; (2) service needs of different groups of workers; (3) alternative service delivery patterns; and (4) social policy and work.

In each area, in addition to identifying the major research questions, we suggest some potential strategies for studying these questions. And in the concluding section of this chapter, we shall explore some of the practical and ethical dilemmas faced by social work researchers attempting to study work-related issues.

Special Aspects of Direct Practice with Workers

As Seymour Sarason has commented:

> How we gain understanding of another person's experience of work should be no easy matter, except for those of that thoughtless cast of mind who turn complexities into banal simplicities, or cannot see substantive issues because everything is viewed as a technical problem. The experience of work, like that of sex, is so extraordinarily complicated and private, so determined by culture and tradition, so much the organizing center of our lives, and so much a developmental process that it is small wonder we as individuals have difficulty taking distance from "our work", i.e., from ourselves.[11]

This comment suggests that before social workers can understand and help clients with work-related issues, they must resolve their own feelings about work. Yet surprisingly little research attention has been given to the experiences of social workers as workers. Although the profession has long been aware of the need for direct service practitioners to come to terms with their own family experiences in order to help with other people's family problems, the relationship between practitioners' feelings about their work and their capacity to help with work problems has never been explored. Therefore, a critical starting point for any research on the practice components of services to workers might be social workers' own work attitudes and experiences.

A simple descriptive study, using written questionnaires as the primary data source, could provide very valuable information about social workers as workers, such as: What are the primary sources of satisfaction and strain in their work? Do these shift at different points in the career cycle? How do their work demands mesh with their family responsibilities and leisure activities? In what ways have their career choices and work expectations been influenced by the experiences of their parents as workers? How do they compare their work to that of their spouses, friends, children, etc.? In what ways do their fields of practice and their professional roles affect their work attitudes? Depending on its purpose and its auspices, a study such as this could focus either on all social workers or on those employed in a particular location or type of setting. Once descriptive information such as this is available, it should be possible to classify the work expectations and experiences of social workers. It would then be important to examine how practitioners' work attitudes influence the type of service they provide to clients with work-related problems.

Another research topic of potential benefit to practitioners is the identification of the critical areas to be explored in formulating what might be termed a work assessment. There has been extensive study of the factors that must be assessed in formulating a family diagnosis.[12] Similar efforts are needed to identify the most relevant and salient aspects of a work history or situation. On a deductive basis, one might surmise that a comprehensive assessment of a worker's problem(s) should include the following variables:

I. Worker
   A. Work History
   B. Current Position—Occupation, Hours, Salary, Fringe Benefits
   C. Job Duties and Responsibilities
   D. Adequacy of Job Performance
   E. Degree and Type of Autonomy and Control in Work Role
   F. Relationships with Colleagues, Supervisors, Subordinates
   G. Specific Work Strains and Satisfactions
   H. Career Goals
   I. Self-Concept as a Worker
II. Work Organization
   A. Size, Location, Function, Physical Setting
   B. General Ambiance
   C. Organizational Structure
   D. Opportunities Provided Workers for Advancement
   E. Expectations ré Loyalty, Performance, etc.
III. Interface between Work and Family
   A. Mesh between Worker's Time and Family Time
   B. Adequacy of Income to Meet Personal and Family Needs
   C. Degree to Which Work Role and Responsibilities Intrude on Family Life

   D.   Degree to Which Family Roles and Responsibilities Intrude on
        Work Life
   E.   Degree to Which Work Role Meets Expectations of Significant
        Others, e.g., Spouse, Children, Family of Origin, Friends
   F.   Overlap between Work and Leisure Activities

This is a research area in which practitioners, especially those in industrial settings, could make a real contribution by suggesting other potentially significant variables and identifying which of these seem most critical in the assessment of work-related problems. Because there has been so little prior investigation in this area, the researcher must rely on anecdotal observations and serendipitous findings, together with logical analysis, to design a systematic exploratory study of significant work-related variables. Yet such an exploratory study is a necessary first step in moving toward the long-term practice research goal of identifying which types of practice interventions are effective, with which types of workers, for which types of problems.

This leads to discussion of evaluation research, another arena in which additional work is sorely needed. Evaluation is a necessary component of practice, regardless of the setting in which it occurs. Social work practice has for much of its history relied upon practitioner and client judgment, either individually or in combination, to establish the effectiveness of their mutual efforts. In addition to these efforts to evaluate services, whether carried out informally or systematically, programs and/or agencies have frequently identified the number and characteristics of clients served by a given number of practitioners and associated these with the details of agency resources. A descriptive analysis of specific program efforts has then been compared with others of a like kind, in an attempt to assess efficiency or effectiveness. In more recent years attempts have been made to evaluate the outcomes of practice in more rigorous scientific terms. Unfortunately, except for a few researchers,[13] who have used experimental laboratory approaches where practice could be controlled in analog treatment situations, most of the practice evaluative efforts have gone into the design and measurement of outcomes. That is, evaluation has been concerned during this period with great efforts to measure the movement that might be observed in client systems directed toward the goals that were presumed to be clearly known or possible of formulation. Less attention has been directed toward the careful delineation and specification of practice inputs related to various theoretical persuasions or of the powerful intervening variables that by themselves might represent a sufficient condition for producing outcomes of either a positive or negative nature.

Social work practice effectiveness research has often been grandiose in its expectations of changing behaviors that could not be affected by the nature of the practice because of uncontrolled psychosocial elements of the client's predicament. Hunger for scientific respectability has often prevented addressing the design considerations necessary either to display success or to bemoan failure. We cannot study in an experimental manner the evaluation of an intervention without concern for who does it, what it is they specifically do, why they do it, and also for controlling the intervening environmental and client-related variables that affect the outcome. Therefore, evaluative research must address practice process issues such as the following:

1. On what theoretical basis is the intervention chosen? What assumptions are involved about the conditions necessary for the intervention to be successful?
2. What specifically is involved in the interventions?
3. How long is the intervention permitted to last? Can goal achievement, no matter whether this relates to internal or external events, be reasonably expected in this time span?
4. Who is delivering the service, and what is the nature of the available skills, knowledge, and competence?
5. Who are the clients, and what are their specific circumstances in terms of the necessity of goal attainment?
6. Toward what end is intervention aimed? What is expected to change? Are such goals feasible? Are the goals stable and unchanging as treatment progresses?
7. What are the signs of recognizing the outcome and effects that are desired and articulated in the treatment contract?

In addition, it is critical to determine whether or not evaluative or pre-evaluative efforts are indicated in the particular setting. Some twenty years ago, Elizabeth Herzog reminded us that it is not profitable to go to the great lengths demanded by evaluative experimental design in such matters as the quality of sample and reliability if the criteria for treatment intervention and outcome definitions are ambiguous and uncertain.[14] Pre-evaluative research that can tell us more about what we are doing, to whom we are doing it, and to what end such doings are directed must precede efforts to learn how well we are doing it. This is no less true now than it was when Herzog wrote it. Rigorous scientific experimental work cannot be carried out without such knowledge. To use quasi-experimental designs, such as Campbell suggests,[15] is within the bounds of acceptability in terms of doing what one can do, even without a perfect sample. It is quite another thing, however, to attempt experimentation without knowledge or control of the independent and dependent variables. Systematic explorations of practice are woefully lacking. Perhaps the relatively new practice in industrial social work settings can provide us with an unbiased approach to that practice, enabling us to delineate more objectively various intervention concepts and processes. Also, we would hope that evaluation studies in other fields of practice will begin to focus more explicitly on the work role as an intervening variable. For example, the Reid and Shyne study of differences between brief and extended casework is a classic example of the type of evaluative research that is needed in social work practice. Their study demonstrated no relationship between social class and outcome.[16] However, they did not examine differences by type of occupation. This is unfortunate, because, given the differences in cognitive style that characterize people selecting different types of work roles, it seems possible that people in different occupations may prefer and/or make better progress in different interventive modalities. Therefore, we would urge that explicit attention be given to work role in all evaluative studies of social work practice.

In order to conduct valid evaluation studies, it is also essential that we reach greater clarity and consensus about the expected outcomes of social work intervention. In any program, public or private, work-related or community-based, competition for scarce resources is likely to increase concerns with cost-benefit ratios. The delivery of social services in private industrial settings may be more conscious of cost-benefit analysis as a part of the profit motive in such settings, but they are no longer alone in that awareness. Public programs are increasingly being evaluated in cost-benefit terms. When this is the direction that assessment of services takes, it is critical to include a wide variety of indexes that will allow for measurement of the potential of social work intervention. Quality-of-life issues related to work are increasingly becoming the central focus in labor-management negotiations. Similar psychosocial issues must be incorporated into the composite picture of benefit to be derived from the direct services provided through social work auspices. These elements are not often reflected in immediate results, such as increased employment or decreased use of alcohol and drugs. Similarly, costs must take into account effects on individuals, families, and communities, when service is not available.[17] For example, the lack of sufficient resources for community mental health services may result in higher hospitalization rates. The costs of hospitalization to worker, family, community, and industry far exceed those of adequate preventive services.

Service Needs of Different Groups of Workers

An issue of primary concern in any community service system is the composition of the population to be served. Work is an impelling force, which joins together those who share a common occupation into a "functional community." This grouping allows for an analysis somewhat comparable to that made possible by the geographic catchmenting associated with the community mental health movement. Workers in a common occupation or industry share an important aspect of their lives, whether they work in the same work site or not. The nature of problems experienced by workers in different occupations and the manner in which they are manifested varies considerably. Hence, research is needed to identify these differences.

Where the location of large industrial work sites constitutes an important segment of the client population toward which a service program is directed, it may be possible to direct a research effort toward the workplace structure and the needs of that particular population. Where this is not so, the task will require a different approach. In this event, a picture of the distribution of occupations in a given community can be the starting point for work-associated need assessment and problem definition. In either situation, it is essential first to determine where different groups of workers live and work. It is then possible to develop a picture of who these workers are, how they live, and what they perceive to be valid and valued. Most of this information can be gathered rather easily. To illustrate, a survey questionnaire can be used to obtain data in the following areas known to be associated with work-related problems and methods of problem-solving:

1. Demographic characteristics
2. Social mobility, aspirations, and achievement
3. Membership and participation in voluntary associations
4. Use of leisure time
5. Family organization
6. Degree of alienation from work
7. Cognitive style

The validity of a needs assessment of any population group rests on the availability of descriptive data such as those outlined above; fortunately, such information is readily obtainable. But since the concepts of problem and need are vague and value-laden, it is a far more difficult research task to analyze the service needs of a specific population. The problems addressed by social workers are by definition transactional in nature. Therefore, no two people are likely to experience the same problem in exactly the same way. The concept of social need is even more complicated, because there are so many ways in which need can be measured.

Yet in order to plan any social service program, it is necessary to make some assessment of the needs of the target population. Moreover, the extent to which similar problems can be identified within particular occupations or work sites determines the degree to which those concerned about the delivery of services can plan effective prevention and early intervention programs. Therefore, determining the nature and extent of the specific problems in psychosocial functioning that are associated with different types of work is a natural direction for research efforts.

A listing of all possible problems associated with psychosocial functioning would be too lengthy for practical use with many different groups of workers. Pretesting in a particular occupation or work site might provide sufficient content to prepare a scale suitable for use with that specific population. However, in the long run, suitable, reliable, and valid social functioning scales, which do not require long periods of time to complete and which can be used as comparable data in studies of different working populations, need to be developed by social work researchers. Such instruments would permit us to mine the rich sources of data inherent in social work settings that serve diverse groups of workers.

The development of knowledge concerning the needs of the working populations requires coherence rather than ad hoc accumulation of bits of information. We might organize such inquiry into the following categories:

1. Discovering the *unity and diversity* to be found in the expression of psychosocial problems identified within the work force;

2. Discovering the *structural aspects* of identified problems through the increasing opportunity to observe job-related environments;
3. Discovering the nature of *coping skills and styles* of different work populations;
4. Discovering the types of *strains* experienced by various groups of workers at different points in the life cycle;
5. Discovering the *meaning of work* for different populations, types of work, and differential rewards; and
6. Discovering how to influence *policy, planning, and practice* so that the information about work-related social functioning may be utilized in the services offered to workers both in the work site and in the community at large.

Within this organization of potential research, the special needs of different populations at risk can be examined. For example, attention to the relationship between healthy growth and development and attitudes toward work may yield understanding of those aspects of socialization and environments that comprise the necessary conditions for youth to develop capacities appropriate to the demands of the workplace. Longitudinal studies can contribute to the understanding of how socialization patterns and role models affect entry routes into the world of work. The way in which individuals move from fantasy choices in childhood about the nature of desirable work to tentative choices in youth, and finally to more realistic choices in adulthood requires further understanding.[18] The sense of competence and effectance constitutes an important developmental line, adding another dimension to ego development and identity formation as ingredients of healthy growth and development.[19] Inquiry into the manner in which the sense of competence and effectance shapes approaches to work would also be of considerable importance to both treatment and planning efforts.

Another issue of special interest to social work is that of the conditions and processes involved in the re-entry into the world of work after a period of absence from such engagement. Problems associated with re-entry into the workplace from various life circumstances—such as time spent in prison, mental hospitals, the Peace Corps, the military, educational and vocational training programs, and child-rearing—need to be identified and made available for interventive and planning purposes. Frequently, the conditions of re-entry into the work world seriously affect the ability to search for work and to maintain it, once found. Restrictions related to either bureaucratic regulations or personal demands of the environment may interfere with a comfortable and productive engagement in work. A lack of trust in those who have been out of the work world is a common community response. Where institutionalization has been involved, the fear of discovery often leads to the necessity to lie about one's background. This in turn lowers self-esteem and not only may interfere with use of self but also may lead to the use of stimulants or depressants in alcohol and other forms as a way to avoid the pain that accompanies such circumstances. Research into the impact of re-entry into the world of work and the special problems associated with specific types of re-entry would have immediate knowledge-transfer potential, and thus practice utility.

The special needs of working women and dual-career families also require continued research efforts. While there is currently a flurry of research activity in these areas, there are many issues of special concern to social workers that need further clarification. Inner conflicts of working women in relation to the pulls of work and family responsibilities continue; and increasing numbers of men in dual-career families are beginning to experience similar conflicts. As women acquire positions of greater responsibility and power in their work roles, they may demand corresponding readjustments in their personal relationships. Changes in both male and female role expectations require resocialization of adults and new patterns of socialization for children. Basic changes such as these are always accompanied by anxiety and may cause some personal and family disorganization. Yet, recent research findings suggest that the overall impact of employment is beneficial for women and their families.[20] Therefore, it seems important to study which aspects or types of work may have negative effects and how these can be minimized.

Recent legislative changes have significantly improved employment opportunities for women, minority group members, and handicapped persons, especially in entry-level positions. However, little is known about the personal satisfactions and strains experienced by individuals participating in affirmative action programs. Moreover, there is some evidence that those who aspire to upper-level positions may experience many structural obstacles.[21] Further research is needed to determine how individuals cope with the blocks that may be encountered later on in their careers.

A related topic that requires additional study is the problem of overqualification and underemployment. This has long been a concern of women and minority men, but it is a problem that is beginning to plague white males as well. The amount of education attained by Americans far outstrips the number of positions available in the economy to utilize that education. In 1900, only 2 percent of the nation's population had obtained a college education. By 1950, this figure had risen to 19 percent, and by 1970, 26 percent of all adult Americans had obtained the once highly exclusive bachelor's degree.[22] This change has led one observer to identify the relationship between education and work as the "Great Training Robbery."[23] The number of highly educated Americans in all social and economic sectors of the country who are either bored with work that is not consistent with their talents and education or who have high expectations about work and its rewards that will go unfulfilled constitute an area of increasing importance and high priority for research and action. These issues are merely suggestive of the direct relevance that research in current social issues related to work issues would have in the field of social work and social welfare.

Two other populations at risk of experiencing psychosocial problems related to work are the unemployed and the retired. Although the members of these groups are not in the workforce, because of the prominence assigned to work in American society, the very absence of an acceptable work role can precipitate many difficulties in social functioning associated with the lack of income, social status, and feelings of self-esteem and competency. Many work organizations have established preretirement counseling programs, in hopes of easing the transition to retirement for their members. However, few provide any services to their former employees once they have terminated their employment. Some union programs have been developed for unemployed and retired members, but these serve a very small proportion of the total population. Unemployed and retired workers are more and more likely to be seen in mental health settings, family service agencies, and programs for the aging. Therefore, researchers in these settings could serve an important function by examining the unique needs of these groups. Work organizations could also make a real contribution by developing a series of small demonstration projects, aimed at identifying the types of services that unemployed and retired workers might use to prevent the diminished sense of purpose, self-esteem, and social status frequently associated with loss of work role.

In this section we have highlighted only the needs of those populations which may be most at risk because of work-related problems. One could just as easily focus attention on other groups of workers, for example, those experiencing mid-life crises, those whose career paths seem blocked, those in dangerous occupations, migrant workers, domestic workers, and those in very routine, monotonous occupations. What is essential for social work research is that efforts be directed toward identifying the specific service needs of each potential target population. As suggested earlier, because the concept of need is so ambiguous, it is difficult to conduct a valid needs assessment of any group. For example, there have been numerous studies of the need for day care services, yet we have no clear picture of real needs in this area. When asked, most working parents of young children will say they would like to have day care services available; however, it has been shown repeatedly that only a small proportion of these parents will actually use the day care program(s) established to meet their alleged needs for such service.

One promising approach to this problem of needs assessment has been suggested by Bradshaw, who distinguishes between four types of social need: (1) normative need, that is, need for which there is a widespread expert consensus that healthy survival demands fulfillment—for example, adequate nutrition; (2) comparative need, that is, need that is being met for other people in the same status—for example, public education for children in the U.S.; (3) expressed need, that is, need for which clients/consumers have expressed a demand—for example, transportation for handicapped persons; and (4) felt need, that is, a need that people would acknowledge if asked whether they would like a particular service, for example, parent education programs. Bradshaw goes on to suggest that service priorities can be established by assessing how many categories of need any particular service is designed to meet.[24] If needs assessments of this type were carried out by appropriate means for each potential target population with work-related problems, it should be possible to establish service priorities within and across different groups of workers.

Alternative Service Delivery Patterns

An understanding of the conditions of life affected by work-related issues may be more critical to the utilization of services by large numbers of the working force than knowledge of the individual resistances often thought to be operative. Whether concern centers around community-based social service systems or industrial social work programs, it is necessary to have knowledge of the work situation in order to plan and organize the types of services needed and the manner in which they may be delivered most effectively. Community services are rarely planned to accommodate the types and conditions of work in which their target populations are involved. Identifying the nature of stress in different occupations—not by guessing what an occupational title involves, but rather by investigating carefully the ethnography of work—may help to direct service programs and interventions in a more appropriate manner. Research on the problems associated with different types of work at different phases in the life cycle might facilitate the establishment of self-help groups for supervisors, forced retirees, women in nontraditional occupations, single-parent workers, and so forth. Accurate forecasting of potential community service needs requires prior investigation of the specific hazards to health, both physical and emotional, in different types of work and at different levels of responsibility. For example, some communities have organized programs directed at promoting self-help groups in the police department to deal with the widely-found fear syndrome associated with this work.

All too often, agency services are planned with little consideration or knowledge of the hours of work in which the consumers of their services engage. Knowledge of the community's work schedule in terms of the numbers of consumers available at various hours of the day would permit social agencies to schedule their time in such a manner as to create the greatest impact in the time zones that promote utilization, while maintaining sufficient service opportunities at less saturated but still necessary time slots. Similarly, greater consideration should be given to the conflicting work and family demands experienced by many clients. Two-worker families continue to increase. What are the implications for family service agencies? How can children's service programs be restructured to obtain the necessary level of parental involvement? Has increased participation in the labor force by mothers of young children resulted in increased numbers of "latch-key" children? What services are needed to prevent some of the potential problems that may result from this phenomenon? Systematic consideration of work-related issues such as these could force massive reorganization of many traditional community service agencies.

In addition to the general service delivery issues identified in relation to community service systems, there are specific issues that must be examined when services are concentrated in the work site or in related union structures. It is probably healthy at this stage of development for the expanding industrial social work services to experiment with a wide variety of methods of delivering the services they are committed to provide. Some services involve contract arrangements by private groups, who find this new venture both exciting and profitable; while other services involve contracting with the industrial setting from the base of existing community services, such as family agencies and community mental health centers. Other approaches involve the development of services within the work organization, whether it be labor, management, or a combination of both that supports the service. Some services are primarily concerned with the direct delivery of service to the workers; while others are mainly a referral source to facilitate utilization of community resources to which workers are already entitled. Some seek to identify the most disadvantaged part of the work population and to develop service patterns for their benefit; while others address a wider variety of workers and therefore require a more extensive spectrum of services to meet their varied needs. (See chapter 9, by Akabas and Kurzman, for a full discussion of social services at the worksite.) No matter which of these patterns is used, it is necessary to monitor and research the consequences carefully. For these services to proliferate without careful attention to the effects of different structural approaches would constitute a form of neglect. If some form of evaluation is not carried out now, as a fundamental aspect of industry-related social work practice, there will be little information with which to counter criticisms in the future. Toward this end, research might be addressed to some of the following issues:

1. How can services be delivered most effectively in a highly political environment, in which interventions may not only be suspect but may actually be in conflict with the approaches approved by conflicting interests within the organization? Without understanding the geography of the particular work environment and the conflicting interests found in any workplace, one enters into what is necessarily a political environment, at peril of one's professional life.

2. How can formal and informal networks of authority within the workplace be used as a part of the service delivery pattern? Foremen, management personnel, and union business agents form a network of knowledge and interventive power that is not always clearly articulated in the formal directives of the association. The discovery of what constitutes quid pro quo arrangements with such persons in the roles they occupy may be one of the most fundamental and critical pieces of understanding necessary to an adequate social service delivery system in the work site. How can these people be served as well as utilized to help serve others?

3. What is the nature of the industrial pattern of work and the specific workplace that will affect the manner in which services can best be delivered to the population served? The presence of services in a given industry is not sufficient to ensure their availability and usability. Research into the special needs, circumstances, and lifestyle associated with a particular kind of work and industry may make the difference between success and failure.

4. What is the best way to manage utilization rates? Should the service actively seek to increase utilization as much as possible, or should it take a more careful and conservative approach to case finding, so as not to be overwhelmed by potential demands for service? This has been a critical issue in most industrial social work programs. Is it a fact that certain classes of workers will not use services that are available, or are the available services not suitably organized for use by these workers? For example, the Retail Clerks Community Mental Health Development Program in Los Angeles, which organized its services in a way that reflected understanding of worker

circumstance, need, and perception of problems, experienced one of the highest utilization rates of any community mental health center in the country. In 1968, there was a 6.5 percent worker utilization rate and a 5.6 percent total family eligible utilization rate. Services were directed toward the problems in a manner articulated by consumers, not by professionals. This is not to suggest that the practitioners gave up their own theories and perspectives, but rather that their knowledge of the consumer group enabled them to utilize their competence in a manner that was compatible with the style and perspective of the client.[25]

5. What are the advantages and disadvantages inherent in the different modes of organizing services at the workplace? Are on-site or off-site programs preferred? Which have higher utilization rates? What are the trade-offs between offering short-time services to a large number of employees and providing intensive services to a smaller, at-risk population? How can access be maximized and stigma minimized?

Many different research strategies could be used to examine the service delivery questions suggested above. Choice of a particular research design always depends on the nature of the research problem; but one advantage to conducting research at the work site is that data are frequently available which permit samples to be stratified on key variables that are not recorded in other more traditional settings, for example, job seniority.

As Finestone and Kahn have suggested, in order to arrive at an appropriate design for a study, one must make a set of planning decisions. Hence, once the problem has been carefully formulated, the researcher must answer the following questions:

1. What are appropriate sources of information? . . .
2. What is the sampling strategy? . . .
3. By what methods will the information be obtained from the sources selected? . . .
4. What is the general strategy for measuring, counting, or classifying the data? . . .
5. How will the process of obtaining data be patterned? . . .
6. How will the data be organized? . . .[26]

To illustrate, if one wished to study worker satisfaction with different service delivery models, it would be possible to design a relatively simple descriptive survey, in which a random sample of former clients in different types of programs were asked to complete a questionnaire, which asked them to evaluate various aspects of the service they received. In such a study, the type of program would be the independent variable; and, depending on the researcher's interest, a decision might be made to control for type of worker, type of problem, or other intervening variables. Level of satisfaction would then be used as the dependent variable.

In contrast, if one wished to study the effectiveness of various service models in dealing with the problem of alcoholism among workers, it would be necessary to design an experimental study in which workers with problems of alcoholism were randomly assigned to different types of service programs. Although it is never possible to control all the intervening variables in a study which involves human subjects over a period of time, an effort would have to be made to identify and limit as many as possible of the external factors that might affect treatment outcome. The components of the independent variable—service modality— would also have to be carefully specified in advance. The researcher would then have to develop a series of carefully selected, adequately pretested, outcome measures, which could be used to evaluate "success" from different perspectives, for example, employer, employee, family, coworkers, physician, and so forth.

Because there has been so little prior research on service delivery strategies for helping clients with work-related problems, the pay-off from experimental studies of this type is likely to be very low. Further exploratory work is needed to insure that: (1) the research is addressing the right questions; (2) critical differences in the independent variable—service delivery model—can be identified and manipulated; (3) significant intervening variables can be delineated and controlled; and (4) valid and reliable measures are available to assess differential outcomes. Therefore, we would suggest that, for the immediate future, research efforts related to service delivery models should be concentrated in two areas.

First, much could be learned from more widespread, systematic use of consumer satisfaction surveys. The model for a client follow-up survey developed by Beck and Jones[27] and later refined by Beck[28] for the Family Service Association of America (FSAA) provides an excellent example of the type of questionnaire that could easily be administered by mail on a routine basis to former clients in a variety of settings. By modifying some of the questions slightly, it would be possible to use this questionnaire to tap client attitudes about the type of help they received with work-related problems. Unfortunately, because this is such a new field of practice, industrial social work programs do not belong to an umbrella organization such as the FSAA, which could assume responsibility for developing and pre-testing a comparable survey instrument. There is no clearly-defined universe of social service programs organized around work issues. Ultimately, in order to compare consumer perceptions of the advantages and disadvantages of different service delivery models, it will be necessary to survey a random sample of clients from the full range of program models. But as an initial step, it would be very useful for an informal coalition of social workers concerned about work issues to develop and distribute, perhaps under the auspices of the Council on Social Work Education or the National Association of Social Workers, a common survey instrument that was designed to measure worker satisfaction with different types of service programs. If these results were then reported to a central source, researchers could begin to develop and test hypotheses about ways in which service arrangements affect client perceptions of outcome.

Researchers concerned about service delivery patterns also need to conduct more extensive qualitative studies aimed at identifying and conceptualizing the ways in which service arrangements shape the nature of practice. As Glaser and Strauss have suggested,[29] in a relatively new and unexplored area, research efforts directed toward developing grounded theory about the phenomenon under study may be more productive than rigorous testing of limited theoretical constructs. Theory that is based on careful observation of the real world is likely to provide a more valid explanation of the research question and to be more amenable to empirical verification than theory that is proposed on a sort of "grand-theory" basis. However, the development of such grounded theory requires that the researcher collect very systematic data and engage in what Glaser and Strauss have termed a constant, comparative method of data analysis, whereby incidents are gathered, examined, and classified until theoretical constructs and relationships begin to emerge and the collection of additional incidents does not reveal any new patterns. This is obviously a costly, time-consuming process, which demands extensive use of participant observation or some other strategy for collecting reliable qualitative data. Yet it is likely to be the most productive means of developing hypotheses about how services can best be structured to meet different types of needs for different groups of workers. Once such hypotheses have been generated, it should be possible to design a series of demonstration projects aimed at testing the viability of various service delivery strategies for different populations.

Social Policy Issues

Formulation of social policy ultimately involves value choices. Hence it is unrealistic to assume that research alone can provide an adequate base from which to make policy decisions. However, research can provide the empirical data necessary to inform policy choices, and research findings can be used to garner support for the approaches that policy-makers have decided to pursue. It therefore seems appropriate to consider some of the types of work-related policy research that social workers might undertake.

In the United States, as Ozawa remarked in chapter 3, ". . . social policy and social welfare programs have revolved around the working status of individuals and families" (p. 36). Consequently, there is no shortage of potential policy research topics. The task is to identify priority issues for social work researchers.

Perhaps the most pressing concern for those concerned about the delivery of services to workers is the appropriate division of responsibility between the occupational and the social welfare sectors. As industrial social service programs continue to multiply, questions must be raised as to how far we wish to turn the responsibility for social services over to the world of work. It seems clear that the workplace is an appropriate locus for the delivery of certain types of services to selected groups of workers. But if responsibility for planning and funding these services is given to the workplace, who will assume responsibility for those who have no formal ties to the world of work?

As Ozawa has documented, non-wage-related employee benefits provided through the occupational sector tend to reinforce existing patterns of stratification, that is, those who do well in their work roles also receive substantial non-wage benefits; whereas those who work at lower wage levels also receive lower nonwage benefits. Prior research has focused primarily on the distribution of fiscal benefits, but it would now seem to be appropriate to study the distribution of social benefits, such as day care, recreation, counseling, and educational programs. What is the range and the extent of the social services now provided through the workplace?[30] Are social services such as these also distributed in ways that enforce existing patterns of stratification? Has the expansion of industrial social work programs been associated with any change in the target populations of community social service programs? If so, who has benefited, and who has lost from the transfer of responsibility?

A cost-benefit analysis of these alternative types of service provision requires careful examination of social as well as fiscal costs. To illustrate, as increasing numbers of workers receive counseling services through their workplaces, is the stigma that is often associated with any type of mental health service decreased? Does the provision of non-work-related services give employers increased control over their employees? Does the provision of social services as an occupational fringe benefit increase a worker's sense of entitlement and equity with service providers? In order to arrive at any rational decision regarding the degree to which public policy should support the development of industrial social service programs via tax incentives, provision of funds for demonstration projects, and so forth, it will be necessary to find answers to questions such as these.

The recent family policy debate has focused attention on another area in which additional policy research is needed, that is, the relationship between work and family roles for men and women. Kanter's monograph[31] outlines the issues so clearly and succinctly that it seems almost redundant to discuss them here. However, she identifies two issues which should be of special concern to social work researchers. First is the relationship between the timing of significant events in the career and family life cycles. To illustrate, because of delayed entry into the labor force, many young men become fathers long before they acquire the jobs that enable them to provide adequately for their children. Women who wish to have children often have to take maternity leaves at the very age (twenty-five to thirty-five) when they should be building their careers. Both women and men are likely to be most absorbed by work demands at the time that their young children (under fifteen) need the most attention. And couples often have to face retirement shortly after they have been forced to cope with the gradual emancipation and loss of their children. Because the biological clock is relatively fixed, further research is needed to identify ways in which work organizations can accommodate to the needs of family life. Two approaches that have been used successfully in several European countries are increased use of flexitime and of paternity as well as maternity leaves. Although some companies in this country have initiated similar benefits, these are relatively limited. Why? What incentives are needed to encourage more worksites to introduce these practices? What are the potential cost benefits to employers and society at large of giving workers a choice as to whether they use some of their social security "retirement" benefits during their early child-rearing years and extend their working years proportionately?

The other policy issue identified by Kanter that should be of special concern to social work researchers is the traditional split between work and family roles. In a discussion of family policy in Sweden, Liljestrom[32] suggests that the traditional specialization of sex roles in home/private/expressive and work/public/instrumental spheres has limited opportunities for personal development for both men and women and has contributed to the lower social status of women. The current rate of female participation in the labor force challenges this concept of role segregation. Yet traditional sex-role expectations persist, creating increased strain in marital relationships. For example, based on their careful analysis of economic factors contributing to marital instability, Ross and Sawhill hypothesize that ". . . Whatever the degree of role specialization in marriage, instability will be greater when there is incongruity between role performance and ideology."[33]

Economic realities, coupled with rising expectations for achievement in the work sphere brought about by the women's movement, make it unlikely that large numbers of women will return to their traditional role in the home. Therefore, research is needed to determine how specialized sex-role expectations can be made more congruent with actual role performance. One strategy might be to conduct a series of in-depth interviews, with a matched sample of couples from different ethnic and socioeconomic backgrounds, in which one group seems to have made satisfactory readjustment in role expectations and the other group holds to traditional views of sex-role specialization. Using the Glaser and Strauss approach to the development of grounded theory that was discussed earlier, it should be possible to generate a series of hypotheses regarding ways in which public policy can influence sex-role expectations. Based on this analysis, a series of demonstration projects could then be designed to different policy options.

To illustrate, Sweden has recently instituted a policy whereby both mother and father must use a portion of the parental leave to which families are entitled in order to take full advantage of publicly-subsidized child-care benefits. Kanter advocates further experimentation with flexitime, joint family-work group meetings, and opportunities for children and spouses to spend time at the workplace.[34] Public education problems and support for the development of self-help groups for men and women who are struggling to modify their role expectations and to find new ways of integrating family and work lives might also result in significant attitudinal changes.

Another area in which further research is needed is the social and personal impact of affirmative action programs for women, minorities, and the disabled at the workplace. The social work profession, influenced by its historical mission and its ethical code, has lent strong support to the development of such programs; and certainly this is an essential first step in the effort to modify the structural obstacles faced by various oppressed groups. However, it is equally important to examine how these programs are implemented and what their long-term ramifications might be for the beneficiaries and for society at large. For example, are those who gain access to entry-level positions as a result of affirmative action efforts promoted at an expectable rate, or do they continue to face discrimination at each critical point in their careers? Does the knowledge that one has benefited from an affirmative action program affect work performance, satisfaction, or expectations? What is the extent of backlash in different types of work settings? How do different groups cope with this? Do affirmative action efforts affect the work attitudes of other employees? To what degree do affirmative action programs at the workplace help to diminish discriminatory practices and/or to create greater social cohesion in other spheres of life? These are very difficult issues to study, requiring innovative research strategies; yet such study is necessary if we are to determine which types of affirmative action programs are most effective and how public policies should be shaped to insure that such programs attain their intended results.

A final area that must be mentioned in relation to work-related policy research is the whole problem of unemployment. Although unemployment per se is primarily a topic for economists, social work research could contribute a great deal in relation to some of the personal and social aspects of unemployment. It seems clear that without a major change in our economic system or in the composition of the potential labor force, there will simply never be enough adequate jobs for those who want or need to work. Therefore, as a nation we must face some very difficult policy choices regarding which groups of people will be encouraged and/or permitted to work, at which times in their lives. In the past, such decisions have been left primarily to the marketplace, permitting healthy, middle-aged, white males to dominate the labor force. However, the traditional allocation of work roles is now being challenged by the demands of various interest groups previously excluded from desirable jobs and by the work requirements of some of the newer fields of employment, in which different types of knowledge and skill are required.

A series of cost-benefit analyses could help to identify the potential social advantages and disadvantages of different employment policies. For example, the social costs of excluding low-income minority youth from the labor force have become all too clear to residents of urban areas. But if this group is given adequate access to jobs, who should be excluded? It would be naive to pretend that such decisions will not be made primarily on the basis of political considerations. However, the policy debate could at least be informed by the careful study of various alternatives. Do some groups suffer fewer emotional and social costs than others when they are unemployed? If so, are there ways to provide necessary financial subsidies to these groups? Rather than crowding the best work opportunities into the midlife period, when many people are also busy with family responsibilities, are there ways to extend career beginnings and endings, providing periodic "sabbaticals" to all workers? Could men and women cope more easily with unemployment during selected mid-life years? If people are given opportunities to participate in selected types of educational, volunteer, and leisure activities during periods of unemployment, will these activities supply the sense of personal competency and social worth that is usually provided through work roles? These again are very difficult research issues to tackle; however, they are areas in which social work expertise could be utilized to make a real contribution to public policy.

Research Dilemmas at the Work Site

Social workers conducting research in work organizations must cope with some special ethical dilemmas and political challenges. Perhaps the first problem confronting anyone planning a work-related study is that of gaining access and support. The development and updating of a knowledge base about workers and work sites may seem to present an added and unnecessary burden to agencies struggling for survival. There is one thing that is certain about this shortsighted view, however. Even if a great deal is known about the people who find their way to social services, little will be known about the needs of the total community unless something is known about its work organizations. In the long run, the base of support will suffer. This is a lesson that is difficult to learn and one that is frequently ignored. Therefore, the motivation to cooperate with such efforts must be developed in terms of the self-interest of the participants, rather than as an obscure contribution to the accumulation of scientific knowledge. The success of such ventures usually hinges upon long-term, intensive efforts to recruit support from community groups, labor and management leaders, and social service personnel.

The problems of gaining access and support for research activities in work organizations are often different from those experienced in more traditional settings. Work, like all other important elements of personal and social organization, is a highly political encounter. Research data can provide enormous political ammunition to be used against, as well as for, the benefit of defined target populations. Management and union officials, as well as workers, tend to be suspicious of the collection of data—all the more so when the collector is an outsider. The outsider or stranger to the workplace is not immediately welcomed with open arms. Professionals of middle-class origins, as well as those who have arrived at their current status through upward social mobility, are suspect to a large segment of the work force. These are difficulties that need to be understood, rather than barriers that cannot be overcome. In fact, programmatic research is more common in industrial social work settings than in many other fields of practice. But researchers must do their homework in regard to the participants in the worksites from which they seek cooperation in their research efforts. Time must be made available and must be utilized effectively to reduce suspicion about the purposes of the research and the manner in which the results will be used. Also, it should be emphasized that *service* is often a point of access for research in these settings. Prior experience has demonstrated that it is usually through providing direct service that social workers establish their credibility, both with the workers and with the organizational gate-keepers who control access to the centralized data and the permission-giving processes that are needed to conduct research.

It is frequently helpful to seek counsel and advice concerning the research instruments that will be utilized in the study. This is strategically wise, and, furthermore, those who are close to the work forces are acquainted with the specific lexicon that is most likely to be understood and not resented. To illustrate, the head of the union participated in the design of a questionnaire used in a research epidemiological survey of a union population.[35] During the process of its development, regular consultations were held with the union leadership, who provided many helpful suggestions. At the same time, it was possible to help the union leadership understand the nature of the questions being posed and their relevance in addressing personal and family adjustments. The final product was felt to be a joint effort, and the head of the union wrote a personal letter to the membership, explaining its purpose and requesting their cooperation. While this particular strategy may not always be the most appropriate, the general principle of mutual involvement cannot be neglected if the barriers to research in such settings are to be overcome.

Another issue that researchers need to address is that of developing procedures to insure that client rights are safeguarded. In addition to statutory regulations providing the rights of human subjects, the code of ethics of the National Association of Social Workers states:

1. The social worker engaged in research should consider carefully its possible consequences for human beings.
2. The social worker engaged in research should ascertain that the consent of participants in the research is voluntary and informed, without any implied deprivation or penalty for refusal to participate and with due regard for participants' privacy and dignity.
3. The social worker engaged in research should protect participants from unwarranted physical or mental discomfort, distress, harm, danger, or deprivation.
4. The social worker who engages in the evaluation of services or cases should discuss them only for professional purposes and only with persons directly and professionally concerned with them.
5. Information obtained about participants in research should be treated as confidential.[36]

The constraints on social workers engaged in work-related research are no different from those engaged in other types of research. However, at the work site, research subjects are often known to those funding the study; hence special care must be taken to insure that privacy is protected. Also, because corporate and union leaders are seldom involved in research with human subjects, researchers in work organizations may have to engage in extensive educational campaigns to persuade those sponsoring their studies of the importance of following professional conventions for scholarly inquiry.

A final concern that needs to be mentioned is the political context in which most work-related research must be carried out. The increasing use of evaluation as a tool for decision-making concerning the development, modification, or cessation of social programs has fostered as much debate about the evaluation of evaluative research as there is about the programs and practices that such research is intended to evaluate. The debate is generally about whether the evaluation ought to use experimental design, along with the rigor of control demanded of such design, or whether evaluation efforts should be directed by a more flexible approach, taking into consideration the timeliness of research findings to program development and change.

Evaluative studies are particularly vulnerable to use in a destructive manner. When decision-makers are advised that *all* programs "reveal no difference" or fail to produce *any* desired effects, there is reason to be cautious, if not suspicious, that there may be problems in conceptualization and design. A well-developed social work program, solidly entrenched in an organizational setting, can profit from a carefully designed experiment that evaluates whether or not a particular treatment approach, based upon a sound theoretical foundation, produces the effects that the theory promises. In programs that do not have such acceptance or support from their organization, there may be a need for more immediate feedback for the purposes of making necessary alterations in the delivery of services. In any event, the delivery of social services deals with critical life circumstances; therefore, from an ethical perspective, it is essential that the information that can improve the program or prevent failure be supplied as soon as it is available. Above all, evaluation research should provide an environment in which interest in learning about process and outcome related to program efforts is enhanced, rather than decreased. The use of a theoretical framework in evaluation research enhances the value of its product. Nebulous objectives must be turned into specific aims, so that they can be measured. Yet the very effort to accomplish this may again reveal the politics of evaluative research. Nebulous objectives are often meant to serve many masters, each believing that his or her viewpoint will prevail. Forcing clarity in regard to goals and objectives requires diplomacy as well as conceptual clarity. In the final analysis, those who evaluate and those who deliver the services must be in agreement about the outcomes to be measured and the manner in which design may affect the practice. Evaluation is best accomplished when it is not viewed as a threat to existence, but rather a way of helping practitioners to do what they want to do more effectively and efficiently.

Goals and objectives related to the psychosocial impact of work have seldom been specified in social work practice. The consequences of such neglect is the limited perception by social workers of the relationship of work and the workplace to social functioning. Work-focused research needs to be expanded, but, even more important, work-related variables need to be included in all research.

Notes

[1] Henry S. Maas, ed., *Social Service Research: Reviews of Studies* (Washington, D.C.: National Association of Social Workers, 1978).

[2] W.S. Neff, *Work and Human Behavior* (New York: Atherton Press, 1968); E. W. Baake, *Citizens Without Work* (New Haven, Conn.: Yale University Press, 1940).

[3] Rosabeth Moss Kanter, *Men and Women of the Corporation* (New York: Basic Books, 1977), pp. 14–15.

[4] Carel Germain, "Casework and Service: A Historical Encounter," in Robert W. Roberts and Robert M. Nee, eds., *Theories of Social Casework* (Chicago: Aldine Publishing Company, 1967), p. 15.

[5] Sidney E. Zimbalist, *Historic Themes and Landmarks in Social Welfare Research* (New York: Harper and Row, 1977), p. 408.

[6] *U.S. Working Women: A Databook* (Washington, D.C.: U.S. Department of Labor/Bureau of Labor Statistics, 1977), Table 19.

[7] *Work in America, Report of a Special Task Force to the Secretary of Health, Education, and Welfare* (Cambridge, Mass.: M.I.T. Press, 1973).

[8] H. Weiner, S. Akabas, and J. Sommer, *Mental Health Care in the World of Work* (New York: Association Press, 1973); A. Kornhauser, *Mental Health of the Industrial Worker* (New York: Wiley, 1965); J. Cohen and H. Hunter, "Mental Health Insurance: A Comparison of a Fee-for-Service Indemnity Plan and a Comprehensive Mental Health Center," *American Journal of Orthopsychiatry,* 42, no. 1 (Jan. 1972), 146–53.

[9] R. King, "Working," *Columbia Forum,* 2, no. 4 (Fall 1973), 2–5; L. Woodcock, "Changing World of Work: A Labor Viewpoint," paper presented to the American Assembly, November 1, 1973, New York.

[10] Studs Terkel, *Working* (New York: Pantheon Books, 1972).

[11] Seymour B. Sarason, *Work, Aging, and Social Change* (New York: The Free Press, 1977), p. 2.

[12] See, for example, H. Parad and G. Caplan, "A Framework for Studying Families in Crisis," in H. Parad, ed., *Crisis Intervention* (New York: Family Service Association of America, 1965), pp. 53–74; and R. O'Connell, "Developmental Tasks of the Family," *Smith College Studies in Social Work,* 42, no. 3 (June 1972), 203–10.

[13] E. Thomas, *Behavioral Science for Social Workers* (New York: The Free Press, 1967); R.R. Miller, "An Experimental Study of the Observational Process in Casework," *Social Work,* 3, no. 2 (April 1958), 96–102.

[14] E. Herzog, *Some Guidelines for Evaluation Research* (Washington, D.C.: Department of Health, Education, and Welfare, 1959).

[15] D.T. Campbell, "Quasi-Experimental Designs," in H.W. Riecken and others, eds., *Social Experimentation as a Method of Planning and Evaluating Social Programs* (New York: Academic Press, 1974), pp. 87–116.

[16] W. J. Reid and A.W. Shyne, *Brief and Extended Casework* (New York: Columbia University Press, 1969), p. 112.

[17] S. Salasin, "From National Security to Mental Health: Making Analysis Count in Government—An Interview with Laurence E. Lynn, Jr.," *Evaluation,* 4 (1977), pp. 165–177.

[18] E. Ginzberg, *Occupational Choice* (New York: Columbia University Press, 1951).

[19] Robert W. White, "Competence and the Psychosexual Stages of Development," in Nebraska Symposium on Motivation (Lincoln: University of Nebraska Press, 1960), pp. 97–141.

[20] Rosabeth Moss Kanter, *Work and Family in the United States: A Critical Review and Agenda for Research and Policy* (New York: Russell Sage Foundation, 1977), pp. 61–62.

[21] Kanter, *Men and Women of the Corporation,* chapter 9.

[22] Carnegie Commission of Higher Education, *College Graduates and Jobs: Adjusting to a New Market Situation* (New York: McGraw Hill, 1973).

[23] Iver Berg, *Education and Jobs: The Great Training Robbery* (New York: Praeger, 1970).

[24] J. Bradshaw, "The Concept of Social Need," *New Society,* 30, no. 496 (March 30, 1972), 640–43.

[25] J. Alexander and K. Kolodziejski, "Unique Aspects of a Union Population's Influence on Service Delivery," *American Journal of Orthopsychiatry,* 40, no. 1 (January 1970), 151–57.

[26] S. Finestone and A.J. Kahn, "The Design of Research," in N.A. Polansky, ed., *Social Work Research,* rev. ed. (Chicago: University of Chicago Press, 1975), pp. 38–39.

[27] D.F. Beck and M.A. Jones, *Process or Family Problems: A Nationwide Study of Clients' and Counselors' Views on Family Agency Services* (New York: Family Service Association of America, 1973).

[28] D.F. Beck, *How to Conduct a Client Follow-Up Study, 1977 Supplement* (New York: Family Service Association of America, 1977).

[29] B.G. Glaser and A.L. Strauss, *The Discovery of Grounded Theory: Strategies for Qualitative Research* (Chicago: Aldine Publishing Company, 1967).

[30] Hans B.C. Spiegel, *Not for Work Alone: Services at the Workplace* (New York: Urban Research Center, Hunter College of the City University of New York, 1974.)

[31] Kanter, *Work and Family in the United States.*

[32] R. Liljestrom, "Sweden," in S.B. Kamerman and A.J. Kahn, eds., *Family Policy: Government and Families in Fourteen Countries* (New York: Columbia University Press, 1978), pp. 19–48.

[33] H.L. Ross and J.V. Sawhill, *Time of Transition: The Growth of Families Headed by Women* (Washington, D.C.: Urban Institute, 1975), p. 47.

[34] Kanter, *Work and Family in the United States,* pp. 94–95.

[35] J. Cohen and P. Wagner, *Mental Health of the Worker: A Study of Symptoms Among Retail Clerks* (Washington, D.C.: Report to the Center for Epidemiology of the National Institute of Mental Health, Department of Health, Education, and Welfare, 1970); Cohen and Hunter, "Mental Health Insurance."

[36] "The NASW Code of Ethics," I.E., 1-5, *NASW News,* 25, no. 1 (January 1980), 24–25.

7

Applying Business Management Strategies in Social Agencies: Prospects and Limitations*

Rino J. Patti, D. S. W.

University of Washington

This chapter explores the lessons from industry and labor that can be applied to the management of social agencies and underscores the need for mastery of organizational theory by social work administrators. Patti utilizes two popular management strategies—management by objectives (MBO) and contingency management—to identify the ramifications for social welfare agencies, both conceptually and operationally.

With respect to MBO, he suggests that technology transfer is more complicated than it might appear. While such business techniques might be objective and neutral in and of themselves, the values in their application (not knowledge or skill) are the vexing issue. Even when business technology and craft might provide an improvement in the administration of a social agency, their use may not be value-free. Can the concepts and techniques be modified in their transfer and implementation to make the ethical implications acceptable to the commitment of a helping profession? As an illustration, industry largely is oriented toward function, but the dilemma—and it is a major one—is that social work is committed to function and cause (or, as Lewis would note, the cause in function).† Measures of "effectiveness"

*The author wishes to gratefully acknowledge the helpful criticisms by Michael Austin and Ronald Dear, on previous drafts of this paper.

†Harold Lewis, "The Cause in Function," Journal of the Otto Rank Association, 2 (Winter, 1976), 18–25.

are more difficult, for we place value on the process (as well as the outcome), on strengthening clients' capacity (not merely serving them well), and on working toward distributive justice (rather than maximizing our share of the market).

As one conferee suggested, social workers would probably reject a norm which implied that

- *participation as such is not important;*
- *we will be reactive rather than proactive, stressing adaptation to situational realities;*
- *we will deal and be responsive only to those who have power; and*
- *profit and financial advantage will take precedence among our goals and multiple commitments.*

Patti does not suggest that business management strategies cannot be applied in the realm of social welfare due to explicit or implicit differences in values. Rather, he advocates the adjustment of technology (such as MBO.) to the organizational environment and the mandates of a helping profession. This presupposes a thorough grounding for social work administrators in organizational theory and an equally thorough commitment to social work norms.

The contribution of business schools and industrial organizations to social work literature and practice is substantial, however, and Patti argues persuasively that the industrial social work experience (which includes our "insiders' " exposure to the corporate world) can promote understanding and comfort with an increasing use of management innovations. Some business innovations, such as management information systems, program budgeting techniques, or organizational development, may be more value-free than others, and, therefore, may require less adaptation when applied in a social welfare institution.

Contingency management, for example, is a good model, because it takes it for granted that the environment will be unpredictable. Although we may act as if the world makes decisions on the basis of MBO., in reality, decisions are made in response to unanticipated crises that threaten to divert us from our objectives. Hence, the notion of contingency management that takes into account variables in the environment is supplementary and complementary. It conditions internal management decisions in a world where objectives are tempered by outside forces, which one may not always be able to anticipate. Deliberately building in flexibility is a required balancing mechanism if our organizations (and their leaders) are to adapt and survive. This is especially true when social work administrators elect to take chances rather than "play it safe," to innovate rather than maintain the status quo, to risk in order to achieve a measure of social change. Advocating subdominant values—including much of what is implicit in social action—places public and nonprofit social agencies at risk of losing support from the key individuals and institutions who control financial resources in a profit-oriented economic system. Patti asks us to borrow, selectively, from labor and industry, to strengthen our services to clients, enhance our ability to engage in social action, *and improve our organizational maintenance and survival skills in a world that may have mixed feelings about our clients and about our mission.*

The industrial social worker's exposure to organized labor provides the author with another set of reference points. What can we learn from a trade union, whose mission is not so different from our own, concerning advocacy and service to people? How do trade unions blend the dual commitment to give service and to promote change that we so often speak of but have not always found a way to fulfill? Or, what (if anything) is different in a social agency when the staff is re-presented by a union; what do labor unions do in our own settings that we might learn from them?

Finally, by looking at business without the cloud of a preconception, Patti bridges the gap between the "hard-hearted" representatives of industry and the "do-gooders" of social work, so that we can take a more objective look at what one can contribute to the work of the other. The prospect of applying business concepts to the common mission of management is promising, provided that social workers understand the adaptations that are necessary in order to make these strategies consistent with the underlying goals of the social work profession.

Introduction

In recent years there has been a growing recognition of the interdependence between the social welfare and the business sectors and a concomitant increase in communication across institutional boundaries. A number of factors are respon-sible for this development. First, the magnitude of the social welfare enterprise, which now accounts for over 20 percent of the Gross National Product,[1] and the increasingly important role it plays in the political and economic life of this country, have required both labor and industry to be more attentive to, and in-formed about, their implications for the general workforce. The involvement of business leaders in voluntary and public welfare programs and the establishment of corporate offices concerned with promoting social responsibility are among the evidences of this trend.[2] Second, the emergence of accountability as a central concern in social welfare has prompted both professional and governmental leaders to look to the private sector for managerial knowledge and technology. The interest in applying techniques like zero-based budgeting, program planning budgeting systems (PPBS), and management by objectives (MBO) to the management of social programs has become more intense in recent years. Third, both labor and industry increasingly have recognized that the personal problems of workers can undermine organizational efficiency and effectiveness unless they are addressed at the work site.[3] As a result, a number of unions and business concerns have introduced personal service programs, and with these have come an influx of social and health professionals, including an increasing number of social workers.[4]

Social work has not been an unwilling partner in these developments. Though there remains some guardedness regarding linkages between industry and social welfare,[5,6] the profession nevertheless has sought to strengthen collaborative efforts. Schools of social work are increasingly interested in preparing practitioners for this arena of practice, and there are indications that a growing number of social workers look upon industrial settings as favorable places of employment. Finally, schools of social work around the country have actively sought alliances with schools of business administration, in order to build curricula that will enhance their capability to train social welfare managers.[7]

Nowhere has this intersystem collaboration been so evident as in the pervasive efforts to introduce business management theory and technology into the administration of social welfare organizations. This trend, while generally applauded as a move toward greater efficiency and rationality in social programs, has also been the object of some criticism. Among other things, observers have cautioned that in the widespread adoption of business management techniques by social agencies, too little attention has been given to the distinctive features of such organizations, including their goals, the political and economic context in which they operate, the services they provide, the clientele they serve, and so on. In general, critics have expressed concern that unless management technologies are adapted to political and organizational realities in social work, they may introduce serious distortions in the purposes and priorities of social agencies.[8]

The purpose of this paper is to inform this dialogue by identifying some of the salient characteristics and processes of social welfare organizations and the issues and problems they pose for management. Since social workers play such a prominent role in administering such agencies, we shall take the perspective of the profession and attempt to delineate the normative posture it has taken with regard to the management issues identified. In developing this analysis, we intend to suggest a preliminary normative framework which might be utilized to assess the relevance and utility of business management contributions for social welfare. It is our hope that the framework will enable practitioners and scholars in social work and business to consider more systematically the problems that must be addressed when transplanting management technology from industry to the social work sector.[9] Having suggested this framework, we shall then apply it to an analysis of two popular management strategies, management by objectives (MBO) and contingency management, in order to explore their potential contributions to the administration of social agencies.

Toward a Normative Framework for Social Welfare Administration

In this section, we attempt to set forth a normative conception of social welfare administration, from the perspective of social work. To derive the elements of this preliminary framework, we start by looking at the attributes and processes that appear to be fairly pervasive among, and distinctive (in some degree) to social welfare organizations. In each case, as we shall see, these characteristics pose special problems and issues for management that can be variously resolved. How they are resolved, in our view, is in part a function of the normative stance held by agency administrators.

For purposes of this discussion we shall confine ourselves to social welfare agencies (also referred to as social agencies) whose primary purpose is to change the behaviors, cognitions, attitudes, or interpersonal relationships of persons who are having difficulty in the performance of social roles. This group of agencies, which variously have been characterized as people-changing, treatment, and rehabilitative organizations,[10] relies heavily on interpersonal modes of therapy, delivered or supervised by trained human service professionals, most prominently social workers. Typical examples include family service agencies, community mental health centers, children's residential treatment facilities, and child protective services.

Norms, in this context, refer to standards regarding the ways in which an agency should function or operate in order to achieve its goals. They are to be differentiated from the outcomes or objectives an agency may seek for clients, such as improved mental health, a reduction in deviant behavior, enhanced interpersonal relationships, or more adequate and responsible social provisions. Normative standards are essentially means to achieving these ends. Our intent here is to explicate certain of the norms that social work traditionally has sought to promote in social welfare agencies and to suggest how these might inform the assessment and selection of management technologies from the business sector. Five such norms are presented in the following discussion: advocacy of subdominate values, responsiveness to diverse community constituencies, staff participation in administrative decision-making, decentralization of treatment authority, and use of evaluation to improve performance. Other norms, equally important in social work's view of how social agencies should operate, might include the development of professional staff, client confidentiality, equality of opportunity regardless of race or sex, equity in the treatment of clients with similar needs, etc.[11] However, due to space limitations, these norms will not be addressed here.

Why worry about developing such a framework? Some would argue that management is management, regardless of the setting, and that social work administrators should get on with the task of incorporating available technologies that have been applied "successfully" elsewhere.[12] It is our position that management technology is seldom neutral, but that it is, rather, based on assumptions regarding the climate, structure, and desired performance of organizations. For example, a strategy or technique based on the implicit notion that problems are largely technical matters, to be solved through information and the application of expert analysis, is likely to be found wanting in a setting where problems are resolved largely through bargaining and negotiation among groups with conflicting interests. If this is so, then it behooves social work administrators to be sure that the technology adopted rests on assumptions that are congruent with their perception of organizational reality.[13]

Agency-Environmental Relationships: Advocating Subdominate Values

Social welfare agencies, like other types of organizations, are open systems, continually interacting with the larger environment in which they exist. Community values, the ideas and attitudes that organizational participants bring with them from prior experiences and current group affiliations, the expectations and constraints imposed by other institutions—these and a host of other elements in the environment do much to condition an agency's goals, structure, and internal processes. This much has become almost axiomatic in thinking about organizations as a class of phenomena. In the case of social welfare organizations, however, relations with the environment take on a special character, because of the fact that agency purposes often are at variance with dominant community values.

Social welfare organizations typically operate in a political climate characterized by conflicting societal values. Particularly in those instances where social problems cannot be attributed to some unfortunate act of nature or to physical cause, society tends to be quite widely divided about whether and how to assist the unfortunate. Tropman's excellent analysis of the ways in which inconsistent American values have influenced the development of social policy suggests the dimensions of the problem confronting social welfare organizations as well.

> In any consideration of American values one must immediately note . . . the value system is characterized by conflicting values. . . . The value of equality is countered by "racism and group superiority themes" . . . . Moral judgments about those who have failed to "make it" in the success/mobility race is [sic] softened by values advocating humanitarian approaches. . . . In particular, our view toward the poor is at once mean and compassionate. Thousands of dollars will be donated to help a poor family if its plight becomes public through the press, yet welfare grants have never been adequate and welfare officials are criticized as working to undermine the "will to work." There exists a basic ambivalence . . . which permits differing, opposed, yet legitimate values to be espoused. And nowhere is this ambivalence more acute than in its application to clients in the social welfare enterprise.[14]

But it would not be accurate to say that these contrasting societal values have had equal valence. Clearly, as Tropman points out, values like cultural homogeneity, individualism, and moral culpability have enjoyed greater legitimacy than pluralism, social responsibility, or service without fault.[15] These sets of values coexist in our society, but the latter, those that social welfare organizations generally seek to promote, have been less dominant than the former. As a result, social service agencies frequently find themselves in an environment of opinion that discounts or stigmatizes the clientele they serve and, by extension, the programs and personnel who serve them. Equally important, social agencies, to the extent that they pursue these "subdominate" value sets, almost invariably experience strain in relationships with the larger community: a strain born of the need to gain support and legitimation for efforts that the larger society does not consider wholly legitimate. The stakes in this scenario can be quite high. On the one hand, an agency can seek a position somewhat closer to the value mainstream (for example, treating more socially attractive clients, emphasizing efficiency and accountability, etc.) in order to establish a firmer base of political and financial support. To do this may mean abandoning or obscuring its commitment to subdominate values. On the other hand, the social agency can continue identification with, and advocacy of, subdominate values. Such a position may enable an agency to remain closer to its mission, but it will also tend to render it vulnerable to public criticism, the creation of competing agencies, and, in times of fiscal scarcity or political reaction, funding cutbacks.

The normative stance in social work traditionally has favored the position that social agencies should seek to act upon, represent, and where possible advocate for subdominate values. Early theoreticians in social welfare administration, such as Spencer and Kidneigh, argued that administrators should seek to inform policy and change community attitudes in the interest of gaining support for more humane and adequate social programs.[16] In their view, it was not sufficient for the social welfare administrator simply to implement policies as they were passed down or to passively reflect community attitudes in agency operations. Rather, in Spencer's words, the agency administrator had an affirmative role to play in "improving, or raising, the community social ethic."[17] In more recent years, reflecting the preoccupation with internal management, less emphasis has been given to the administrator's role as advocate; but, as the profession emerges from its intense concern with managerial technique, it appears once again to be turning to this conception. Gummer, for example, in a recent paper posits a model of administration that requires the practitioner to "have an explicitly and systematically developed view about the purposes of social welfare" and "expertise in the promotion and protection of values."[18] The position taken by the National Conference on Social Welfare task force report, *Expanding Management Technology and Professional Accountability in Social Service Programs,* while less explicit on this point, also tends to support this view of the administrator's role.[19]

The position taken here is that the social work administrator plays, or should play, an active role in promoting the subdominate values to which Tropman refers. The administrator, perhaps more than anyone else in the social welfare enterprise, is in a position to articulate these values and martial evidence to support them. Failing this leadership, social agencies will lose their ability to act as a countervailing force against the antiwelfare biases in this society: to act as informants and advocates in the policy dialogue. In the last analysis, given the political and fiscal realities, we may seldom see these values fully reflected in policies and programs, but it is no less important that such values be given public expression. One might note here that social work administrators could benefit from the marketing experience of business. This is not to suggest that marketing products is the same as promoting values. Yet there would seem to be much that could be learned from marketing and public relations in the for-profit sector about how to communicate with an indifferent public.

This leads us, finally, to the formulation of the first guideline in a framework for assessing potential contributions from business management: *Strategies or techniques adopted from industry should, at the very least, not detract from, and optimally should contribute to, a theory and practice of social work administration that recognizes the centrality of value advocacy.* Specifically, the strategies and techniques adopted should foster attention to conflicting societal values, enable administrators to systematically document need in support of more adequate and humane services, and facilitate their capacity to argue for causes that may not have widespread support.

The Task Environment: Responsiveness to Diverse Constituencies

Social welfare agencies typically exist in a task environment consisting of groups and organizations that have a vital interest in how they operate. Legislatures, planning and funding bodies, unions, business concerns, professional schools and associations, other agencies that provide complementary or parallel services, and client or consumer organizations are some of the most prominent in this respect. In varying degrees, the social agency is engaged in interdependent relationships with this network, characterized by exchanges of program resources, information, personnel, clients, and the like. In this sense, it is not unlike other types of organizations. In the field of social welfare, however, where goals are heavily influenced by ideological considerations,[20] it is not uncommon for groups and organizations in this network to have quite different and sometimes conflicting expectations regarding an agency's proper function, including who should be served, to what ends, and in what manner. For example, a legislative body may emphasize the treatment of chronically and severely disabled patients in allocating funds for a mental health agency; while at the same time other community groups are insisting that the agency do more in the way of community education, prevention, and crisis-oriented treatment. To be sure, some of the groups may be more powerful than others in pressing their conceptions of purpose on an agency. But an agency that is inattentive to the values and preferences of other constituencies, even those with relatively little influence, runs the risk of provoking counterreactions that can be disruptive to its operations and damaging to its credibility. Strikes, organized protests by consumer groups, withdrawal of support by cooperating agencies, and unfavorable publicity are some of the consequences that may be incurred when an agency consistently fails to respond to the values and interests of constituencies. This is not to say that agencies can build support by merely reflecting these diverse expectations, because doing so inevitably brings problems of its own. The point is that the social welfare agency confronts the ongoing task of balancing the need for program integrity and internal coherence with an equally compelling need to be responsive to the sometimes diverse interests and values of groups in its task environment.

The manner in which this issue is resolved does much to determine the goals that an agency will pursue. According to Hasenfeld and English, an agency may seek to avoid alienating groups in its network by casting its goals in terms sufficiently abstract to encompass varied expectations. It may also reduce goals to the "lowest common denominator," thereby providing services that are minimally responsive to the interests of many groups. It may also pursue multiple goals or seek to align its aims with the interest of those groups that are most important or powerful.[21] Observation suggests yet another strategy, in which an agency adapts new goals or shifts priorities among those already established, in order to forestall conflict with, or a loss of support from, groups whose expectations or interests are being violated. Each of these strategies, as the literature attests, can have problematic secondary consequences.[22]

Though social work long has recognized the enormous difficulty of developing rational, internally consistent goals in the face of a task environment with such ideological diversity, it nonetheless has nurtured the idea of widespread community involvement in agency decision-making.[23] This posture, sometimes honored more in rhetoric than in practice, has rested on a belief that social agencies can be most effective when they are alert and responsive to a wide range of ideas, interests, and values. The time and energy given to building representative and informed boards, to community needs assessment, to consumer participation, and to interagency coordination, though often inspired by external mandate and/or the need to cultivate political support, also has grown out of the conviction that social agencies are instruments for affecting the community will. Agency administrators often have difficulty making good on this commitment and frequently resort to ways of conditioning and even sometimes neutralizing the influence of community groups.[24] But there are few, one suspects, who would choose to insulate the agency from community inputs, even if that were possible.

A related point on community involvement concerns the importance attached to the interests of unofficial and frequently less powerful groups in the task environment. In recent years there has developed a substantial professional concern with accountability. For the most part, however, this concern has been directed at those bodies which provide official legitimacy, policy direction, and funding, for example, federal agencies and state legislatures. Though this move to greater accountability often has been burdensome to social agencies, there has been little dispute over its basic desirability. At the same time, there are those in social work who are uncomfortable with the fact that increased responsiveness to official bodies sometimes has meant reduced attention to the needs and interests of other constituencies, most notably client organizations. Professionals recognize that the interests of authoritative public bodies and those of clients are sometimes not parallel. This has led to the view that even while agencies are attempting to be more accountable to the former, they must remain attentive and responsive to the expectations of the latter.[25]

In assessing potential contributions from management in the for-profit sector, the foregoing discussion would suggest that social welfare administrators should look for *strategies and techniques that permit practitioners to address an array of ideological perspectives and expectations. Such techniques should strengthen the administrator's ability to discern the goals and expectations of diverse constituencies and systematically assess the tradeoffs that must be made in attempting to balance various interests.*

The Nature of Agency Membership: Building Commitment through Participation

Just as the value preferences and expectations of external groups are likely to vary, so, too, will those of participants within the organization. There are many sources of this diversity. Clients come with idiosyncratic needs and individualized ideas about what the agency might be able to do to help them. Workers at several hierarchical levels in the organization are likely to have quite different educational backgrounds, prior work histories, and social class affiliations, all of which will influence their perceptions of, and preferences for, agency goals. Employees with extended professional training, in particular, often are committed to norms and ethics that contrast sharply with organizational policies and procedures.[26] Similarly, board members often come to their responsibilities with views on agency purpose that may differ from those of the management and staff.[27]

All this might be said of many other types of organizations as well. What tends to distinguish social welfare agencies is the fact that there is seldom an objective standard (profitability, for example) against which to test competing conceptions of agency purpose. Moreover, with few exceptions, the relationship between how things are done and outcomes is usually unclear and less linear, so that even when goals are agreed upon, people may reasonably differ over the best means for achieving them. Under these circumstances, one might expect participants in social welfare organizations to pursue courses of action that maximize their value preferences. To some extent this occurs, but in the last analysis, an organization must develop means for narrowing and/or reconciling the range of diverse views regarding agency goals or risk an unacceptable level of internal conflict and fragmentation.

Among the most important mechanisms for reducing ideological dispersion within the agency are selective recruitment, orientation and training, supervision, promotion, and the like. These efforts are useful for developing a commonality among organizational participants, but they are seldom sufficient in themselves for building commitment to agency goals and ensuring compliance with policies and procedures. It is here that administrative leadership plays a crucial role.

In the broadest sense, agency administrators have two options available (more a continuum than discrete alternatives) for dealing with the value diversity that is likely to characterize the various subgroups in an organization. On the one hand, they can establish a system of centralized decision-making—which prescribes goals, policies, and procedures for organizational members—and use the authority of office to enforce them. This strategy may recognize different points of view, but generally it does not provide a forum in which they can be actively promulgated in the decision process. Under this option, emphasis is placed on providing clear direction from above and upon management control to ensure conformity. Conversely, at the other end of the continuum, administrators may choose to treat the value diversity that exists among members as the focal point of the decision-making process. Without abrogating the responsibility for making decisions, administrators who employ this strategy actively elicit the opinions and views of agency employees and seek, in an ongoing process, to negotiate compromises that reflect varied interests. This style of leadership relies heavily on information and persuasion. It assumes that participation and influence in the decision process will promote commitment to agency goals and cooperation in the implementation of programs.

Social work long has recognized the need to combine elements of both of these leadership styles in the administrative process. Indeed, there is a growing appreciation that the indiscriminate application of either the centralized or the participatory approach can produce negative consequences for individual as well as agency performance.[28] Increasingly, the trend is toward specifying the circumstances, both internal and external to the organization, under which one or another of these approaches is likely to be most effective.[29] At the same time, it is safe to say that both the theory and the practice of administration in social work have tended to emphasize the participatory strategy more consistently and on a broader range of issues than is true of management in profit-making settings. This is not to imply that participatory management is neglected in other types of organizations, or that social work's experience in this regard is unique. Indeed, it is clear that the profession has drawn heavily upon the theory and experience of business, and especially labor, in formulating its own stance on this issue.[30]

Nevertheless, though social work draws upon a theoretical heritage common to managers in other settings, some observers have felt that participation is too widely and indiscriminately employed by social welfare administrators. Others have criticized the time-consuming and often ritualized nature of this approach to decision-making.[31] No doubt these criticisms often are justified, yet such a position often fails to recognize the many ways in which organizational members can subvert or neutralize agency efforts if their views are not given expression. Perhaps, more importantly, the professional stance on participation grows out of a recognition that much of what transpires in social welfare organizations cannot readily be observed or evaluated by management. Informed policy, therefore, requires that workers share their experiences in service delivery with their superiors, and such sharing is only likely to occur if subordinates have meaningful access to decision-makers and the decision-making process. Finally, only the most myopic administrator believes that managers are not prone to the kind of external pressures that may cause them to neglect the interests of their staff and clients. Recognizing this possibility, social work has emphasized the value of participation as a vehicle for maintaining administrative accountability to those who give and receive agency services.

This discussion suggests a third guideline for assessing the relevance and utility of business management technology to social welfare administration. *In general, such technologies should support managerial efforts to elicit the views and experiences of subordinates and give them active consideration in the decision-making process. Moreover, management techniques should aid administrators in understanding the diverse values and interests found among social agency participants and strengthen their ability to reconcile these views in the formulation of agency goals, policies, and procedures.*

The Nature of Service Delivery: Decentralizing Treatment Authority

In a general sense, social agencies share with most other types of organizations the functions of converting raw materials that are introduced and exporting them in modified form to the environment. However, while this analogy is accurate in one sense, it is misleading in another. Words like "raw materials," "converting," and "exporting" convey an image of inert, malleable matter, which can be manipulated at will. Money is converted to investments, pig iron to steel, and meat to sausage. In no case does the raw material complain, refuse to cooperate, or suggest alternate methods of conversion.

Clearly, this is not the case with clients who seek help at social agencies. On the contrary, they present an array of quite different problems and capabilities, and they are likely to have their own ideas about how to ameliorate these difficulties. The outcomes to be sought, even if they can readily be defined, normally cannot be imposed on the client, but rather must grow out of a process of contract setting in which the client's values, preferences, past experiences, and aspirations are central considerations.[32] The negotiations between worker and client necessarily occur in a context defined by agency goals, program objectives, and resource availability. Still, the active cooperation of the client is an essential element in the change process, and workers find it necessary to fashion interventions that are responsive to their unique problems and capabilities. Moreover, in order to maintain symmetry of purpose, treatment arrangements frequently have to be renegotiated over time. The means and ends in service delivery are seldom held constant. The variability of clients and the necessity of tailoring interventions to individual needs and capabilities make it difficult for agencies to prescribe a single change process. If uniform prescription were possible (or indeed desirable), its application by social workers no doubt would vary because of different educational and experiential qualities and personal predispositions.[33] The net effect of these interacting variables is to produce a service delivery or change process that is likely to be characterized by uncertainty and variability.

The character of service delivery in social agencies poses a number of critical problems for managers. However, the one we will focus upon is the question of how much authority and discretion to delegate to front-line workers. This is a troublesome area for management, since it involves reconciling the need for equity and reliability in the delivery of services with the need for individualized treatment arrangements. Each is a compelling norm for social agencies, and each can only be fully actualized at some cost to the other. The dilemma can be resolved to some degree, however. Managers can avoid the need for discretionary authority at the front line by adopting simplifying assumptions about the nature and range of problems presented by clients (for example, troubled children need discipline), by narrowly defining the types of services the agency will provide (vocational training, for example), or by promulgating extensive organizational rules and regulations (such as manuals of procedure).[34] In each case, variability for the clientele is reduced, as is the need for highly particularized treatment responses.[35] Managers also may attempt to resolve the dilemma by allowing workers substantial autonomy, trusting to their judgment and competence that client needs will be met in a professionally responsible manner. The problems inherent in each of these positions are readily apparent. One stance increases the agency's ability to prescribe uniform treatments, but at some obvious costs to flexibility and individualization. The other facilitates flexibility, but introduces potential problems of reliability and consistency in service delivery.

A normative stance taken in social work has tended to favor the delegation of treatment authority to front-line workers. There has, of course, been a parallel preference for supervision to ensure that inexperienced workers, or those without sufficient training, exercise this discretionary authority in accordance with agency rules and principles of the profession. Nevertheless, the type of intervention, level of intensity, frequency, and duration are within broad agency guidelines, generally thought to be best decided in the context of an intimate, trusting relationship between worker and client. Lewis, for example, argues that service

> . . . requires sufficient personal contact to permit the recognition of differences and idiosyncratic attributes. It requires a feeling and knowing interface between client and agency. Anonymity masks client differences and seeks to assure uniform treatment. It minimizes worker judgments.[36]

A somewhat similar posture has been taken by the National Conference on Social Welfare. Its task force report urges that the worker be given greater control over resources and "authority to make decisions necessary to implement service plans that he [sic] has developed with clients."[37]

The rationale for decentralized authority has been somewhat weakened in recent years, as studies have revealed an apparent lack of treatment effectiveness. In some agencies, this has occasioned a move toward making service more uniform and reducing the discretion exercised by workers. At the very least, the question about the efficacy of service has promoted greater attention to monitoring and evaluation. Through all of this, however, there has remained a widespread professional commitment to the notion that agency services should be responsive to individual needs and circumstances, and that these determinations should be made in the context of a relationship in which the provider exercises considerable professional judgment.[38]

Thus we come to a fourth guideline for evaluating the contributions of managerial technology from the field of business. *Strategies or techniques incorporated into the theory and practice of social work administration should strengthen the manager's ability to identify conditions which require the delegation of authority to service providers and to devise organizational arrangements that support the responsible use of discretion in the treatment process.*

Accountability: Using Evaluation to Improve Performance

Information, it is said, is the lifeblood of management. Certainly, the manager must know what is being done in an organization—at what costs, and with what effect—in order to budget intelligently and allocate resources, to plan, modify, and implement programs, and to account to external sources. Social work managers, like those in other kinds of organizations, therefore, spend a good deal of time and energy in monitoring and assessing the activities of subordinates.[39]

In a time of scarce resources and increasing competition for available funds, this management function has taken on increasing importance and is likely to become even more critical in the foreseeable future. Unfortunately, in the press for more and better information on which to base management decisions, too little attention has been given to the characteristics of social welfare organizations that condition both the nature of the information that can be collected and the means for doing so.

Much that has been said of social agencies so far also can be applied to understanding the special problems attendant to monitoring and evaluating performance in social agencies. For example, as we noted previously, in order to win legitimacy and support from groups and organizations with diverse viewpoints, social agencies often adopt goal statements that are sufficiently broad and abstract to encompass a range of value positions. Alternately, agencies sometimes incorporate goals that appeal to different groups in the environment, even though such goals conflict with one another. We also have commented upon the fact that social welfare organizations deal with the kind of largely nonroutine service events that require a good deal of ad hoc problem-solving and the concomitant exercise of discretion by front-line staff. Monitoring and evaluating social service activity are facilitated by standardizing treatments and prescribing levels of effort. Such steps can be taken, of course, but the willingness of workers to deliver, and clients to receive, services under this format is likely to pose serious problems. Given the private nature of these transactions, workers who disagree with treatments that have been prescribed can vary them, or can comply in a ritual manner.[40] Clients can, of course, reject interventions or, more typically, pressure the service provider to modify them.

Another constraint to monitoring and evaluating in social agencies inheres in the professional norms to which social work practitioners tend to subscribe. By and large, reporting requirements, especially if the worker perceives them to be of little or no value, are likely to be seen as a diversion from direct service. Worker resistance to recording and filling out forms and their perfunctory treatment of monthly statistical reports are some of the obstacles that managers encounter when they seek to establish extensive and sophisticated information systems that have little apparent relevance for front-line staff. A related norm regarding autonomy grows out of the belief that professional training and experience have equipped the social worker to be the best judge of the nature and intensity of the service to be provided and whether outcomes have been achieved. Consultation with other professionals who possess similar expertise generally is valued, but efforts by managerial personnel, especially those with no professional credentials, are likely to be resented as an intrusion on professional prerogative. Finally, in some instances, social workers resist providing sensitive information about clients when there is a possibility that it may be used for purposes other than originally intended.

There is little question that social welfare agencies will find it more and more necessary to enhance their evaluative capabilities, both to support internal decision processes and to account to external policy-making and funding bodies. There is a widespread recognition of this reality in social work, and in recent years theory and practice in social work administration increasingly have focused on means for improving accountability. Many of the gains made in the field have resulted from innovations pioneered in the business sector and adopted by social agencies. Management information system technology, computer-assisted decision-making, productivity management, project planning and control systems (PERT, for example), are some of the technologies that have buttressed the evaluating and monitoring capabilities of social agencies.

At the same time, having struggled with efforts to systematically evaluate agency performance, social work administrators are beginning to find that efforts to improve accountability are not an unmixed blessing. There are several areas of concern. First, such efforts tend to focus on the most readily quantifiable elements of service delivery. Faced with the difficulties of measuring the quality of service and its effectiveness, variables like time, cost, units of service, and numbers of clients served tend to become the central criteria used in measuring the performance of individual workers and agency programs. When this occurs, it is not uncommon for service providers to emphasize (at least in their reports) the activities that are best reflected in this system.[41] Second, where evaluation concentrates on outcomes that are easily measurable (recidivism, job placement, return to community, etc.), direct service workers may have a tendency to "cream" those clients who are most likely to succeed in these terms. Under these circumstances, program success often is achieved at the cost of neglecting clients who are hard to reach or more profoundly disturbed.[42] Third, there is some concern that monitoring and evaluating schemes have little developmental payoff for direct service workers. Ideally, such efforts should provide corrective feedback to front-line workers, in order to help them assess and improve their practice. Unfortunately, such systems frequently do not serve this purpose. In part, this seems to occur because the demands for external accountability take precedence over the internal needs for evaluation that are aimed at supporting knowledge and skill development. Finally, there is a concern that the preoccupation with evaluation sometimes obscures the fact that organizational performance is as much a function of existing policy and of what resources are available to the agency as it is of agency practices, good *or* bad.[43]

Experience with these problems has alerted academics and practitioners in social work to the fact that monitoring and evaluating have important implications for how an organization sets priorities and delivers services. Clearly, social work administrators cannot shrink from the responsibility of accounting for agency performance. At the same time, there is a professional commitment to the notion that evaluation also is a tool that should be used in the service of program improvement: a supportive resource for planning and decision-making at all levels in the organization and a means for enhancing service provision and identifying areas requiring social change.

This normative posture suggests a final guideline for assessing the relevance of managerial technology to social work administration: *Techniques for monitoring and evaluating social service activity should facilitate the manager's ability to assess the substantive nature of practice, rather than simply its extrinsic characteristics.* Such technology should further enable the administrator to construct evaluation systems that can generate the kind of performance-related information that will be useful to actors at various levels in refining and improving their practice and agency programs.

Analyzing Contributions from the Business Sector

Up to this point, we have presented selected characteristics of social welfare organizations, some of the typical problems and dilemmas that beset such agencies, and the normative stance that social work has taken with regard to how these problems might be resolved. One could argue with the profession's normative posture on these issues (or with our formulation of it). There are wide differences of opinion on these matters, both within and without the field of social work. For the sake of discussion, however, we will assume that the norms suggested earlier are subscribed to by most social work administrators, most of the time. Given this normative stance and the guidelines derived, we turn now to assessing the relevance of selected managerial technologies to social work administration.

In recent years, a steady stream of ideas, strategies, and technologies that were originally developed and applied in for-profit organizations has been proposed to and/or adopted by social welfare agencies. Indeed, as previously mentioned, social work and social welfare agencies are heavily indebted to business administration for many recent advances in management practice. One need only list some of the better-known strategies and techniques that were developed largely in the for-profit sector to appreciate how much social work administration has been influenced:

- Management by Objectives (MBO)
- Program Evaluation Review Technique (PERT)
- Cost-benefit analysis
- Performance budgeting
- Zero-based budgeting
- Cost accounting
- Contingency management
- Matrix organization
- Behavioral management
- Work enlargement, enrichment
- Flexitime
- Stress management
- Operations research
- Time management
- Organizational development

This list could be expanded and elaborated at length, but it is long enough now to suggest how profoundly social administration theory and practice have been affected by this technology transfer.

Having acknowledged this debt, it is important to note that social work has not always been a discriminating consumer in the marketplace of management ideas. In the final analysis, it is the profession's reponsibility, growing out of its intimate familiarity with (and leadership role in) social welfare, to select and adapt those technologies that are best suited to promoting the essential character of the field. In what follows, therefore, we select two major contributions from business administration, management by objectives and contingency management, in order to test their "goodness of fit" with the norms espoused by the profession. Our intent here is to assess how the application of these strategies may aid or detract from the social work administrator's ability to run an organization in accordance with the norms specified earlier.

Management by Objectives (MBO)

Of all the managerial developments in the for-profit sector, perhaps none has been so widely touted and applied in social agencies as management by objectives (MBO). Since it was first formulated by Drucker in 1954, MBO has been extensively employed in busines and industry.[44] As with any popular innovation, it has been refined and adapted continuously for various uses, but its fundamental purposes are as follows: (1) to orchestrate the objectives of actors at several organizational levels and across units or divisions, so that each is rationally linked to the central formal goals of the organization; and (2) to evaluate performance at individual, unit, and organizational levels, in terms of the degree to which explicitly stated and measurable objectives are achieved. The MBO process, according to one popular formulation, entails four essential elements: goal setting, action planning, self-control, and periodic review.[45] The process begins with the formulation of overall organizational goals, which subsequently are translated into increasingly narrower and more specific subgoals or objectives, at successively lower levels in the organization. "The process is repeated at every management level until a clear and integrated hierarchy of objectives exists throughout the entire organization."[46] The next stage involves formulating detailed action plans, which specify how the objectives are to be accomplished, as well as when, by whom, and so forth. Having formulated the objectives and the means for achieving them, each unit in the organization exercises responsibility for assessing its own implementation and taking corrective action as needed to adjust action plans. Finally, at periodic intervals, the performance of units in the organization is reviewed in relation to established goals, problems are identified and resolved, objectives are revised, and, where necessary, steps are taken to reinforce or improve upon the skills needed to perform effectively. All of these steps in the process are, of course, interactive, so theoretically there are continual adjustments made between goals and performance at various levels in the organization.

This is only the most skeletal overview of MBO, but it is enough to suggest its potential implications for the normative stance that social work attempts to further in social welfare organizations.[47]

Advocating for subdominate values. The application of MBO in social welfare organizations would seem only indirectly related to the promotion of this norm. Indeed, it should be noted that MBO is not intended as a means for advocating values that are not widely supported in the community. Rather, its purpose is to martial resources more effectively in the service of agency objectives, whether or not these are congruent with the value mainstream of society. Within this context, however, MBO may have important secondary consequences for an agency's ability to represent subdominate values. To the extent that this management approach fosters the development of measurable, concrete goals and objectives, social work administrators may be better able to represent their agency's purposes in public forums and to argue more effectively the need for programs and policies serving groups that are stigmatized or devalued in our society. This consequence may be important, since organizations whose goals conflict with the values of the dominant society frequently are attacked not on these grounds, but rather on the basis of their inability to state clearly what it is they intend to accomplish and when and how they expect to do so. In short, diffusion of purpose or seeming lack of direction becomes the target of opportunity for community groups who oppose the values and interests served by social welfare agencies. The rationality that MBO can bring to agency goals and objectives will not eliminate the strain between dominant community values and those advocated by social agencies. However, it may increase the tolerance of the general community for such agencies or reduce the latter's vulnerability in times of political reaction.

Responsiveness to diverse constituencies. Successful application of MBO requires, among other things, the most precise possible statements of agency goals and objectives. Moreover, it appears necessary that such goals remain fairly constant in the near term if there is to be any reasonable chance of assessing whether performance has had the desired effect. These requirements for MBO may not be reconciled easily with the norm of agency responsiveness for three reasons. First, it seems quite likely that this system will force agency management to commit itself to a narrow range of external expectations, in order to achieve the goal clarity and specificity required. Diffused and/or conflicting goals are an anathema to MBO. Second, the expectations of groups or organizations in the task environment that are less easily operationalized (for example, humane treatment of clients, reduction of racism) may not be given the same hearing as those which focus on concrete objectives (such as cost or output units). One should not dismiss the possibility that agencies under MBO may respond to those values that most readily translate to measurable outcomes. Last, there is some evidence to suggest that where agencies operate in an unstable environment, characterized by unanticipatable crises and unpredictable funding, MBO is difficult to implement.[48] This appears so because of the need for long-term planning and continuity. By extrapolation, we may surmise that in a task environment consisting of groups or organizations with conflicting values and very nearly equal power vis-à-vis the agency, MBO may not be a workable management system.

Building commitment through participation. Much of the literature on MBO emphasizes the importance of staff participation in formulating the goals and objectives to be pursued by the organization. In at least some of this literature, however, participation occurs in a sharply hierarchical context, such that personnel at successively lower levels formulate objectives within parameters narrowly prescribed by their superiors.[49] Some have referred to this as the "deductive" approach to MBO.[50] Experience in social welfare agencies suggests that MBO can be implemented most effectively in an "inductive" manner, building from lower-level to higher-level goals and objectives. Raider, for example, comments:

> Goal development should be an inductive process in a social agency. General departmental or unit goals are constructed from many specific individual worker objectives. After compiling individual worker objectives, members of the department would collectively seek to ascertain what common goals could be formulated and what plans could be developed.[51]

Some combination of both deductive and inductive processes probably is required in social agencies, but there seems little doubt that the latter must be a central component if an agency wishes to encourage the norm of participatory decision-making. When implemented in this way, MBO would seem to be a useful means for explicating the diverse perspectives of management and staff and providing an opportunity for agency members to negotiate and reconcile their differences. There is a widespread belief (and some empirical evidence) that would suggest that where there is opportunity for this kind of involvement, the commitment of staff to agency goals and objectives is increased.[52]

Decentralized treatment authority. MBO also would seem a potentially useful management strategy for facilitating the ability of front-line workers to deal flexibly with the diverse needs of clients. When MBO utilizes an inductive process, responsibility for formulating social service objectives devolves largely upon direct service practitioners. Although these objectives are negotiated with and agreed to by superiors, there is an assumption that workers have access to the information and experience that confer a particular expertise with regard to service delivery. Theoretically, therefore, under an MBO system one would expect program objectives to grow out of the interaction of front-line workers and their immediate supervisors, instead of being decided at the top and unilaterally imposed downward.[53]

MBO also encourages decentralization by focusing attention on outcomes rather than means or processes. Action plans for the accomplishment of objectives are a central requirement, but the emphasis is placed on the relationship between activities and objectives, not on activities per se.

> Inherent in the [MBO] process is the notion that the individual, not his superior, will control his own behavior and the activities required to implement the action plan and to achieve the objectives.[54]

Under such a system, then, front-line workers should have considerable latitude to adopt the intervention strategies they consider most useful to achieving treatment outcomes. Workers are monitored and held accountable, but the emphasis is not on whether they have followed standardized procedures, but rather on whether their actions have achieved the desired result.[55]

There are some potential pitfalls. Agencies of any complexity are likely to have several distinct units or divisions whose functions are interdependent. To the extent that competing or noncomplementary objectives are developed at the program level, MBO may generate a potential for conflict and competitiveness among units.[56] There is some reason to wonder if the same system that allows for decentralized and supposedly more responsive programs of service also may stimulate intense and perhaps parochial loyalty to particular organizational units.

Using evaluation to improve performance. One of the potentially attractive features of MBO is the capacity it provides for periodic performance appraisals at both individual and organizational levels. The individual or organizational unit formulates objectives and action plans, and these are assessed jointly with superiors at periodic intervals with a view to determining the relationship between what has been done and the outcome. Since the objectives and plans have been generated at least partly by the person (or unit) being evaluated, the assessment and feedback are likely to be considered relevant to professional performance. Some writers on this subject stress the importance of using these periodic assessments as a problem-solving device, which can focus on professional development goals as well as on performance effectiveness.[57] Here the focus is not only on performance and outcome but also on the knowledge, skill, or experience that subordinates may wish to acquire in order to improve their competence.[58] In this context, the assessment of performance is intimately linked with the professional aspirations of staff.

Under the best of circumstances, then, MBO affords an approach to evaluation which can be used in the service of improving performance and developing staff capability. This has not always occurred. Among the criticisms that have been leveled at this system of management is that it tends to emphasize only the most quantifiable elements of service delivery. There also has been a tendency in some settings to impose objectives and action plans on subordinates, thereby bypassing the painstaking and time-consuming processes of discussion, negotiating, and joint goal setting, which are essential to effective MBO in social agencies.[59] When this occurs, subordinates are not likely to develop a commitment to the evaluation process or to perceive it as useful to their growth and development. Finally, one of the common problems that beset MBO systems is the tendency for them to become laden with procedures, paper work, and excessive reporting requirements. Often associated with this procedural overlay is negative staff reaction. Even where MBO has value as a mechanism for evaluating and improving performance, excessive formalism can render it ineffective if staff members perceive the system as too burdensome.[60]

Contingency Management

Until quite recently, much of the thinking about organizational design and administrative leadership has been characterized by one-dimensional prescriptions, which argue a "best way" to structure and manage organizations. This tradition, exemplified in schools of thought like "scientific management," "human relations," and "management process," has emphasized the search for universal principles to guide students and practitioners in understanding and directing organizational behavior. In the past two decades, this search for a "best way" has given way to the view that organizations are complex, multivariate entities, which may not be amenable to monolithic explanatory or intervention models. Instead, the position taken—frequently characterized as the contingency approach—is that managerial activities must be tailored to fit the specific characteristics of the organization and the environment in which it operates.[61] Blau summarizes the broad outlines of this approach:

> The contingency view seeks to understand the relationships within and among subsystems as well as between the organization and its environment and to define relationships or configurations of variables. It . . . attempts to understand how organizations operate under varying circumstances and in specific situations. Contingency views are ultimately directed toward suggesting organizational designs and managerial actions most appropriate for specific situations.[62]

There are two specific expressions of this general approach, pertaining to organizational design and to administrative leadership, respectively. Both expressions have gained considerable attention in the general management literature. Each draws upon a complex body of theory and research to which we cannot fully do justice here.

The contingency approach to organizational design is concerned with finding the optimal fit between the distribution of authority in a system and the nature of the technology it employs. Stated simply, the central question concerns the circumstances under which tasks can be most effectively carried out. There seems to be some agreement that where technology (that is, the techniques employed to accomplish the work of the organization) is repetitive, standardized, routine, and easily programmed, decision-making is best centralized in the upper reaches of the hierarchy. Under these contingent circumstances, managers should decide what is to be done and when and how it is to be done and should prescribe the actions of subordinates through direction, rules, manuals of procedures, and the like. Conversely, where technology is nonroutine (that is, variable, complex, and indeterminate), contingency analysis suggests that authority should be delegated to subordinates, so as to permit flexibility and discretion.[63]

The contingency notion has also been applied to leadership behavior. Vroom's work on the extent to which managers should share decision-making authority with subordinates illustrates the application of this approach to leadership. Vroom's research suggests that leadership style (on an autocratic-participatory continuum) should vary, depending on the nature of the decision at hand. In his model, a manager is "neither universally autocratic nor universally participative, but utilizes either approach in response to the demands of the situation as *he perceives them.*"[64] Situational properties that determine the appropriate leadership style, for example, include the nature of the problem to be solved, the information needed, the extent to which subordinates must accept the decision in order to implement it, time constraints, and so on. Empirical evidence suggests that the model of leadership proposed by Vroom is useful for predicting successful decision outcomes in a high percentage of cases.[65]

There is little documented experience with the contingency approach in social welfare, though one suspects that some administrators have long employed elements of this model in day-to-day practice. Nevertheless, at this writing there is little descriptive or empirical evidence upon which to draw in assessing the implication of this model for the normative stance that is promoted in social work. What follows, therefore, must be considered speculative. Contingency management would seem to have immediate implications for three norms that were identified earlier.

Responsiveness to diverse constituencies. One of the critical situational variables considered in the contingency model is the nature of the environment in which an organization operates. In general, both theoretical formulations and research evidence point to the notion that organizations tend to perform most effectively when there is a "fit" between organizational design and leadership patterns, on the one hand, and the nature of the organizational environment, on the other.[66] Thus "organic systems" (that is, less stratified, open, two-way communication, consultative leadership style, etc.) are thought to be more effective in the face of unstable task environments, characterized by change and uncertainty. Conversely, "mechanistic systems" (that is, stratified, top-down communication, extensive rules and procedures, etc.) are thought to be most appropriate when the environment is relatively unchanging, and when expectations and demands are clear and constant. Research on this question is ongoing, but this approach to organizational design and leadership would seem to be promising for social agencies.

Given the diverse and changing nature of the task environment in which most social agencies operate, and the normative posture regarding organizational responsiveness that was referred to earlier, the contingency approach should help social work administrators to deliberately design organizations that are appropriate to the circumstances. Too often, managers maintain structural arrangements and leadership styles that are better suited to relatively stable environments. The persistence of the bureaucratic form among social agencies is one indication of this. The contingency approach directs attention to the relationship between internal structure, climate, and external conditions and should, therefore, alert administrators to design and leadership alternatives that will better equip their agencies to respond to a dynamic task environment. Among other things, one would expect contingency-oriented management to make much greater use of structural arrangements that permit quicker response time, flexible planning, and cross-program integration. Task forces, teams, linking roles, and matrix organizations are some of the available options that might help agencies to be more responsive to external constituencies.[67]

Building commitment through participation. Participatory management, as we indicated earlier, has long been important in social work. Although administrators have sometimes been criticized for adopting this leadership style, a widespread belief has persisted that meaningful participation in the administrative process is an important way of building commitment to agency goals. What has been lacking is an explicit theoretical and empirical rationale for this posture.

The contingency approach to leadership may offer a useful tool to social work managers who seek to promote the norm of participation. Application of the contingency model could provide managers with a systematic means for identifying those situations in which participatory decision-making is likely to increase the quality of the decision made and/or the probability that it will be implemented effectively. To this extent, one would expect participation to be used more purposefully by administrators. It is one thing for managers to involve subordinates in decision-making because they feel that better-quality decisions *may* result. It is quite another for managers, based on their analyses of the problems, to conclude that participation of staff is *essential* to a high-quality decision. In short, contingency management may strengthen the rationale for, and investment in, participatory decision-making where that style of leadership is preferred. Some years ago, Herman Stein spoke to the importance of "relevant" staff involvement if participation were to have meaning for administrators and subordinates.[68] Contingency management provides a framework for determining the question of relevancy and rationalizes the relationship between participation and decision outcome.

While the contingency approach to leadership may help to foster meaningful participation, it may also create a dilemma for administrators. One possible outcome is that different departments, units, or levels in the organization will have quite different degrees of involvement in administrative decisions. For example, employees dealing with relatively routine problems, using a standardized repertoire of responses (for example, secretarial and custodial staff and professional staff administering concrete social services), are likely to be little involved in decision-making if the contingency model is consistently applied. This is true to some extent now, but the use of the contingency approach may make differential rates of participation even more visible in agencies and perhaps increase power disparities among subgroups in the organization. Lowered morale and conflict among staff, as well as increased stridency from those who perceive themselves losing power to affect the work environment, may be undesirable secondary consequences of this approach to leadership.

Decentralizing treatment authority. In recent years, there has been a decided shift toward standardizing service delivery to bring it under closer management control. Counter-arguments, based on the need for professional autonomy in order to permit the exercise of discretion, generally have not been persuasive. The application of the contingency model in social agencies may assist managers in systematically analyzing service transactions to determine the organizational structure best suited to facilitating task performance. Mullis' analysis of service delivery in income maintenance, medical, and social service programs in public welfare (and the degree of decentralization appropriate in each of these areas) is an example of the contingency approach applied to social welfare. Social services should be centrally monitored and evaluated, in Mullis' view, but the nature of client problems and treatment methodology lead him to conclude that:

> . . . decisions as to which service to provide and the method of provision are most properly made at the local level by truly professional staff. Local decision making provides the variety and the rapid response necessary to cope with the very individual approach required.[69]

This kind of analysis is only beginning to appear in social work, but as it is developed further, it should help to rescue the issue of organizational design from the tug-of-war that has existed between those who insist on centralized control under all circumstances and those who argue for decentralization based upon the need for differential assessment of client need.

Conclusion

This paper is only a first step toward a normative framework that may help social workers to assess the relevance and utility of managerial technologies for social welfare organizations. It has not been our purpose to exhaust either the organizational norms that social workers pursue or the managerial technologies that might usefully be transferred from business to social welfare. Rather, our purpose has been to suggest a line of analysis, which is based on the premise that the responsible utilization of knowledge and skill from other fields requires clarity about the values and goals that social work holds important and about just how well or poorly these values and goals are served by the available tools. A failure to do so invites the indiscriminate application of business technology in social welfare, with its unanticipated and often negative consequences for social agencies and the clients they serve. In short, whether one agrees with the particulars presented here is not important. Far more critical is the notion that social work be a proactive consumer as it shops in the managerial marketplace. Our hope is that this discussion may stimulate a more productive dialogue between business and social work regarding new management technology for social welfare organizations.

Notes

[1] These are figures for 1974–75 and include public expenditures for income maintenance and for certain health and education programs. See *Encyclopedia of Social Work* 2, 17th ed., (Washington, D.C.: NASW, 1977), p. 1639.

[2] The close ties between United Way and leaders in the business sector are well known, of course. For example, through its National Corporate Development Program, United Way has recruited executives in 101 of the Fortune 500 companies to promote charitable donations in these firms. Ron Chernow, "Cornering the Goodness Market: The Uncharitable Doings at United Way," *Saturday Review* (October 28, 1978), p. 17.

[3] Stanislav Kasl, "Work and Mental Health," in James O'Toole, ed., *Work and the Quality of Life* (Cambridge, Mass.: M.I.T. Press, 1974), p. 196; and Michael Austin and Erwin Jackson, "Occupational Mental Health and the Human Services: A Review," *Health and Social Work*, 2, no. 1 (February, 1977), 93–118.

[4] See, for example, Rex Skidmore, David Balsam, and Otto Jones, "Social Work Practice in Industry," *Social Work*, 19, no. 4 (May 1974), 280–86; Andrew Weissman, "A Social Service Strategy in Industry," *Social Work*, 20, no. 5 (September 1975), 401–03; and Sheila H. Akabas, Paul A. Kurzman, and Nancy S. Kolben, eds., *Labor and Industrial Settings: Sites for Social Work Practice* (New York: Columbia University, Hunter College, CSWE, 1978).

[5] Robert Jacobsen, "Industrial Social Work in Context," *Social Work*, 19, no. 6 (November 1974), 655–66.

[6] As the principal profession in social welfare, social work has far too long been content to think of the industrial system as the "perpetrator" of social ills, a set of forces and interests that create "diswelfares" on societal, familial, and individual levels, in order to promote its selfish purposes. To the extent that this conception was shared, social work tended to think of itself as a bulwark against inhumane practices in the industrial sector. Social welfare agencies were left with the task of tending to the needs of persons who the industrial world would, or could not accommodate, or, at worst, of those who were the victims of unfair or exploitative practices. But while much of the social work profession bemoaned the plight of those who were not part of the market place, or criticized the social irresponsibility of industry, it was clearly unequal to the task of correcting these inequitable and injurious practices. Social work thus embraced the notion that government should be a countervailing force to the inhumane and exploitative practices in the industrial sector. By interposing government between industry and itself (or, more properly, the clients it served), social work could avoid direct involvement with this economic institution. Unfortunately, this adversarial posture had the effect of "distancing" social work and social welfare programs from the social and psychological problems encountered by persons in the world of work and obscuring the potentials for social prevention that were presented by these settings. Just as importantly, the distance between social work and industry has fostered stereotypes, which have served as impediments to information and technology exchange.

[7] For a description and analysis of these efforts, see *Administration in Social Work*, 2 (Summer 1978), and George Brager and Megan McLaughlin, eds., *Training Social Welfare Managers: Social Work Business Cooperation* (New York: Columbia University School of Social Work, 1978).

[8] Ida Hoos, *Systems Analysis in Public Policy* (Berkeley, Calif.: University of California Press, 1972); Rino Patti, "The New Scientific Management: Systems Analysis for Social Welfare," *Public Welfare*, 33, no. 2 (Spring 1975), 23–31; Murray Gruber, "Total Administration," *Social Work*, 19, no. 5 (September 1974), 625–36.

[9] For an informative discussion on barriers to collaboration, see "The Manager vs. the Social Worker," *Public Welfare*, 36, no. 3 (Summer 1978), 5–10.

[10] For a more complete discussion of this kind of agency, see Yeheskel Hasenfeld and Richard English, eds., *Human Service Organizations* (Ann Arbor, Michigan: University of Michigan Press, 1974), pp. 33–50 and Alfred Kahn, *Social Policy and Social Services* (New York: Random House, 1973), pp. 27–33.

[11] It is important to note here that although social work generally has advocated these norms, there are differences among professionals in the field regarding the extent to which such conditions and processes are necessary to the delivery of effective social services. Some will argue, for example, that advocacy of subdominate values or responsiveness to disease constituencies can be detrimental to agencies that are seeking to establish credibility with policy-making bodies. Others differ over the emphasis given to staff participation, on the grounds that the time and energy given to these activities often can divert an agency from its service objectives.

We should also point out that while the profession has promulgated these norms, they are seldom fully realized in agency practice. Funding constraints, time pressures, externally imposed requirements, and a host of other political and economic considerations frequently require agency administrators to compromise these norms, however desirable they may consider them to be. Notwithstanding this discrepancy between what is espoused and what is practiced, it is our view that the normative stance described below continues to exert a significant influence on how social work administrators believe they and their agencies should function.

[12] There has been a tendency in social work to assume that because a management technology has been widely employed in industry, it must have been successful. Gruber and others have made it quite clear that this is not always so. See Gruber, "Total Administration."

[13] Leo Miller, of Polaroid, and others have argued that many norms previously thought distinctive to social welfare are increasingly characteristic of business concerns as well. For example, norms such as responsiveness to "less-power" groups in the task environment, participation in management, and the delegation of authority to lower levels in the organiza-

tion apparently have increasing currency in many for-profit firms. The extent to which there is a convergence in these areas and its implications for the transfer of management technology are matters that deserve serious consideration.

[14] John Tropman, "Societal Values and Social Policy: Implications for Social Work," in John Tropman and others, eds., *Strategic Perspectives on Social Policy* (New York: Pergamon Press, 1976), p. 69.

[15] Ibid.

[16] Sue Spencer, "The Administrative Process in a Social Agency," in Harry Schatz, ed., *Social Work Administration* (New York: Council on Social Work Education, 1970), pp. 135–44 and John C. Kidneigh, "Social Work Administration: An Area of Social Work Practice," *Social Work Journal*, 31, no. 2 (April 1950), 57–61, 79.

[17] Spencer, "The Administrative Process," p. 139.

[18] Burton Gummer, "Social Planning and Administration: Implications for Curriculum Development," in Simon Slavin, ed., *Social Administration* (New York: Haworth Press, 1978), p. 19. Archie Hanlan reflects a similar view in "From Social Work to Social Administration," in Slavin, *Social Administration*, pp. 57–59.

[19] *Expanding Management Technology and Professional Accountability in Social Service Programs* (Columbus, Ohio: National Conference on Social Welfare, 1976), p. 17. A similar point of view is expressed by Bernard Neugeboren in "Evaluation of Field Instruction for Social Welfare Administration," *Report of the Western Conference on Social Welfare Administration*, University of Washington, 1977, pp. 35–36.

[20] Hasenfeld and English, eds., *Human Service Organizations*, pp. 9–10.

[21] Ibid., pp. 10–11.

[22] Gilbert Smith, *Social Work and the Sociology of Organizations* (London: Routledge and Kegan Paul, 1970), pp. 1–12.

[23] See, for example, Herman Stein, "Board, Executive and Staff," in Slavin, ed., *Social Administration*, pp. 212–16; Spencer, "The Administrative Process," pp. 140–43; and Harleigh Trecker, *Social Work Administration* (New York: Association Press, 1977), pp. 85–94.

[24] See, for example, James Senor, "Another Look at Executive-Board Relations," in Mayer Zald, ed., *Social Welfare Institutions* (New York: Wiley, 1965), pp. 418–27; Edward O'Donnel and Otto Reid, "Citizen Participation on Public Boards and Committees," in Slavin, ed., *Social Administration*, pp. 134–48.

[25] Harold Lewis, "Management in the Nonprofit Social Service Agency," in Slavin, ed., *Social Administration*, pp. 12–13.

[26] Richard Scott, "Professional Employees in a Bureaucratic Structure: Social Work," in Amitai Etzioni, ed., *The Semi-Professions and Their Organization* (New York: Free Press, 1969), pp. 82–140.

[27] Ralph Kramer, "Ideology, Status, and Power in Board-Executive Relationships," in Ralph Kramer and Harry Specht, eds., *Readings in Community Organization Practice*, 2d ed. (Englewood Cliffs, N.J.: Prentice-Hall, 1975), pp. 307–14.

[28] *Expanding Management Technology*, pp. 11–14.

[29] Herman Stein, "Administrative Leadership in Complex Service Organizations," in Schatz, ed., *Social Work Administration*, pp. 288–93.

[30] For example, research of the human relations school and much of the recent work on participation have been conducted in industrial settings. Social work literature reflects this emphasis. See Trecker, *Social Work Administration*, pp. 162–69; Kenneth P. Fallon, "Participatory Management: An Alternative in Human Service Delivery Systems," in Slavin, ed., *Social Administration*, pp. 169–76; Cornelius Utz, "The Responsibility of Administration for Maximizing the Contribution of Casework Staff," *Social Casework*, 45, no. 3 (March 1964), 137–43.

[31] Richard Steiner, *Managing the Human Service Organization* (Beverly Hills, Calif.: Sage Publications, 1977), p. 25.

[32] Hasenfeld and English, eds., *Human Service Organizations*, p. 8.

[33] Steiner, *Managing the Human Service Organization*, pp. 21–22.

[34] See Paul A. Kurzman, "Rules and Regulations in Large-Scale Organizations: A Theoretical Approach to the Problem," *Administration in Social Work*, 1, no. 4 (Winter 1977), 421–31.

[35] See Hasenfeld and English, eds., *Human Service Organizations*, pp. 13–14. For an interesting discussion on how the agency's definition of client problems influences the nature of the services provided, see Charles Perrow, *Organizational Analysis: A Sociological View* (Belmont, Calif.: Brooks Cole Publishing Co., 1970), pp. 28–37.

[36] Lewis, "Management in the Nonprofit Social Service Agency," p. 10.

[37] *Expanding Management Technology*, p. 6. A similar view is reflected in Robert Vinter, "The Social Structure of Service," in *Issues in American Social Work*, Alfred Kahn, ed. (New York: Columbia University Press, 1959), pp. 261–65, and Trecker, *Social Work Administration*, pp. 103–107.

[38] This position is reflected in the "NASW Working Definition of Social Work Practice." See discussion in Nina Toren, "Semi-Professionalism," in Etzioni, ed., *The Semi-Professions and Their Organization*, p. 160.

[39] Rino Patti, "Patterns of Management Activity in Social Welfare Agencies," *Administration in Social Work*, 1, no. 1 (Spring 1977), 5–18.

[40] Peter Rossi, "Some Issues in the Evaluation of Human Service Delivery," in Rosemary Sarri and Yeheskel Hasenfeld, eds., *The Management of Human Services* (New York: Columbia University Press, 1978), pp. 235–61.

[41] George Hoshino, "Social Services: The Problem of Accountability," in Slavin, ed., *Social Administration*, p. 306.

[42] Rossi, "Some Issues," p. 243.

[43] Arnold Gurin, "Conceptual and Technical Issues in the Management of Human Services," in Sarri and Hasenfeld, eds., *The Management of Human Services*, p. 292.

[44] Peter Drucker, *The Practice of Management* (New York: Harper and Row, 1954).

[45] Anthony Raia, *Managing by Objectives* (Glenview, Ill.: Scott, Foresman, 1974), pp. 15–22.

[46] Raia, *Managing*, p. 17.

[47] In analyzing the strengths and weaknesses of MBO in relation to the norms promoted by social work, the author is not suggesting that social agencies should abandon efforts to specify goals and objectives. Agencies, of course, must be clear about what they are attempting to accomplish, in order to rationally allocate resources, monitor and evaluate results, and be accountable to clients and funding sources. The question here is not whether to set goals, but whether this particular technique will aid the administrator who seeks to realize the norms that were discussed earlier.

[48] Melvyn Raider, "Installing Management by Objectives in Social Agencies," in Slavin, ed., *Social Administration*, pp. 283–92.

[49] Raia, *Managing*, p. 17.

[50] Vernon Wiehe, "Management by Objectives in a Family Service Agency," in Slavin, ed., *Social Administration*, pp. 276–82.

[51] Raider, "Installing Management by Objectives," p. 288.

[52] Maryanne Vandervelde, "Correlates of Participatory and Influence Based Decision Making in Human Service Organizations," unpublished Ph.D. dissertation, University of Washington, 1979.

[53] *Expanding Management Technology*, p. 24.

[54] Raia, *Managing*, p. 17.

[55] See also Donald Granvold, "Supervision by Objectives," *Administration in Social Work*, 2, no. 2 (Summer 1978), 199–209.

[56] Raider, "Installing Management by Objectives," p. 284.

[57] Ibid., pp. 290–91.

[58] Granvold, "Supervision by Objectives," pp. 200–201.

[59] *Expanding Management Technology*, p. 25.

[60] Raider, "Installing Management by Objectives," p. 289.

[61] Fremont Kast and James Rosenweig, *Organization and Management: A Systems Approach* (New York: McGraw-Hill, 1974), pp. 505–19.

[62] As quoted in Kast and Rosenweig, *Organization and Management*, p. 505.

[63] Perrow, *Organizational Analysis*, pp. 75–91; Jay Galbraith, "Organizational Design: An Information Processing View," in J. Richard Hackman, Edward Lawler, and Lyman Porter, eds., *Perspectives on Behavior in Organizations* (New York: McGraw-Hill, 1977), pp.207–15.

[64] Victor Vroom, "Can Leaders Learn to Lead?" in Hackman, Lawler, and Porter, eds., *Perspectives on Behavior in Organizations*, p. 401.

[65] Vroom, "Can Leaders Learn to Lead?" pp. 401–402.

[66] Kast and Rosenweig, *Organization and Management*, pp. 507–18 and Wendell French and Cecil Bell, *Organizational Development* (Englewood Cliffs, N.J.: Prentice-Hall, 1973), pp. 185–91.

[67] Galbraith, "Organizational Design," pp. 211–13.

[68] Stein, "Administrative Leadership," pp. 290–91.

[69] Scott Mullis, "Management Applications to the Welfare System," in Slavin, ed., *Social Administration*, p. 50.

8

Taking Account of the Workplace in Community Organization Practice

Jack Rothman, Ph.D.
University of Michigan

In reviewing the labor and industrial experience for its applications to traditional social work settings, Rothman observes that many successful corporations and trade unions maintain substantial social action, social planning, and community development functions to meet their primary goals. It can be argued, therefore, that we should staff departments of "Health, Education, and Welfare" in labor and management settings, as we have traditionally done in the governmental sector. Albeit what we can learn from the experiences of these institutions in performing these functions can be valuable for strengthening our "community-directed" performance ·in the primary and host settings in which we practice.

Using a tripartite schema—social planning, social action, and locality (community) development—Rothman draws primarily on the lessons from the large-scale corporations, where planning—not just for next year, but for the next five to ten years—is an essential function. Regardless of the social organization's current success (without such a focus), it would be risking loss of competitive advantage if it were not simultaneously anticipating the future. How many social agencies in the public or voluntary sector, he would ask, are consciously planning for 1985–95, like IBM or General Motors? If IBM can plan for computers two to three "generations" in advance, can we not anticipate and gear up for meeting the needs of client populations a generation ahead? Moreover, how can one make a resource commitment in an agency setting to planning for the future without sacrificing the present need of clients for service? Are the two functions competitive (or even mutually exclusive) in times of limited human and fiscal resources, or are they complementary, wherein one activity actually reinforces and supports the other? Our agencies often are so unstable in their mandates and funding that we cannot figure out how to adopt a long-range focus.

Frequently we are so involved in the "doing" and so overwhelmed by crises of coping that our principal agenda is survival in the here and now. Rothman suggests, however, that this is not a wise solution—not even a "satisficing" one (in Herbert Simon's formulation), for it ensures (by omission if not commission) that one will mortgage the agency's future to its present. This is not a favorable tradeoff for the agency, its staff, or its clientele. The lesson from work institutions is that through the planning function, one must attempt to shape events rather than be shaped by them, to take the initiative in charting the future rather than waiting to be reactive, to merge one's service delivery in the present with a pledge to planning for the future.

Similarly, Rothman looks to the trade union movement for lessons in social action. Social workers, for example, often decry their powerlessness in host settings vis-à-vis other professions in administrative control or toward competitive systems when working in primary settings. Social workers can learn from unions, where social action is a way of life tied to competition and organizational survival. Campaigns that mobilize union members on behalf of organizational interests build loyalty to the elected leadership and to one another and remind outsiders that the members are a collective unit to reckon with, a source of actual and potential power to influence decisions in the larger community. Agency advisory boards and occasional movement activities notwithstanding, rarely do social workers harness the clout of their clients, board members, and professional organizations to influence the legislative and executive process that governs our ability to serve our clients well. Agencies must learn how to take on a social action function to accomplish better services for clients and community.

Finally, we come to Rothman's concept of locality development, with its emphasis on the process goals with which the profession historically has been most comfortable. In developing the concept, he reminds us that one needs to focus on functional and geographical definitions of community. We often fail to do what labor and industry do routinely, that is, identify relevant communities, conduct needs assessments, and develop community-based constituencies to support the agency function. We must recognize that communities are multiple, not singular, functional as well as geographic, and always relative to our own location and our own function. Differential assessment, emphasized in professional education, is the skill that can ensure individualization of our programs to meet the particular needs of our agency and its multiple publics.

The interrelatedness of companies and trade unions to their geographical communities also suggests a lesson for social work as an agency-based profession. As employers and organizations depending on satisfied "customers," it is in the interest of social agencies to attend to the needs of the "markets" in which they "do business." Rothman's examples of the intimate relationships of labor unions to the communities in which their members live and of employers (such as utilities and banks) to the neighborhoods in which they do business and hire their workforce make a point that is useful to social agencies as well. A social agency's interdependence with the community may not be very noticeable, but the consequences of being inattentive to the inherently symbiotic relationship of client and community can become very noticeable.

The industrial social work experience highlights some of the issues of social work practice. Much of our success depends on the negotiation for our own function in relation to experts who control the organization. Industrial social workers often face resistance to their value framework, which may be new (or even alien) to the manager of a profit-making corporation. Rothman suggests that the experience (and achievements) of industrial social workers could be useful to the large number of social workers who practice in other host (or primary) settings.

There is no question that the value base—of loyalty in labor, and of profit in industrial organizations—places a strain on a social worker's primary commitment to social change and social service. By sifting the dilemmas and solutions and the coping and success of our colleagues in industrial social work through the sieve of their nontraditional setting, we can learn a great deal about how to adapt their findings to the increasing number of proprietary, for-profit institutions in which we practice (health settings such as proprietary hospitals, nursing homes, and home-health care agencies, for example). Abdicating the social work role to another profession (or to those without formal training) hardly seems an adequate solution. The community organization worker's trained sensitivity to such organizational issues, and his or her experience in achieving ethical and "satisficing" solutions, pushes forward the state of the art in this arena and is an additional insight from the industrial social work experience that can make a contribution to the work of the profession.

In sum, Rothman takes an interesting and novel approach toward helping the reader understand the importance of community organization in traditional social work practice. By delineating in some detail the nature of such practice in labor and industrial organizations, he offers an opportunity to translate the insights from this field to community organization practice in the public, voluntary, and proprietary settings in which we more frequently practice.

Introduction

Community organization practice takes as its main point of departure the local community and becomes operational through engagement with a multiplicity of social units therein. It is interesting to observe that the workplace generally has been excluded as a social unit of relevance. Typically, social units encompassed by practice have included block clubs, small neighborhoods, public housing projects, churches, schools, ethnic enclaves, social agencies, and others. For some reason, industrial plants, trade unions, and proprietary service establishments have escaped the attention that has been bestowed on other social units. They have not been prominent either as beneficiaries of or as participants in the community organization process. When working people have been involved, it usually has been as residents or citizens, rather than through their occupational roles or their identities as part of the functional community of work.

In this paper we discuss some implications for community organization practice of taking the workplace into account as a salient social unit within the community. As an aspect of this undertaking, we endeavor to conceptualize the community of work as a functional community, with distinct characteristics. Such an analysis has two sets of consequences for community organization practice. In the first place, there are implications for typical social agencies and planning organizations *based in the community at large,* such as family service agencies, community mental health centers, or settlement houses. Secondly, there are implications for practice *within the workplace setting itself.* While the former is the chief concern of this paper and publication, the latter also will be touched upon.

The separation between social work and the community of work has been remarked upon by a number of observers. For example, Titmuss, in his *Commitment to Welfare,* states that the occupational social welfare system existing within the world of work is walled off from other community-based welfare programs:

> What goes on within and as a result of one system is ignored by others. They are appraised, criticized or applauded as abstract, independent entities.[1]

Weiner and others concluded that the "world of social welfare and the world of work are relatively estranged from each other."[2] Gorson, Kalter, and Nann, in their historical study,[3] found this estrangement to extend over a period of a hundred years. The causes of estrangement appear to be multiple. In the first place, there are the views of social workers themselves. Googins points to skeptical social work attitudes regarding a "sell out to the evils of capitalism."[4] Gorson, Kalter, and Nann also make note of the concerns of social workers about the difference between their values and those of industry.[5]

Trade unions and workers have not always extended themselves in an accommodating manner, however. According to Deutsch,[6] labor has remained aloof because of the view that social work is a creature of the upper classes and because in its inner-directed struggle to become established, labor has not formed close working relationships with all relevant institutions. Labor's attitudes have been exacerbated by the fact that in certain periods social workers have been used by industrialists to monitor and control workers and to thwart trade union organizing endeavors. In addition, Form and Miller suggest that voluntary agencies have been more responsive to management than to labor concerns, as economic support and "philanthropy" have emanated from business elites.[7]

Nevertheless, management has not grasped social work with full fraternal embrace. Industry, according to Leeman, Moore, and Cohen,[8] has tended to be distrustful of social work and to resist overtures made by social work professionals. Management is aware that historically some elements of the profession have identified with the trade union movement and provided service and support, as typified by Jane Addams' relationship with the Amalgamated Clothing Workers of America.

Perhaps the one exception to this description is the participation of both management and labor in United Way programming, especially fundraising in plants and businesses. Although this is an important activity, it is not sufficient to offset the general division between social work on the one hand and the community of work, composed of both management and labor components, on the other.

The analysis that follows may serve to lower some of these barriers. A clearer conception of the workplace as a functional community, and of its relationship to the broader geographic community, could serve as a vehicle of rapprochement.

The Workplace as a Functional Community

The workplace may be viewed as a subsystem, having specific functions, role relationships, norms, and patterns of operation. It is clearly a significant social unit within the broader community. The prominence of economic functions among community processes is recognized in sociological writings. Max Weber,[9] for example, defined the city as a settlement with a market. Cox[10] indicates that early rural sociologists sought to identify the boundaries wthin which people traded. One of the most widely accepted formulations of community is the social system conceptualization of Warren, as presented in *The Community in America.* Warren defines community in terms of a set of five "locality-relevant" functions. He states:

> The first major function of the community is to provide the local organization of individuals and systems which facilitate productive effort and to provide for the distribution and consumption of what is produced.[11]

It is of interest to note that Warren sees the economic function as affording the opportunity for remunerative work as well as making goods and services accessible for local consumption.

The workplace is the chief form of social organization through which economic functions are performed. For our purposes here we will conceive of it as a functional community, a concept which has had a long-standing place in the community organization literature. Ross defines a functional community as one which "includes groups of people who share some common interest or function, such as welfare, agriculture, education, or religion."[12] It is obvious that the work, fraternal organization, and economic functions described by Warren could be encompassed by this definition and added to Ross' listing. Ross emphasizes that a functional community is a delineated subpart of the broader community; it does not "include everyone in the geographic community but only those individuals and groups who have a particular interest or function in common."[13] He also indicates that it is not necessary for such a social unit, consciously or explicitly, to designate itself as a functional community in order for that designation to be applied to it. Moreover, a particular functional community ordinarily is not the only community with which individuals identify or in which they participate. Persons hold multiple identifications and conduct their affairs in a variety of different subsystems with community and organizational characteristics (neighborhood, ethnic group, church, union, etc.). While work and the workplace do not hold a monopoly in this connection, writers such as Perlman,[14] McNew and DeYoung,[15] and Olshansky and Unterberger,[16] among others, have underlined the importance of work in the lives of people, and Terkel has dramatized this in his popular book *Working*.[17] The way the workplace operates to constitute a significant functional community in this regard has been portrayed by Weiner and others in the following passage:

> The particular industry in which an individual labors becomes, for him, a community which defines many dimensions of his existence. The kind of job he performs, the hours he works, the union he joins and the friends he makes may all flow from the place in which he spends a major portion of his waking hours. Any particular working individual, therefore, is effectively a member of the functional community of work.[18]

The workplace as a subcommunity can be located usefully within contemporary community theory through an analysis by Tropman, Erlich, and Cox.[19] These authors have developed a "Triple Community" theory for understanding community phenomena. In their view, the community can best be perceived in terms of territory, subculture, and formal organization. The first, territory, is related to place or physical space, ordinarily one's residence. Subculture is related to interpersonal associations, which can be ethnic, religious, or racial in nature. Formal organization is related by these authors to the workplace community. Elsewhere, Johnson and Tropman spell this out:

> A majority of Americans spend a good part of the day there, derive most of their income from it, and build their social lives around it. Much organizing goes on there, including that undertaken by industrial unions, trade unions, professional associations, and trade associations.[20]

This community is seen by Tropman, Erlich, and Cox as perhaps the strongest and most solidified of the three modern community types. "The organizational [or work] community has grown vigorously, in fact almost overwhelming the other aspects of community."[21] They state that this both offers a tangible vehicle for community organization efforts and also raises concern about the degree of influence on individuals of different community entities:

> . . . the organizational community is the most "organized" and has perhaps the greatest clarity of membership (rights, responsibilities, etc.) of the three types. Some of the most salient questions arise from the control the organization has over the worker's life. It is perhaps because of the strength and pervasiveness found in the workplace that fresh organizational efforts there are so laden with conflict. Measures of power, money or prestige are often at stake.[22]

This discussion leads to a necessary qualification in describing the workplace as a functional community. The workplace has certain features of a community that are useful to acknowledge for both analytical and practice purposes. At the same time, the workplace constitutes a formal organization, having a center of bureaucratic control at the top, clear bases for entry (joining or being hired), means of losing membership (being fired), and designated rules and procedures guiding behavior while participating in the community (hours of work, job tasks, paying dues). In other words, an organizational community is a tighter, more definitive and controlled environment than the geographic community of residence.[23] For heuristic purposes, it is advantageous in functional terms to conceive of a university as a community of scholars, a mental hospital as a therapeutic community, and a factory as an economic or production community. At the same time, to stretch the point and to ignore the strong formal organizational attributes of these subsystems is to invite conceptual misunderstanding and error in intervention.

Analyzing the Functional Community of Work

The functional community we have been describing has some attributes that are similar to community subsystems in general and other attributes that are somewhat unique. In approaching the functional community of work, it would be useful to do an analysis equivalent to that which would be made in engaging with any new community entity. Social workers need to be particularly aware of the ambiance of the industrial settings—with their characteristics of hierarchy, productivity and profit-making—features which are distinctly different from typical human service organizations. It is important to recognize that the typical worker in the plant functions as a member of two systems. In one, the corporate structure, authority emanates essentially from the corporate board and flows down in hierarchical fashion through middle management, the foreman, and finally to the worker on the line or in the office. In the other system, the trade union, the source of authority ideally is the worker as part of the collective membership, and authority flows up to the top leadership of the union organization. Thus, the workplace community is a complex social organism, composed of a dual structure, in which the worker is situated at the bottom of one authority chain and (in principle) at the top in the other.

It is appropriate to conduct a systems analysis and needs assessment early in one's association with such a community. What, for example, are some of the typical human problems in the stuation? A function and technology involving heavy manual work will likely result in a younger population, experiencing numerous physical disabilities and having a rapid burn-out rate. Such a group may need assistance in the medical area, as well as aid in making employment changes. Tedious, repetitive work may lead to a high incidence of alcoholism, drug abuse, and nervous disorders. As part of the assessment, both internal resources (services and benefits offered by the company) and external resources (services provided by general community agencies) need to be determined. Those controlling access to and employment of these resources must be identified.

The Functional Community of Work and the General Community: Reciprocal Relationships

To designate the workplace as a functional community is not to imply a self-contained unit, isolated from the broader geographic community. The community of work is of necessity an open system, with many linkages to its surrounding environment. In their excellent treatise, *Industry, Labor and the Community,* Form and Miller state: "Modern cities are fashioned by their industrial bases . . . . Union officials and businessmen realize that industry and the community are interdependent."[24] Both management and labor have needs that must be met by the community. At the same time, the community is dependent upon the workplace for its own stability and well-being. These mutual interdependencies will be explored, drawing upon Form and Miller's analysis.

What Management Requires of the Community

Management requires, in the first instance, a place to locate. It needs land or space, facilities, and road access to conduct its operations. Additionally, it requires a pool of employees that is adequate to the functional and technical tasks of production or service. This implies both ample numbers and sufficient technical skills in the local workforce.

It is also important to have efficient local services that support the economic operations. Here management is concerned with substantive aids, such as water supply, sewage, lights, and rubbish disposal, as well as amenities, such as schools, welfare services, recreation, and cultural attractions. The latter set relates to attracting and retaining the work force, the former set to economic growth. Finally, management seeks an atmosphere of community acceptance, including opportunities to participate in and influence local institutions so that they will be responsive to workplace production needs. Management wishes to obtain these accomodations and services in a way that will maximize economic gains, namely at the lowest possible cost.

What Labor Requires of the Community

Organized labor wishes of the community an adequate level of health and welfare services to meet the needs of workers. In labor's view, there should be a fair and equal distribution of civic services. In other words, working class neighborhoods and citizens should receive the same treatment as wealthy areas in connection with police protection, street maintenance, schools, etc.

Labor desires community acceptance of the right to organize, to negotiate on wages and working conditions, and to use legitimate trade union weapons, such as the strike. It seeks the same opportunities as management to participate in local affairs and to influence the policies of governmental agencies, recreation and welfare programs, and family serving institutions.

What the General Community Requires of the Functional Community of Work

The outside community wishes, first of all, its economic well-being to be enhanced by the functional community of work. This means the availability of jobs, an adequate supply of goods and services, and the attracting of monies, investments, resources, and amenities to the community. The community wishes the world of work to share in meeting economic responsibilities, such as paying adequate taxes and providing fees for civic services.

There also is a desire for the community of work to assume social responsibilities in the creation and maintenance of community institutions, such as a good school system, fine churches, modern playgrounds, and a broad range of cultural activities, as well as a physically attractive and ecologically healthy environment.

Interdependencies around Social Work and Social Welfare

Mutual relationships and expectations also pertain specifically to the area of social welfare. As was indicated earlier, the community of work and the social work community to some degree have had a separate and at times an antagonistic existence. Still, each has resources and benefits that may be of value to the other. An application of exchange theory can be useful in understanding the significance of this dynamic and the reciprocal rewards. From the standpoint of social work, the availability of economically viable and psychologically satisfying jobs has both a preventive and therapeutic consequence for its clientele. Corporate philanthropic funds supplement government-supported services. As Form and Miller state, social workers wish from the work community a "continual flow of funds to maintain adequate services according to professional standards."[25]

Workplace members from both labor and management provide a range of supports for the social work field: volunteers for providing services; membership and leadership for policy-making boards; recruiters and public relations agents for social agency programs; fund raisers. Additionally, the work community constitutes a population group within an institutional setting, offering an available clientele to receive professional social work services. In this sense it allows for an emerging field of practice within social work.

In addition, the social work community is powerfully affected and shaped by the form and extent of service provisions in the occupational social welfare system. Existence of pensions, medical care fees, recreational programs for retirees, and so on all impinge on the kinds of services that need to be provided by community social work agencies. Expansion and contraction of the services provided internally within the occupational welfare system has a reciprocal impact on the extent and character of broader community social services. In addition, as Titmuss has noted and Kurzman has elaborated,[26] availability to employees of third-party payments for mental health and social services can have an expanding and enriching effect on general social work services. It generates additional clients and financial resources through fees.

For management, there are a variety of benefits that can be derived from an effective social work system in the community. Most importantly, these services can affect the mental and physical functioning of the workers, so that they perform their tasks at maximum efficiency. Such service may result in curtailing absenteeism, reducing on-the-job injuries, minimizing disruptive behavior in the plant, eliminating crises due to drug abuse or alcoholism, and cutting the training costs that are necessitated by heavy personnel turnover. When workplace members perform at optimal levels of psychological health, this is correlated with optimal levels of profit. At least, increasing numbers of workplace establishments seem to assume such a relationship, and some research supports the assumption.[27] Moreover, companies want good services in the communities in which they locate their offices and plants, in order to attract and hold the best personnel.

From a social work point of view, there can be compatible goals in such a situation, as the profession works for the enhancement of mental health and of productive use of one's self socially and economically. Easy access to people needing service is a plus factor. However, there also is a danger, from a social work position, that concern with efficiency and production can run counter to the interests of employees and to social work values.

From the standpoint of labor, a responsive social work community can be a tremendous asset. Unions are desirous of a range of programs and services to benefit their members. Such services help protect workers and build their loyalty to their union and its elected leadership. Some of these services are provided by the unions themselves, some by or in conjunction with management. In addition, external services can supplement what is not attainable within the community of work. Form and Miller state that union people are:

Concerned that welfare funds are adequate for the task, irrespective of their source. . . . In general, union officials are more inclined to back an expanding welfare program to fit "community" needs as defined by professional welfare workers. Businessmen, on the other hand, are somewhat suspicious of the expanding definitions of "needs."[28]

It is likely that in the current period of Proposition 13 retrenchment, both labor and management want social services to be delivered in a highly accountable and cost-efficient way that allows containment of expenses. Within that common frame of reference, however, labor is more likely to view community social services as a necessary and usually insufficiently available resource for its members.

With the interplay between the community of work and the general community explicated, it would be useful to point out some broad conceptual implications for community organization practice.

The Workplace and Community Organization Practice

The previous discussion established the workplace as a significant social unit, constituting a discernible functional community within the broader general community. This creates new perspectives for community organization practice, both outside of and within the functional community of work. For typical community agencies *on the outside*, such as community mental health centers, family service agencies, settlement houses, and welfare planning boards, the workplace may be seen as a target of intervention. When viewed in this way there are at least four intervention implications:

1. The workplace comprises a valid client system or population, for whom services should be planned. Community agencies, accordingly, should endeavor to include this functional community as a type of catchment area to be reached and accommodated. This is an organizationally encompassed population, engaged in designated occupational roles. Hence, the agency may come to view its clientele as overlapping two realms: the community of work as workers, and the residential community as family members and citizens. Experiences and roles in the two realms are mutually interactive. The meaning of this for practice has been expressed well by Googins:

> In turning its attention toward the work establishment, social work could use an already established framework—the concept of "person-in-situation"—which relates to the whole human being within a fluid real-life situation. Looking at the person constantly moving between home and work offers a new perspective to achieve proper functioning and equilibrium while focusing on additional entry points to effect change. Problems that show up in the work environment often have causal or symptomatic links to the outside environment. What can be

hidden within the privacy of the home often will show up in a declining or irregular job performance. Likewise, problems not apparent to the existing social services delivery network manifest themselves in the not-so-private site of the job.[29]

According to this view, the services that take account of the workplace and of the work role would be expanded to give specific attention to people in getting jobs, in maintaining job performance, and in job mobility. More concern for programs dealing with job preparation, occupational skill development and career counseling would be called for among all clients served by the agency, especially young people and those subject to discrimination (minorities, women, and the disabled, for example). In addition, agencies would be required to form more and firmer linkages with institutions engaged in manpower services, vocational rehabilitation, and occupational health and safety and to engage in collaborative planning with them. At the current time, such linkages are weak compared to other collaborative social work arrangements.

Serving the community of work requires adaptation to certain normative features of that environment, necessitating changes in style of service delivery.[30] For example, it may be necessary to deal with a range of different problems, to respond to new forms of service requests, and to utilize both short-term and long-term service interventions. Services would need to be provided in a flexible and easily accessible manner: both at various times throughout the day and at evening, on demand, within the workplace situation or at an alternative convenient location. Responsible and accountable linkage and continuity of care (rather than "referral") would be required;[31] if the agency is not able to provide the service, the client would expect the agency to advocate for service provision by a competent collateral source. Consumer satisfaction would be a much more salient consideration, especially with union people, who function as members and sponsors as well as consumers. This calls for vigorous men and women, who are not desk bound and who can accommodate the aggressive, adversarial atmosphere of the workplace and confront personal and organizational issues head-on when necessary. They should be able to give tough, caring service as "good doers" rather than "do-gooders."[32]

2. The workplace may also be viewed as a structural client system, rather than as an aggregation of individuals requiring common services. As a corporate system, the workplace may need help with certain organizational problems. Such services involve aid in dealing with system-disturbing phenomena. This may require a commitment to respond on call to administrators with short-term, intensive, clinical intervention; or, it may necessitate consultation to administration on relationship problems between organizational units, individuals, or competing subsystems. In an organization characterized by a high level of pressure, an educational program might be mounted on ways of coping with stress. This could entail systemwide seminars and discussion groups. Organizational consultation could also entail diagnosis of structural problems, which tend to dehumanize the workplace and create unnecessary

stressful conditions. The point here is that the *troubled organization,* rather than the *troubled individual,* may be the client, and the definition of the presenting problem is put in organizational terms. Any cause of stress, dysfunction, or ill health, such as a toxic agent in the plant atmosphere, becomes the focus of professional intervention. If we have learned to use ourselves in this way with work organizations, so too can we transfer these principles and skills to other organizations of significance within the communities in which our agencies function.

3. As a target, the work community may be seen as an arena for social action. This could lead to community pressure on management regarding ecological and environmental matters. Another approach would be to enter into alliances and coalitions to enhance the environment and/or improve the economic conditions of workers. The possibilities here are numerous. One question to be dealt with is whether the outside agency wishes to deal *only* with the issues that are general or neutral in the functional community of work or whether it wishes to back one or another of the subsystems, either variably or consistently. Neutrality makes for overall good relations, but limits severely the scope and character of action. Support of management may result in distrust and resistance from the broad client population and from union officials. Partisan aid to labor may disturb the elites who control access, affect social welfare policies, and disperse funds to agencies. These obviously are politically sensitive issues, which need to be dealt with and which mirror the very same community organization issues with which we in our agencies must come to grips.

4. The workplace may be viewed as a relevant social unit for purposes of representation or participation in the agency's program. Currently, few workplace communities are involved in this organic way. When representation exists, typically it is from Big Labor or Top Management, rather than from other workplace entities. Involvements of workplace units in agency programs might include participation on agency governing boards, advisory panels, planning committees, program task forces, and so on. Broad community needs assessments would include interviews in or analyses of the workplace as a relevant source of information or focus of concern. The conflict skills of labor and the political resources of management could be called upon in community-wide social action programs. Their managing and planning sophistication could be drawn on for social planning and program development. Many of these things occur now, but not in the systematic and sustained way that this formulation suggests, and surely this is a lesson from the workplace for our practice in public and voluntary settings.

Practice within the Workplace

When focusing on the workplace as a setting for practice, a number of potential initiatives are apparent. In this conception the functional community of work becomes a field of practice with a particular set of focal problems, structural arrangements, and population characteristics. What occurs is a reversal of the previous position.

1. Outside community agencies become resources and targets to be utilized to serve the needs of the functional community. An important community task is making such agencies accessible and responsive to functional community members. This may involve aspects of both planning and social action. Needs assessment should be carried on within the functional community in order to determine what services and programs to offer to community members, either by acquiring these from the general community or through the establishment of special programs within the functional community of work.
2. The general community becomes a target for obtaining resources and for providing services to it by the functional community of work. Provision of such services can serve different purposes: enhance the broad social environment within which the work community functions, improve outside receptivity toward the work community, or meet certain expected standards of service or social responsibility.
3. Internal practice also opens up opportunities for enhancement of the work environment. Practice within the community can make this a legitimate goal to be pursued organizationally through social planning and community development modalities.

Internal practice again involves decisions about relations with the subsystems of the functional community and where to locate the community organization capability. There are management sponsored programs, trade union sponsored programs, and joint programs. They can be based in different functional units—medical, industrial relations, education departments, health and benefit units, or personnel, etc. Level of hierarchy is another consideration. Particularly for community organization roles, location as close as possible to the top policy level offers leverage and initiative.

While the emphasis in industrial social work is often on direct services to individuals, a multiplicity of planning and organizing roles and functions also exist. In a study of students in industrial social work field placements, it was noted that,

> The data revealed that the placements were fairly evenly divided between direct service (case and group work) and program development, community liaison and administration.

This report states that,

> Social workers, unlike other helping professionals, are particularly trained to work with the community, linking individuals to resources they need. In other areas, in corporate social responsibility, affirmative action, and organizational development, social workers bring appropriate, if not unique, skills in planning and program development, organizational maintenance and community relations.[33]

Lessons from Community Organization Practice within the Workplace

A more specific description of community organization roles within the functional community of work follows, using the three models of community organization that this author has previously formulated.[34] These are empirical examples, illustrating the community organization roles and activities that are currently being carried out by social work practitioners, and they are presented so that the reader can extrapolate lessons and implications for practice in traditional social work settings from the community organization innovations at the workplace.

Social Planning

Planning and organizing the delivery of mental health and personal services. Perhaps the most widely practiced industrial social work function is planning and organizing the delivery of services. It involves a direct service to "troubled" employees (or members) through a Personal Service or Employee Assistance Program. The community organization functions here involve establishing the program and then managing an interorganizational service delivery system. A description and analysis of a prototypical program is presented by Erfurt and Foote.[35] In their model scheme, the delivery system entails linkage and coordination among three subsystems: the parent organization (industry, union), the employee assistance staff organization (usually a diagnostic and referral unit), and the relevant treatment agencies in the community (inpatient care, outpatient care, related social services, and self-help groups, such as Alcoholics Anonymous). Linkage between the first two subsystems includes such tasks as publicity, training of referral agents in the parent organization, and evaluation of program procedures. Linkage between the second two entails locating and screening treatment resources in the community, reviewing working arrangements between the program and the agencies, and assessing performance of the treatment agencies. Negotiation of various kinds with units in the community agency system is required.

Planning and organizing a variety of other personal and social services. Some programs visualize employees or members as a client population or community possessing multiple needs, which should be serviced. Any problem that impedes members of the client system is fair game. An example of this approach is the planning of a legal services program for District Council 37, the largest trade union in New York City. Here, a broad needs assessment approach by the union's Personal Service Unit uncovered legal difficulties as an unmet need that was of great concern to members. The staff followed through, using a classic social planning methodology to recommend and then help establish a community-based legal services program, involving coordination among a large number of community institutions and resources.[36] Similar programs have been established in areas such as health and gerontology (retired workers and their problems). Also falling into this category are the planning and policy-making roles that are associated with pensions and other occupational social welfare system provisons.

Industrial development and planning. Here social planning becomes a counterpart of broad industrial planning. In one instance, large-scale industrial development overseas was being undertaken. A community social worker was asked to assist in planning for the movement of a large number of families to an overseas nation and to suggest arrangements and facilities that would facilitate their adjustment and assimilation in the new environment. In another instance, a firm was expanding rapidly in a small community, to the extent that the community would quadruple in size within a short period of time. In this instance, this writer was asked to propose a community social work program that would optimize stability and integration within the community as it grew and to suggest ways of attending to the well-being of the original inhabitants. The company felt that its economic position and attractiveness to employees would benefit if the community remained stable and a "good place to live." Recruiting and retaining personnel was at stake. Contemporary demands on firms for assessments of environmental impact require the kind of perspectives that similarly fall within the professional scope of community organization practice.

Corporate social responsibility. Since the urban disorders of the 1960s, corporations and businesses have felt compelled to make commitments to the social and economic well-being of the communities in which they operate. Good examples are seen in the banking, utility, and insurance fields. One function is advising on the disbursement of investments, so that minority and poor communities are given economic consideration or advantage. In another type of program, proposals for corporate gifts are received by the company and reviewed by the staff for their appropriateness and merit. Recommendations are made concerning disbursement of corporate funds, which are earmarked as contributions to community health, education, and welfare. In some respects, this is similar to the budgeting process that takes place in United Way allocation agencies. Programs in social responsibility and other social areas are described well by the *Human Resources Network*.[37]

Personnel affairs. There are a number of different personnel areas that can be considered in social planning:

1. Affirmative action programs. Many social workers are involved in programs that promote minority needs and interests within their firms.[38]
2. Staff development and training, including a range of training roles and functions. Of particular interest is one instance at Chrysler, where the firm trains handicapped workers under a contract with the government. Some of the rehabilitated trainees are placed within the firm and others in outside positions.
3. Long-range personnel planning, which includes looking at trends, projecting personnel needs, and assisting in recruitment and training. Industries and trade unions take their short- and long-term planning seriously. They apply

considerable money, time, and expertise to it. Many have developed a high level of competence in this area, including techniques that could be borrowed with benefit by community social work agencies.

Community Development

In community development, social workers are concerned with activities that elsewhere have been referred to as "locality development."[39] The prime interest is in bringing people together to help cope with their own needs, to educate them along substantive and organizational lines, and to facilitate the building of a cooperative, self-improving, social system.

Self-help groups. Various examples of self-help groups can be given, particularly from union settings. District Council 37 in New York City has established a group of widows and widowers that has provided a great deal of mutual support for its members. The union has also conducted family life education programs, held educational seminars on credit problems, and distributed self-help kits on legal matters, stressing preventive law and early detection of potentially serious legal problems. Unions, because they are membership organizations, feature these types of programs. Other examples, that have been developed by corporations as well as unions, include groups dealing with weight loss, divorce, new work roles for women, and job stress.

System enhancement. Improving the environment or quality of life of the workplace, both in terms of the climate of interpersonal relations and the structural arrangements that affect workers, can be considered the function of system enhancement. Organizational development (OD) is one aspect; another is consultation with a variety of department or division heads concerning the social dimensions of their responsibility. In some firms, arrangements for social affairs, such as boating trips or picnics, might also be involved. Career planning and preretirement counseling constitute another facet. There is an overlap here with basic union interests (in organized settings) in representing members around issues pertaining to working conditions. Hence sensitivity and care must be exercised in this arena. Any action by social workers that damages legitimate union roles in representing, serving, or organizing workers should be scrupulously avoided, as the trade union is a principal instrument in contemporary society for advancing the welfare of workers. Locality development, a seemingly inefficient, process-oriented endeavor, is seen as important by both tough union leadership and enlightened management. There should indeed be lessons for traditional social agency-based practice in management's and labor's commitment to such efforts.

Advocacy and Social Action

A number of examples can be given of the types of advocacy functions that are found in workplace settings. Through management's employee-assistance programs and union labor agencies, pressures have been placed on community agencies to make their services more responsive to members and employees. Especially when third-party payments and United Way payroll deductions are involved, a financial club can be used to bring agency services in line with client needs.

Other examples come mainly from union settings. Retired members have been organized to lobby for better legislative programs for the aged. Agencies have been pressured to make more generous application of Hill-Burton funds for members. In one instance, a "food stamp alert" campaign was conducted. Programs also have been carried out in the area of consumer affairs: union staff members were trained to act as consumer advocates in specific instances of fraud, and consumer guidebooks for members were published. A social worker has played an important role in carrying out an economic boycott against an industry refusing to enter into collective bargaining.

The union as a natural focus for social action has been commented upon by Johnson and Tropman as follows:

> The development and maintenance of union organizations is a very important setting for community practice, and one which has been less emphasized in schools of social work than one might expect. Not only is the organizing process central to union activity, but the ideological orientation is one which is often harmonious with that espoused by many practitioners. . . . Local union organizing and contract negotiation provide opportunities for those who enjoy social action. For those students of community organization practice who are interested, local union organizing is one of the few places to make a contribution, gain experience and plan a career in social action.[40]

Social action is essential to the survival and growth of trade unions, since large numbers of members and a collective resolve are the main resources available to achieve organizational goals. But the use of political and economic "clout," as demonstrated by both corporations and trade unions, can also provide clues to be adopted by social workers in the more conventional organizations and agencies in which we practice.

Conclusion

This has been a preliminary attempt to conceptualize community organization practice for an extrapolation from the world of work to social work practice in more traditional primary and host settings. As the extent and character of industrial social work practice are still emergent, this paper is tentative and exploratory. We have sought to identify the workplace as a social unit within the community that is of high relevance for community analysis and intervention. The community of work was described as a functional community with distinct structural and operational features that must be understood by all those who hope to appreciate their implications for social work based in public and voluntary agencies—as well as by those who are to be specialists within the community of work itself. Not only does this paper delineate a concrete place for community organization practice within the arena of industrial social work; it also argues that much can be learned from such practice to strengthen community organization practice in more traditional settings.

As larger numbers of social workers become professionally engaged in the industrial sector, value dilemmas and conflicts become apparent. The values of business and the values of social work cannot be said to coincide in any exact way. There are points of divergence and others of overlap. Valid and ethically suitable practice, however, can take place within the area of overlap: Industry has an interest in keeping an experienced worker on the job, and social work is concerned with helping people to earn their livings and maintain their dignity as self-sufficient individuals. At certain times, inhumane and/or physically dangerous circumstances of the workplace may outweigh the economic gains acquired for a given employee/client. Also, conflicting perspectives and interests of management and the trade union may converge on the social worker in a fashion that makes for profound value conflict. With all the opportunities offered by the workplace for expanded and better service, social workers in the workplace also will be faced with ethical and equity concerns not found in all other settings, but the relevance for *current* practice in host settings and an *expanding* social work presence in proprietary service settings is compelling. These issues need to be addressed in an affirmative fashion.

The emergent definition of the social work role must take into account, in an intellectually tough and responsive way, the prevailing social and moral climate. The profession does not need to become subservient to that climate in a supine and uncreative way. Social work must find its own way and stake out its own claim among the various forces at play in the workplace, as in other host settings, such as hospitals, schools, and mental institutions. There are two traps for the social worker to avoid. One is to be so independently smug as to become irrelevant through isolation or exclusion. The other is to be so submissive and uncritical as to become the captive of forces that are inimical to social work goals—which is another form of irrelevance. What we have learned is that organizational sophistication and cool-headed analysis—including a professionally sound definition of our role and of conditions for ethical and effective practice—should precede full-blown incursion into fields where there is a profit motive, where we have not been before, or where we do not govern.

Notes

[1] Richard M. Titmuss, *Commitment to Welfare* (New York: Pantheon Books, 1968), p. 194.

[2] Hyman J. Weiner and others, *The World of Work and Social Welfare Policy* (New York: Industrial Social Welfare Center, Columbia University School of Social Work, 1971), p. 23.

[3] Elaine Gorson, Beverly Kalter, and Richard Nann, "Social Work in Industry," New York: New York School of Social Work, unpublished Master's thesis, May 1959.

[4] Bradley Googins, "Employee Assistance Programs," *Social Work,* 20, no. 6 (November 1975), 464.

[5] Gorson, Kalter, and Nann, "Social Work in Industry."

[6] Albert Deutsch, "American Labor and Social Work," *Science and Society,* 8, no. 4 (Fall 1944), 289–304.

[7] W.H. Form and D.B. Miller, *Industry, Labor, and Community* (New York: Harper Brothers, 1960).

[8] Cavin P. Leeman, John T. Moore, and David Cohen, *A Community Service Program of the Beth Israel Hospital Psychiatric Services,* Quarterly Report No. 4, Boston, Mass., August 3, 1970.

[9] Max Weber, *The City* (Glencoe, Ill.: The Free Press, 1958), translated and edited by Don Martindale and Gertrude Neuwirth.

[10] Fred M. Cox, "Alternative Conceptions of Community: Implications for Community Organization Practice," in Fred M. Cox and others, eds., *Strategies of Community Organization: A Book of Readings,* 3d ed. (Itasca, Ill.: F.E. Peacock, 1979), pp. 224–34.

[11] Roland L. Warren, *The Community in America* (Chicago: Rand McNally, 1972), p. 168.

[12] Murray G. Ross, *Community Organization: Theory, Principles, and Practice,* 2d ed. (New York: Harper and Row, 1967), p. 42.

[13] Ibid.

[14] Helen Harris Perlman, *Persona: Social Role and Personality* (Chicago: University of Chicago Press, 1968), chap. 3, "Work," pp. 59–86.

[15] Emily McNew and Anne DeYoung, "Field Instruction at Marywood: It's Micro, Macro, and Modular," *Journal of Education for Social Work,* 6, no. 1 (Winter 1970), 29–40.

[16] Simon Olshansky and Selma Unterberger, "The Meaning of Work and Its Implications for the Ex-Mental Hospital Patient," *Mental Hygiene,* 47 (1963), 139–49.

[17] Studs Terkel, *Working* (New York: Pantheon Books, 1972).

[18] Weiner and others, *The World of Work,* p. 4.

[19] John E. Tropman, John L. Erlich, and Fred M. Cox, "Introduction," in Fred M. Cox and others, eds., *Tactics and Techniques of Community Practice* (Itasca, Ill.: F.E. Peacock, 1977), pp. 1–13.

[20] Harold R. Johnson and John E. Tropman, "The Setting of Community Organization Practice," in Cox and others, eds., *Strategies of Community Organization,* p. 215.

[21] Tropman, Erlich, and Cox, "Introduction," p. 4.

[22] Ibid., p. 6.

[23] Edward O. Moe, "Consulting with a Community System: A Case Study," *Journal of Social Issues,* 15, no. 2 (1960), 29–35.

[24] Form and Miller, *Industry, Labor, and Community,* p. 1.

[25] Ibid., p. 301.

[26] Titmuss, *Commitment to Welfare*; Paul A. Kurzman, "Third-Party Reimbursement," *Social Work,* 18, no. 6 (November 1973), 11–22.

[27] C.J. Schramm, ed., *Alcoholism and Its Treatment in Industry* (Baltimore: Johns Hopkins University Press, 1977).

[28] Form and Miller, *Industry, Labor, and Community,* p. 30.

[29] Googins, "Employee Assistance Programs," p. 464.

[30] Antonio Blanco and Sheila Akabas, "The Factory: Site for Community Mental Health Practice," *American Journal of Orthopsychiatry,* 38, no. 3 (April 1968), 43–52; Eileen Corrigan,

"Linking the Problem Drinker with Treatment," *Social Work*, 17, no. 2 (1972), 54–61; Rex A. Skidmore, David Balsam, and Otto Jones, "Social Work Practice in Industry," *Social Work*, 19, no. 3 (1974), 280–86; Roslyn Yasser and John J. Sommer, "One Union's Social Service Program," *The Social Welfare Forum* (New York: Columbia University Press, 1975), pp. 112–20; Judson L. Stone and Virginia Crowthers, "Innovations in Program and Funding of Mental Health Service for Blue-Collar Families," *American Journal of Psychiatry*, 128, no. 4 (1972), 1375–80; Robert E. Gould, "Dr. Strangeglass: or How I Stopped Worrying about the Theory and Began Treating the Blue-Collar Worker," *American Journal of Orthopsychiatry*, 37, no. 1 (1967), 78–86.

[31] Andrew Weissman, "Industrial Social Services: Linkage Technology," *Social Casework*, 57, no. 1 (1976), 50–54.

[32] We are grateful to our colleague, Professor Irving Miller, for bringing this distinction to our attention.

[33] Nancy Kolben, "Graduate Education for Social Work Practice in Labor and Industrial Settings: An Interim Report," New York: Council of Social Work Education, January, 1979.

[34] Jack Rothman, "Three Models of Community Organization Practice: Their Mixing and Phasing," in Cox and others, eds., *Strategies of Community Organization*, pp. 25–45.

[35] John C. Erfurt and Andrea Foote, *Occupational Employee Assistance Programs for Substance Abuse and Mental Health Problems* (Ann Arbor: Michigan Institute for Labor and Industrial Relations, University of Michigan–Wayne State University, 1977).

[36] Yasser and Sommer, "One Union's Social Service Program."

[37] Human Resources Network, "Selected Readings: Corporate Social Responsibility" (Philadelphia: Information Center at the *Human Resources Network*, March 7, 1979).

[38] Charles W. Fleming, "Does Social Work Have a Future in Industry?" *Social Work*, 24, no. 3 (1979), 183–86.

[39] Rothman, "Three Models of Community Organization Practice."

[40] Johnson and Tropman, "The Setting of Community Organization Practice," p. 222.

9

The Industrial Social Welfare Specialist: What's So Special

Sheila H. Akabas, Ph.D.*
Columbia University

Paul A. Kurzman, Ph.D.
Hunter College, City University of New York

The theme of this volume is the ways in which social work knowledge and practice skills may be affected by awareness of work, workers, and work organizations. Throughout, contributors have examined the impact of such an awareness on the lives of clients, the experiences of groups and communities, and in the formulations of social policy. In this chapter we turn to Industrial Social Work itself, as that special area of practice where the focus is on the individual in the status of worker, the environment as defined by employing organizations and trade unions, work as the goal of functional performance among client populations, and social policy as a recognition of the interconnection between social welfare and the world of work.

The chapter includes a historic perspective identifying Industrial Social Work as a field of practice that has a past, albeit one of ebb and flow. We suggest, however, that Industrial Social Work now appears to be expanding rapidly for reasons that combine and reflect the parallel interests of the sponsoring auspices (trade unions and employers) and of social work in which the knowledge and skill of the profession fit the changing demands of the setting. Included are the unions' need to increase membership loyalty and commitment, and the employers' need to provide a workplace where performance will flow naturally in a setting that

In view of our equal contributions we have listed our names alphabetically.

values workers and where the quality of work life is congruous with an individual's feeling an "investment" in production goals. These needs increase the interest of work organizations in social work. At the same time, the profession identifies the world of work as a place in which some of our longstanding professional traditions, like self-determination, can be put into practice alongside some of our newest professional concepts, like universal services provided in a functional community to consumers with power.

We note that service through the workplace provides access to large numbers of persons and to organziations with influence. The resultant opportunities, which are multiple and multi-layered, can be a strain as well as a strength. We argue that for the practitioner, and for the profession in general, entry into these institutions may be best accomplished through the core social work practice function of direct service. This role allows the social worker to become invested in helping, establishes the professional as concerned with individuals, reduces the danger of promising more than can be delivered and delineates a turf that may not have been staked out earlier by other persons in the workplace. From this solid base of internal power, derived from professional expertise, the social worker then is able to build trust and make use of the profession's full repertoire of knowledge and skill—the key assets of which, in the world of work, are its understanding of person and environment in interaction, its commitment to individual growth, and to social change.

Throughout the chapter we caution the practitioner to be mindful of the significance of auspices. The world of work is an adversarial setting where the parallel interests of the individual and those of the organization may not be readily apparent. Issues around whose agent the practitioner is, confidentiality of information, and protection of clients' jobs sometime strain professional role and function in such a setting. Cooptation, especially around the goal of productivity, is understandable and tempting, but, given the mandate of our professional code of ethics and our dedication to individuals and their needs, it must be avoided. Such avoidance may be more difficult for those who choose to work for management than for those working with trade unions where organizational self-interest is more likely to be akin to protection of the individual's needs than in the profit-making organization. This is a solvable practice problem, but one of which professionals must be constantly aware if they are to resolve the issue in a way that will avoid some of the pitfalls of the past when social workers became the handmaidens of either management or unions and were trusted by neither, thereby displacing their professional ability to help.

The good news, however, is compelling in this field of practice. Employing organizations and trade unions are powerful forces. Social workers working with them may derive external power to marshall the broader community in the interest of important social welfare policy and service delivery goals. We suggest that this field of practice opens important doors for organizational impact and social change. Although entry may be focused on direct practice, we observe more and more settings in which ongoing relationships offer vastly expanded opportunities for use of one's professional self in the service of organizational change.

Thus, there are two potential and often overlapping employment tracks—as purveyor of direct service and as a policy-related practitioner involved in such areas as corporate social responsibility, affirmative action, or legislative analysis. By proving that we know what we are expected to know, in an organization that values competency, we can expect to be asked to expand our function regardless of the point of original entry. Most institutions in the world of work are faced with a vacuum wherein there exists a dearth of knowledgeable analysts of how people and their environments interact in the interest of social well-being. Knowledge and skill enable the industrial social worker to fill this organizational gap.

Consider the following: Members' and workers' problems are varied. Often the source of difficulty rests with their situational inability to cope or deal with the systems they encounter. Their needs may require practice that hinges on individualization, advocacy, mediation, systems negotiation, and linkage as the primary components of the helping process. Their needs, not unlike many other client populations, often reflect the gaps in community-based social services and the poverty of our social policy. For example, imagine for a moment the odds that a working mother is up against in a society such as ours in which social policy does not provide for adequate daycare, does not offer any family allowance, and manifests pervasive sexual discrimination in work access, advancement, and compensation. Marshalling supportive structures and services as well as documenting inadequate provisions are the responsibility and opportunity of industrial social work practice. The industrial arena as catchment area gives access to work and nonwork personnel and resources that would not be readily available in traditional agency settings. Using them in the interest of social and organizational change is the challenge of industrial social work.

We would leave the reader with a notion of a professional role in evolution. This is, after all, the field of practice from which Reynolds* gathered both the theoretical and experiential conviction that social workers must be stationed at the "crossroads of life." The workplace, as such a crossroads, allows the professional to see groups as well as individuals, to move from case to class, and to identify how the change within the organization can benefit workers, work organizations, and communities.

Unions seek members, and employing organizations seek workers. Both inevitably end up with human beings. How these human beings function in relation to the primary goals of the organization (productivity and output, in the case

---

*Bertha Reynolds, Social Work and Social Living, *(New York, Citadel Press, 1951). (Reprinted in paperback: Washington, D.C.: NASW, 1975).*

of the employing organization; unity and mutual support, in the case of the union) is intimately related to organizational survival. Increasingly, · these work-related organizations have found that their constituent populations require services and raise social policy issues that carry the organizations into unfamiliar turf. This movement away from the indigenous expertise within work institutions is quickened by a changing legislative environment (Affirmative Action, Worker's Compensation, Occupational Safety and Health, Comprehensive Employment and Training Act) and mounting accountability demands from consumers, stockholders, environmentalists, and other interested publics.

In response to these varied pressures, industrial organizations have quite logically turned to social workers, the professionals who are most concerned with such issues. This emergence of industrial social work, although relatively recent, has already had an impact on the industrial organizations in which it is practiced, on social work education, and on the present perspectives and future prospects of the profession. This chapter will look at the conceptual rationale and assumptions behind this development and will define the nature of the practice, particularly those aspects of it that are special to industrial social work.

Job Description

Although formal representations do not convey the significant informal arrangements that develop around a particular job and its occupant, it seems worthwhile in starting a review of the industrial social welfare specialist's activities and relationships to begin where the industrial organization is likely to begin—with a job description. Large industrial organizations, with formalized personnel functions, customarily have an extensive battery of job descriptions, a listing of promotional opportunities defined by well-established career ladders and a picture of structured interactions, all captured on organizational charts.[1] (This is, after all, the birthplace of such concepts as the division of labor, time and motion study, personnel appraisal, span of control, and line and staff function.) A comparable situation is increasingly characteristic of employment situations in not-for-profit organizations and in large trade unions, which tend to mirror the organizational arrangements of their industrial counterparts.

Such job descriptions are based on analysis of the work that must be done. They comprise a statement of objectives, duties, relationships—including lines of responsibility and authority, coordination, and facilitation—and expected results. They are explicit and concrete, indicating the interdependencies of any particular position to others within the organization. They usually also translate the task description into a statement of the desirable training, experience, and characteristics of an appropriate candidate. In an effort to attract employees, the description may spell out promotional opportunities, compensation range, hours, and other working conditions and benefits.

Duties

For an industrial social work specialist, a job description might list duties and expected outcomes as follows:

- counseling and carrying out activities with troubled employees to assist them with their personal problems and to achieve maintenance of their productive performance;
- advising on the use of community services to meet client needs and establish linkage with such programs;
- training front-line personnel (union representatives, foremen, line supervisors) to enable them to (1) identify when changes in job performance warrant referral to a social service unit, and (2) carry out an appropriate approach to the employee that will result in such referral;
- developing and overseeing the operation of a management information system, which will record service information and provide data for analysis of the unit's program.

The direct service function is used as the basis for a job description here, because our surveys show that this has been the most significant entry route for the majority of social workers in labor and industrial settings. There are, however, job descriptions of entry positions in these settings which would focus on the knowledge base, skills, and experience of professionals trained in community organization and for management and administration. A narrowly defined function, as described above, will imply the recency of the program. To the experienced eye, an organization's job description for an industrial social welfare specialist will convey data about social welfare program development within the organization, as well as information concerning the specific job opening. Expansionary roles for social workers imply a social welfare function of longer tenure, one that has achieved the development of trust, both between social worker and worker and, more importantly, between social work and management. In such a role, the social worker's boundaries of activity begin to merge with—and look like—other organizational functions (corporate giving or legislative analysis, for example), rather than like direct practice social work functions in such customary host settings as hospitals and schools. Thus, a listing of job duties for an industrial social welfare specialist in a more firmly established program might include one or more of the following long-range tasks:

- developing a plan for future programmatic direction and staffing;
- offering consultation to management decision-makers concerning human resource policy;
- helping to initiate community health, welfare, recreational, or educational programs for employees/members;
- assisting in administration of the benefit and medical care structure and helping plan for new initiatives;

• advising on corporate giving and on organizational positions in relation to pending social welfare legislation.

Boundaries

As these potential functions suggest, the interdependencies between the goals of social work practice and the interests of the world of work organization are numerous. Often, since there is no other professional within the system who is better equipped by knowledge or experience to deal with these social and human issues, trusted and valued social workers can find themselves with expanding job descriptions, which move away from their own professional expertise and into that No Man's Land where all have interest but none a clear stake. In many ways, such expansion is a legitimate path for social work. Since it is a profession that deals with people and the environment in the interest of social well-being, and a profession with an evolving definition of its identity and turf, new task assignments should help to clarify the nature of the profession. Experiences of industrial social workers suggest that therein lies a hazardous route, however, for although the turf is "available" it may be "uninhabitable."

No profession can fill such a broadly drawn role. Ambiguity is endemic to all boundary-bridging functions, and social work holds that position in the world of work.[2] Role definition presents a dilemma to social workers in industry and labor settings. There is a temptation to accept definitions and expectations conveyed by organizational gatekeepers, who have little knowledge of social work and its training and practice dimensions. These gatekeepers are all too willing to assign to the industrial social welfare worker the responsibility for solving the imponderable problems and making the difficult human decisions that are outside their own areas of managerial expertise. Social workers in world of work settings have been, and will continue to be, plagued by the hazards of promising too much in the face of such challenges.

Although survival within the setting is contingent on expanding roles, undertaking tasks for which a social worker has no particular expertise can be self-defeating. The importance of remaining close to the "core" competencies of the profession has been confirmed many times over. Successful industrial social welfare specialists have resolved the conflict by participating in, but not assuming total responsibility for, the program development and decision-making that is at the boundary of the profession's knowledge base and skill. The professionals who apply for such jobs need, therefore, to be aware of their own limitations and to "test" assigned functions against the mainstream of social work training and values.

Experience and Skills

Incumbents and applicants for positions in the world of work may have other human service training, including psychology, guidance counseling, and psychiatric nursing. Unlike social workers, however, their education often falls short in relation to the experience, special background, and skills required.[3] The social worker's ability to mediate between the individual and the environment is a case in point. Yet, though graduate training in social work may be a necessary preparation for the industrial social welfare specialist, it is by no means sufficient. These practice settings are highly visible; experience in both direct service and administrative functions is essential for even a beginning worker. The language and style are so specialized that course work in economics, organizational behavior, trade union history, and labor market and manpower policy may also prove helpful. Further, competence in alcoholism and drug abuse counseling and in research and computer technology are useful skills for successful practice.

Industrial social welfare specialists also have a distinct "mind set." They value work as an activity for their clients, understand the demands of jobs, and grasp their potential for accommodation to the emotionally troubled and physically disabled person. To this they add facility with mediating technology and coalition formation, the bridge-building functions of the profession. To achieve their goals, they must have knowledge of community resources and the skill to make and follow up appropriate referrals. In addition, they must strive, through training, not to make all organizational personnel human service participants, but rather to equip persons throughout the organization to perform the aspects of their usual functional roles that are complementary to the activities of the human services program.[4]

Additional linkage talent is also needed to allow a specialist to communicate ideas to management. Consultation becomes the avenue for enabling organizational representatives to utilize the services of the industrial social welfare specialist. Value, as well, is placed on the writing and verbal communication skills needed to interpret and feed back the unit's activities. When combined with competence from computers, these skills allow the specialist to understand a management information system, advise on its functions, and make it operational in terms of analysis and policy determination. Finally, all this must be undertaken in a setting where the demands often are compounded by the natural tensions that exist between management and trade union, between employer and employed.

It would be possible to enumerate a list of necessary skills so inclusive as to eliminate all candidates. Indeed, we appear to be on the way—but that is not the purpose here. We do, however, wish to convey a job description for the industrial social welfare specialist that will give pause to all but experienced professionals, those who have acquired ancillary skills and who exemplify an aggressive attitude about what is possible within the projected practice of social work in large-scale, volatile, nonservice-oriented industrial organizations.

Promotional Opportunities

For the individual who becomes a social work provider in a trade union or employing organization, the dilemma, previously posed in terms of programmatic expansion into peripheral endeavors, may become a personal issue as well. Just as a program that works well may become expansionary, so professionals who offer quality service may expand their opportunities. The promotional routes for industrial social welfare specialists in both trade unions and employer settings are frequently managerial careers. Here a division occurs. Some move toward management of the organization's social welfare or human service function, continuing in their social work practitioner roles, for example, as director of the benefit system or manager of training and staff development. Others take a step onto a career ladder that involves leaving the profession and function for which they were trained. They may use their social work knowledge and skill but be sufficiently removed from the core social welfare and service function that they are no longer practicing social workers. We know a former practicing social worker who is an outstanding bank manager. Her sense of process, her knowledge of human behavior, her understanding of interaction—all her professional knowledge and experience—combine to help her function well as a bank manager. But she is no longer working as a social worker. We know a hospital administrator who is successful at his job, in part because of skills acquired from years as director of a hospital social service department, but he is no longer practicing distinctly as a social worker. We know a public relations director whose earlier work as a community liaison representative for the social service department of a large corporation provided the experience necessary to qualify him for his present job in terms of background and experience requirements. But he is no longer working as a social worker. We know a manager of a union local whose responsiveness to members' needs first brought her to the attention of the nominating committee and continues to help maintain her in elective office. But she is no longer working as a social worker.

Direct service may be the most frequent, but not the only, route to entry as a social work professional in the world of work. Industrial social welfare specialists also occupy—and continue to function as social workers in—such varied job titles as community development or social responsibility director, equal employment opportunity or affirmative action officer, corporate giving analyst, retiree or educational program director. If these suggest a broad definition of industrial social welfare specialists, the listing has accomplished its purpose. The criterion that is applied is whether or not the primary focus of the incumbent's activity is within the social welfare arena and makes use of social work expertise.

Definitions

Auspices. It seems appropriate, at this point, to move toward an overview of industrial social welfare, in order to provide a definitional and historical context for our further discussion. Anyone attempting to define industrial social welfare is immediately confronted with the fact that the title selected is, in itself, a partial misnomer. Consider the auspices under which this specialty is practiced: trade unions and employing organizations. Among the forty-eight international unions in the United States with at least 100,000 members, more than a dozen have no one working in industry (unless one defines "industry" as all sites where paid employment occurs).[5] So, too, employing organizations are not, in this view, restricted to the goods-producing sector (which is customarily identified as "industry"), but rather include all employers—the not-for-profit schools, hospitals and other health institutions, and government jurisdictions, as well as profit-making service and distribution organizations from all economic sectors. By definition, then, the auspices for industrial social welfare are the major institutional arrangements in the world of work as they affect their own constituencies and the social policy concerns of their local communities and of the nation. Rarely is a social worker in contact with auspices in which power is so inherent. To survive in an arena of power, and to mold that power to the concerns of social welfare, become the awesome and demanding responsibility of social work in the industrial setting.

Target population. If the auspices are defined as all trade unions and employers, then the target population becomes the 100 million Americans who are in the labor force, including those who, although unemployed or never employed, seek entry.[6] Such a broad population definition, particularly if one includes—as most competent social workers would—family members, places most American domiciliaries in the relevant target group. It is obviously necessary to focus on the "at-risk" grouping within the total frame, that is, those for whom maintenance of worker status may in some way be problematic. It is here that we identify both the universal and the particular about industrial social work. Anyone in the world of work may, at some point in time, become a person in need of service (universal), but at one particular time, a small proportion actually are immediate service recipients (particular):

- those who need assistance with problems in order to continue functioning on a particular job (for example, a person who experiences extreme stress when a promotion places her in a "token position);
- those who need assistance with problems to maintain their status as a general labor force participant (for example, a working parent whose day-care arrangement breaks down);
- those who need referral for assistance with problems that involve their general well-being, but not immediately their continued job performance or labor force participation (for example, a worker involved in marital discord).[7]

Note that *status change,* both for the individual and for whole groups of persons, may distinguish "high-risk" groups. The women who recently have entered the labor force in unprecedented numbers may bring with them new adjustment problems as well as those needs that formerly brought them to social agencies. Minority members, struggling for recognition and acceptance in a world from which they had previously been barred; immigrants, who seek to adjust to a new country and to its work world; teenagers, ill-prepared for the transition from educational institutions to the demands of the work settings; older workers. facing inevitable (or desired) retirement; promoted employees, especially those who are partners in dual-career marriages when a promotion offer means a transfer for one member—all these individuals in transition experience the tensions and ambiguity that may need attention at the workplace.[8]

Although work, in and of itself, does not cause all of these problems that warrant attention from a social worker, those workers who experience excessive change and therefore stress in their lives will use a disproportionate amount of the union- or employer-sponsored service at the workplace. Even within a high-risk population, further distinctions must be made. Individual service will not solve all the problems. For example, if we find consistent absenteeism of single parents with children under the age of five, some form of planning with the community to develop better day-care arrangements might solve the company's problem, along with problems for many others. Or, imagine that many disabled persons who are hired seem to fail on the job—after a few weeks they resign. An exit interview might identify that simply establishing alternative work schedules, so that these disabled workers did not have to travel at the height of rush hour, would resolve the problem. Furthermore, such a solution might become an opportunity to look at how rescheduling for *all* workers could reduce turnover and contribute to the solution of other less drastic but costly personnel problems. Some firms have faced transfer turn-down rates among executives that threaten efficient corporate operation. Family-oriented services—finding an educational facility for a retarded child at the new location, helping members "mourn" the loss of friends, offering job-search assistance for the "displaced" spouse—have alleviated the severity of the problem, as have recommendations for longer tours of duty or changes in the criteria for transfers.

As can be seen, high-risk groups are identifiable not only by demographic factors but also by casually associated common determinants, which precede a given situation in time and have a consistently strong association with the occurrence of the problem. The needs of these persons are not necessarily derived from the workplace, nor are the solutions likely to come from the work setting. But because the groups are heavily into the workplace—women competing in unusual numbers, teenagers with problems because of no entry, immigrants who have come to the United States in search of employment, executives experiencing conflict between work absorption and family need—the workplace institutions must participate in the dialogue as parties to, and potential developers of, a solution for those problems. This, then, is why industrial social welfare specialists must be concerned not only with populations and with providing services for their direct needs but also with social policy issues and the way in which trade unions and employing organizations develop policy and express their positions in the general community. Recognizing populations as being "at risk" not only helps identify those people to whom preventive services should be directed but also helps illuminate other aspects of the role appropriate to the industrial social welfare specialist.

Occupational Social Welfare System

Furthermore, the interconnections between industrial social welfare and general social welfare go beyond definitions of population and auspices to the impact of that vast third social welfare system which Titmuss has referred to as the "occupational welfare structure."[9] This system is comprised of:

> benefits and services, above and beyond wages directed at social and health needs, provision for which is not legislatively mandated. Entitlement to these benefits and services results from affiliation with a job in a particular company or membership in a particular union, or a dependent relationship to an entitlee.[10]

The impact of this system is considerable. Some suggest that the welfare pie is of a fixed size, and that benefits channeled to occupational welfare reduce those available to the more needy. Others view the amount as expandable, but suggest that, to the extent that the social welfare demands of workers are met in the occupational system, there is less pressure for general social welfare benefits in the public and voluntary sectors and that this may interfere with the achievement of increased equality in society. Whatever position one ascribes to, it seems clear that the system affects general welfare and accounts, to some degree, for the need for the industrial social welfare specialist to be able to make the connections between direct service, in-house policy issues, and the general concerns of social welfare in the larger society.

A Social Welfare View

Woven through our discussion is the theme that organizational self-interest is served by introducing social work practitioners into the world of work. The employer needs a functioning labor force. Replacement cost of even the least skilled worker is high, given the need to recruit, train, incorporate within a work group, and develop experience. To the extent that we can assume that individuals may, in the course of their working lives, develop problems, there is a need to provide services to assist people with those problems if they are to be maintained at the workplace. In addition to the organization's own internal operational needs, its public image as an employer warrants the inclusion of an industrial social welfare function.

If the need of an employing organization for such service is apparent, the rationale for a trade union to have it appears even more so, involved as it is in the primary pursuit of membership. The ranks of the organized swell in correlation to how well the union represents its members and provides services to them. Thus, utilization by the target population, whichever auspices is the sponsor, is almost guaranteed. This is so because workplace services, destigmatized, easily accessible, and available based on broad definitions of eligibility, automatically encourage high levels of demand. But social workers must be wary; they must maintain their roles as providers of service and consultants on the allocation of social resources and guard against becoming a means for employment arrangements or unions to exert sophisticated control of workers' organizational loyalty and performance. Caught in the possible cross-fire between the needs of individuals and the interests of organizations, or between the conflicting interests of organizations, or between the conflicting interests of employer and trade union, the professional may find independence to be illusive indeed. For professionals to be well-rooted in their profession's role and values constitutes the best protection for avoiding this cross-fire.

Historical Overview

Although the industrial social welfare specialist may be a new occupational role, social work has had an interconnection with work, workers, trade unions, and employers throughout its professional development. Unfortunately, many of these relationships have been fraught with antagonism, suspicion, and mistrust. It is important to recognize that, in many ways, the world of work is an adversary setting. A lengthy expositon would be required to begin to detail all of the situational nuances, but suffice it here to recognize that wages to workers are expenses to the employer. The same dollar is not available for profit and for expense. Although all parties need each other to accomplish common goals— employment, production, income—survival for many employing organizations depends on keeping expenses at the lowest level possible in order to compete, while survival for trade unions may be dependent on achieving the highest possible wage level.

Into this uneasy coexistence, social work historically has entered without careful consideration. There are times when tension and mistrust are pervasive in these settings, and where the interests of the parties are *not* reconcilable. Although one might think that at such times the social worker, based on professional values, would find herself more comfortable in alliance with labor than with management, this has not been the consistent historic behavior of the profession.[11] During wartime, when ideology is put aside and labor shortages exist, labor and management have had the least degree of conflicting goals. Social work has been able to flourish in the industrial arena and make a significant contribution to service delivery and organizational policy. On other occasions, however, it has "taken sides." Inevitably this has meant alienation of the "other" side! Consider some historic patterns. The early social worker was like a Lady Bountiful, dispensing the charity and moral judgments of her capitalist donors/supporters. This image left little room for an affinity to develop between the social work profession and the working-class client of the late nineteenth century. When workers, who rarely earned enough to support their families, used the strike as a weapon in the early struggle to organize trade unions, the official social work body took the following position:

> Every man has the right to work or not to work as he may choose. But no man has the right to refuse to support his family and himself when he is able to do it; and no one has a right to prevent others from working as these strikers persistently attempt[ed] to do . . . those who refuse to work when offered in order to sustain their combination are, as a general fact, neither entitled to sympathy or aid.[12]

This attitude, coupled with the social workers' affinity for capitalists (whose contributions provided agency funds), helped maintain a zone of silence between social workers and the workers and their unions into the twentieth century. The silence persisted despite the activities of social workers such as Jane Addams, founder of Hull House, who ably assisted the Chicago garment workers in their drive for organization and recognition. (During early union efforts in the men's clothing industry, Jane Addams is reputed to have confronted the owner of Chicago's largest firm and asked him to examine the living conditions his wage scale made possible. Recognition of the union, and wage increases, were the reported results.) Ties between organized labor and social work did not occur until World War I, when the unity of purpose that pervaded the nation made it possible for all parties to overcome their suspicions and allow social work to help resolve some of the human problems at the workplace that had hampered productivity and thus endangered the war effort.

This new alliance was dissipated in the general probusiness atmosphere of the 1920s, as social workers moved from their jointly-sponsored wartime roles to new jobs as the "welfare secretaries" of modern industry. Their efforts often were divided between securing better conditions for workers and greater productivity for management. "The motives of this welfare movement were seen as paternalism, philanthropy, the desire to get more out of the worker and, in some cases, to restore the old personal relations."[13] Workers often viewed the welfare secretary as a violator of privacy, an absence investigator. Unions asked whether it was possible to serve more than one master and concluded that, in general, welfare workers were an antiunion component in the workplace. Samuel Gompers, the president of the American Federation of Labor, called for justice, not charity, and identified the welfare secretary as the "hellfare worker" of modern industry. Summing up this period, Dulles wrote,

> The amplifications of welfare capitalism knew no limits . . . Yet the entire program remained wholly subject to the control of the corporation sponsor, and there was no reality to employee representation under such conditions. It was not without significance that

those corporations which most generously provided for the workers' welfare were also those most strongly anti-union in their basic policies.[14]

In the depression of the 1930s, welfare capitalism collapsed. Corporate supporters of social agencies ceased to be able to finance charity on a scale that could make any inroads into the scope of the problem. Social work moved from its long-term sponsorship by business to a closer relationship with the burgeoning labor movement, partly because of what appears to have been an ideological position that social change, not individual intervention, was the necessary response to economic chaos on the scale experienced in the 1930s. In essence, the depression served as a unifying force between social work and organized labor.

To foster this connection, social workers had to unlearn their attitudes toward strikers and develop an understanding of the revulsion toward a scab in the trade union culture. They had to overcome the persistent image, held by working people, that to need help, from a social worker or anyone else, was a sign of inadequacy, charity, and defeat. But America in the '30s was a country in search of solutions. Although confrontations were frequent, the order of the day was survival; groups had time to be concerned about professional social workers to the extent that they might hold out an additional lifeline, as they did in the numerous public welfare agencies established at this time under the able leadership of Harry Hopkins.[15] Slowly, the commonality of interest was identified. Social workers were called on by their leaders to "bear witness" to the importance of regular employment, a living wage, decent housing, and medical care. Employers began, as a result, to view social workers as sentimental and biased. On the whole, however, the depression era was a period during which suspicions were diluted, setting the stage for another joint honeymoon era during World War II.

With the war, industrial settings returned to the philosophy that workers will be more productive if personal problems are reduced. Management introduced social workers in great numbers to help solve the war-induced manpower problems. (Apparently the employer community believes that, at a time of crisis, it is good business to spend dollars to develop latent possibilities in employees.) Significant developments also took place between organized labor and social work during this period. The outstanding service developed by Bertha Reynolds[16] for the National Maritime Union is the best-documented example. The working class became the new "donor" class for United Way and Community Chests, as contributors were organized by labor representatives at every workplace.

Once again, the wartime collaboration of trade unions, employers, and social work did not survive the peace. Although employers' behavior had given evidence during the war that they considered it good business to spend money to understand their workers' needs and to help develop, strengthen, and hold their employees, these same employers reverted to firings as a means of handling troubled workers at the end of the war, when a large civilian labor force became available. When workers are scarce, recruitment and training costs are high. When the supply of workers is excessive, recruitment and training costs decline. Social intent did not survive the employers' cost-benefit analyses, which suggested to them, in the postwar era, that the marginal cost of social work services was greater than the marginal cost of new recruitment.

For its part, the labor movement took its new-found fringe benefit dollars—those health and welfare benefits provided as an alternative to wage increments during the war—and assigned to individual members the responsibility for purchasing needed services, instead of providing them directly. Linkage was promoted between workers and the appropriate community facilities through the development of an indigenous cadre of union counselors, trained volunteers who acted as referral agents for fellow members in trouble. The social work profession added momentum to this disengagement process by becoming introspective, moving closer to Freudian psychoanalysis, and focusing on professionalization, thereby losing its newly-found credibility with the working class. Thus, since the period almost immediately following World War II, social work has been relatively isolated from the world of work; the two have passed each other like ships in the night.[17]

Present Development

That situation is now in the process of being reversed. Optimism over the future growth of social work in the workplace derives from this historical overview. The hypothesis seems to be warranted that the greater the unity of purpose of the organizational auspices (labor unions and employing organizations), the more likely the development of a social work role in the industrial setting. Recent events suggest that workers, their unions, and their employers have an increasingly powerful and long-term mutuality of interest. The Occupational Safety and Health Act has given legislative recognition to the symbiotic relationship between worker well-being and employer behavior. The mandates of equal employment opportunity and affirmative action have fostered awareness on both sides of the needs of a varied workforce and of some commitment to meeting those needs. The quest for the right to a job and security in it appears to have quickened in the recent period, for many reasons. To wit: the possibility of increased real income seems less likely, and the Age Discrimination Act suggests that worker, union, and employer are wedded for a longer portion of a lifetime than they have formerly been, at the discretion of the member/worker.

From these changing conditions of the ecological system, new responsibilities and relationships emerge, to which the organizations and participants have no pre-existing capacity to respond. The expertise of the social work professional can fill this void. As confirmation, but not by chance, the idea of the "human contract" has been promoted by the AFL-CIO. It calls for joint labor, management, and social work effort in building services at the workplace to meet the needs of the labor force participants,

> The human contract, developed by labor and management around
> the conference table in a climate of cooperation, should concern it-
> self with those personal and family problems which are not covered
> by the union contract . . . professionals, equipped with a special ex-
> pertise, can help both management and labor . . . focus attention on
> the needs of the individual. . . . What every joint union-management
> committee needs (in every department, on every shift, depending
> on the number of employees involved) is a professional trained in
> industrial social work.[18]

It is possible to assess the stage of development of a social endeavor in much
the same way that Rostow suggested could be done for an economy. He laid out
a paradigm for looking at economic growth, which seems equally applicable to
social developments. His stages include the "traditional" period, the "development of preconditions," the "take-off," the "drive to maturity" and the period
of "high mass consumption." Considering the development of industrial social
welfare, it is our sense that the preconditions are in place and that we are now in
a period of take-off.[19]

A historic event took place in June 1978, confirming this assessment. The
first national conference for social work practitioners in labor and industrial settings provided an opportunity for 100 practitioners to come together and lay
out a collective view of the state of the art at this time.[20] They saw a field in
a state of take-off. The enormous variety of models suggested an experimental
stage of development. Not only were definitive models lacking, but the multiplicity of questions raised and the sparsity and indefiniteness of answers confirmed
the recency of the development.

Conferees completed questionnaires concerning their programs. The result
was ninety-seven discrete efforts, located all over the United States.[21] The
criteria for inclusion was that the program have at least one graduate social worker,
with a majority of her work time assigned to industrial social welfare practice.
The auspices under which practice occurred included private companies, government agencies, and unions, in that order of frequency. There were also a handful
of consultants operating out of individual and group private practice, community mental health clinics, or social agencies, all of whom provided contracted
fee-for-service programs.

The union programs were most often free-standing activities, reporting to the
chief executive officer or health and welfare director. In corporate and governmental settings, the personnel department was the most frequent umbrella, with
the medical department the next most usual location. Apparently, most of the
consultant activities were funded by companies. Nonetheless, a few programs
not situated in government facilities were funded by the government (not surprising, in view of the National Institute on Alcohol Abuse and Alcoholism's major
effort to encourage the development of occupational programs).

Although the practitioners themselves reported extensive experience since completing their graduate work, their employment at the present industrial site was relatively recent, over half having been at the site two years or less. The program models were diverse: in-house units, sponsored individually by employer or union, or jointly by both; contracted services, in which the provider— individual or community facility—delivered services to one, several, or a consortium of sites, on workplace locations or at neutral offsite facilities. During conference discussions, each alternative emerged as having both advantages and disadvantages.

Almost without exception, the practitioners were offering and the programs were geared toward direct service, and almost all to training as well. What proved surprising was the diversity of other functions involved in the industrial social welfare effort—all those expansionary activities discussed earlier were enumerated and many more besides, including stress control, debt, and preretirement and career advancement counseling. Organizational consultation was widespread. Several described roles that did not include direct service functions, for example, community development director, trainer in the organizational development department, and manager of corporate giving. Confirmed was the diversity and complexity of practice that is experienced by an industrial social welfare specialist.

Attendees also agreed on the tentative nature of this development and on the numerous organizational constraints that had to be lived with or negotiated to assure an ongoing presence and freedom for practice. Most specialists experienced relative isolation, that of being the only social worker on site, or one of very few, and each reported constant pressure to explain the nature of the profession to unschooled colleagues whose stereotypical notions of social work were often disconcerting. And yet, each reasserted the excitement of the settings, the expansive nature of the opportunity to help individuals and influence systems, and the constant challenge of surviving and growing in a professional outstation. Not one was looking for a job in another field of practice.

Underlying Characteristics

One need only look at the characteristics underlying program development and service delivery in the industrial setting to know that this is, indeed, a special arena for social work practice. The world of work is viewed as a functional community of work, where some of our fondest professional goals can be realized. It provides easy access to 100 million primary participants who are eligible for service as a right, by virtue of their membership as workers in the functional community. Thus, a system of universal service delivery is possible, not one just for sick people, or old people, or poor people, but for all people.

The location of the service, furthermore, like the school, the neighborhood, and the church, is within the natural life space of the potential client. As a result, the delivery system can be viewed as a destigmatized service, one that provides help in a setting physically and personally close to the worker. If everyone is eligible, the service can carry a label of "Help without Hassle," encouraging early case-finding, often achieved by self-referral or the referral by a trusted associate. Secondary prevention is therefore possible, making successful help more likely.

Not only is the location part of the natural life space, but perhaps, most significantly, it is a site where a systems approach to service delivery and program development is possible. The organizational resources are impressive, including the formal fiscal occupational welfare structure discussed earlier and extensive human resources as well. These resources may include representatives of the formal structure, who are in a position to provide transfers, short-term leaves, protection of the right to return, and accommodation of a particular task or worksite; and also include the informal supports which come from the mutual aid and self-help network in any functional community or membership organization.[22]

The systems approach to social work practice in the world of work offers other enticements. It provides access to the joint power and interest of trade unions and management for the accomplishment of internal change. For example, in a recent study to determine how well OSHA (the Occupational Safety and Health Act) was being institutionalized, the significant contribution of joint plant safety committees to the achievement of public policy goals was identified:

> OSHA is achieving changes in attitudes and behavior at the plant level, . . . there are some "integrative" issues within the bargaining relationships over which the parties share common goals . . . safety is one of these issues . . . [when] unions and employers . . . develop a capability for engaging in cooperative problem-solving on safety issues in the context of their overall bargaining relationship . . . [it] provides a climate that fosters safety and health. . . .[23]

The welfare of employees/members appears to be another "integrative" issue. Collaboration of labor and management is available, therefore, to the industrial social welfare specialist. Enlisting such collaboration helps in problem-solving for an individual, and allows the professional to use a case as an opportunity to influence change in the internal system or environment.

Activity with labor and management at a particular employment site sets the preconditions for enlisting these powerful forces toward achievement of more broad-based social welfare goals. The industrial world is the world of power. The social work profession has been so dedicated to its mission to aid the powerless that at times it has acted as if it should avoid the powerful. Yet, all our understanding of constituency building and organizational change refers us to the importance of enlisting the powerful in our mission. The industrial social welfare specialist can help labor and management become an informed public. Devoted to social welfare concerns, labor and management then may be encouraged to use their power in a ripple effect throughout the society.

Support by both labor and management almost guarantees success on the legislative front. It is a coalition against which there are few negative votes. Mitchell Sviridoff, a vice-president of the Ford Foundation, suggests that the most effective way to approach advocacy for human service is "in the context of common interests in our society." He notes that the only social programs that have increased in their resource allocation into the 1970s are Social Security and Unemployment Insurance. "The more social programs are related to work, the better their chances for success in the political process." Although he recognizes (as we do) the disdain with which some idealists may look upon a coalition/political process of the kind we have suggested above, he concludes that such idealists have only their virtue intact. Human needs are unattended. "The lesson in the Social Security–Unemployment Insurance countertrend phenomenon should be obvious and instructive."

It is not farfetched to conclude that the fallout of the systems approach practiced by the industrial social welfare specialist will be to build understanding and support for social welfare goals on the part of labor and management. It will remain for those concerned with human welfare to achieve fulfillment of this potential by more attention, understanding and sensitivity to the political process and by taking the "interests and values of other sectors of society into account at the very outset, in the design of human resource programs."[24] It is possible that the systems approach available in the world of work can influence social welfare. Professional behavior will determine whether it is probable.

Commonalities with Other Areas of Social Work

When one looks at what is special with respect to industrial social work, one also is reminded of what is standard and what ties this field of practice to the experience of the profession. The assessment process still focuses on individuals, families, groups, communities, and organizations. As in most of the fields in which social work is practiced, clinical intervention is the most frequent method currently deployed in labor and management settings, although excellent opportunities are available for group, community, and administrative approaches. Mediating technology, which leads one to see person-in-situation and the situation in a larger environment, is useful both for working with clients and for negotiating with significant others within the labor or industrial organization.

As in more traditional social work settings, clients have difficulty dealing with major service systems in the community: hospitals, landlords, schools, banks, and the justice system. Interpretation, negotiation, brokerage, and advocacy on behalf of individuals and groups of clients sharing a common problem are essential service skills here. Similarly, one needs to be able to negotiate for a client and for particular client populations (single parents, handicapped workers, new workforce entrants, preretirees) in order to ensure that appropriate provisions are made to meet their special needs. While we usually deal with clients who have a lot of strength, they frequently do not have the specific skills or time to advocate for themselves in a world where time is money.

Client advocacy is an essential skill when mediating approaches are not appropriate or sufficient. Government bureaus that deny clients their entitlements, loan and credit institutions that take advantage of a client's naive or trusting nature, professionals who appear to be acting less on behalf of client welfare than out of self-interest, schools and landlords who seem to be taking unjustified and arbitrary actions—all of these call for skill in advocating on behalf of an individual or a class of workers (or members). Outside of the legal profession (whose services are often very expensive), there are very few advocates for working people in a world that is increasingly interdependent, complex, and difficult to navigate alone. Social workers may also advocate with public and voluntary organizations for the provision of *new* benefits and services, which are not currently available for workers and their families.

As in most other social work settings, clinical practice here requires relatively brief and responsive models of intervention. Waiting lists are a problem in the world of work, since the uniqueness and advantage of the industrially-based service is its accessibility to the client and to the problem, which is frequently of a crisis nature. Task-centered intervention, as suggested by Reid and Epstein, has been found helpful in many settings, particularly due to its direct involvement of the client in problem resolution.[25] Planned short-term treatment, discussed by Parad and Parad, is useful in making explicit what might be achieved by client and worker within the context of a time-limited contract to deal with the presenting request for service.[26] The growing literature by Rapoport and others on crisis intervention has proved helpful in work settings, where the request for service is based on job jeopardy or some other family crisis.[27] The ability to recognize the special nature of the crisis, intervene quickly, and stabilize the situation is a useful construct in workplace settings.

Finally, labor- and management-sponsored settings lend themselves to the use of self-help groups as a primary or secondary mode of intervention. Natural helping networks have been established around issues from weight-loss to widowhood, from stress management to questions facing women in nontraditional occupations and titles.[28] The trade union, itself, is a self-help network, with an extensive mutual-aid system characteristic of a membership organization. Similarly, organizational work at industrial sites has intervention modes analogous to those Rothman suggests for community work: action, planning, and community development.[29]

World of work settings share with much of social work practice a central concern for a social functioning perspective. The social worker must assess the sources of limitation (as well as strength) that the client brings to problem resolution, but the focus here is less on questions of "illness" versus "health" than it is on enhancing the client's ability to function more effectively in the critical arenas of life—work and family. Such a social functioning perspective is consistent with what Carel Germain terms

> the "life model," which "defines problems not as reflections of path-ological states but as consequences of interactions among elements of an ecosystem including other people, things, places, organizations, ideas, information, and values. They are conceptualized as problems in living, not as personality disturbances. . . . Help is matched to the problem as the client defines it for the model recognizes that few people actually seek casework service for personality change and that insight itself can be a burden."[30]

There is an essentially preventive focus inherent in industrial social work practice. Recognizing the importance of work and family systems in the lives of most people, the approach looks at potential populations at risk at the workplace and seeks to strengthen the services and enhance the opportunities that will prevent such workers from falling out of the world of work. Hence, there is an element of primary prevention intrinsic to industrial social work practice. As Goldston notes:

> Primary prevention encompasses those activities directed to specifically identify vulnerable high-risk groups within the community who may have not been labeled as psychiatrically ill and for whom measures can be undertaken to avoid the onset of emotional disturbance and/or to enhance their level of positive mental health.[31]

For those workers who must leave the workplace, even temporarily, due to stress, injury, illness, or family crisis, an effort is made to protect the job, obtain services, build indigenous supports, and ensure options for a return if the client chooses. A rehabilitation approach to service delivery generally has been less stigmatic than in most other settings, perhaps because it implies existing membership in (or attachment to) the world of work, and suggests departure primarily due to illness or injury, or as a victim of a catastrophe or "act of God". In this regard, a rehabilitation and social functioning perspective would appear mutually consistent and supportive, in an ecosystems approach to intervention.

In addition to knowledge and skill, the worker in work settings must bring professional values. Ethical issues are present in even the most commonplace policy and practice situations, and the judgment of the social work practitioner must reflect how the value elements inform, condition, and modify the nature of intervention.

Distinguishing Features and Special Opportunities of Industrial Social Work

Our society ties special meaning, support, and rewards to two concepts: family and work. We know a good deal about the former and offer special courses directed at "parent-child relationships" and "family treatment"; we even have a national network of service outposts, called family service agencies, in recognition of the special priority that we attach to support and preservation of the family.

It therefore seems most appropriate for the social work profession to consider work issues and work systems by placing policy and service outposts in the world of work as well. One hundred million Americans spend almost half their waking weekday time at work, sometimes with pain, sometimes with pleasure, but usually with some mix and measure of the two, and, inevitably, work and family blend and the pains and pleasures of one are brought to bear on the other. As Rubin has noted: "What happens during the day on the job colors, if it doesn't actually dictate, what happens during the evening in the living room—perhaps later in the bedroom."[32]

We need to understand work institutions—their needs, goals, and special features—if we are to function effectively with workforce participants. We need to fathom and comprehend trade unions and employing organizations as well as we have come to understand the family. Moving into the world of work is analogous to moving into a new community (functional here, rather than geographic). We have to learn how the system operates, what are its rewards and sanctions, what are its opportunities and constraints. What is the nature of its formal and informal organization, power structure, decision-making, and networks of communication? For the world of work is not only a "host" system—to which we are accustomed—but—unlike hospitals, schools, and justice systems—it is outside of the human service tradition.

Essential to social workers' survival in these settings will be their attention to the needs of the gatekeepers of the organization and their understanding of the central importance of collaboration. Working with other professionals may at times seem difficult, especially when they are accountants and engineers, rather than physicians and teachers. Even when social work's knowledge and skills are respected, its values may be questioned, if social workers are not sufficiently attentive to production, efficiency, and the "bottom line" of profits in corporate settings and to the primacy of loyalty within trade unions.[33]

We must not view "indigenous" personnel—such as foremen, supervisors, and shop stewards—as paraprofessionals with regard to troubled workers and mental health issues (as we might in traditional settings), but rather we must respect the functional differentiation that is characteristic of an "alien" or non-human-service setting. In reaching out and helping workers, the nature of our interdisciplinary collaboration will imply not a hierarchy of functions that moves from physician, to nurse, to attendant, but recognition that each person—

manager or president, foreman or shop steward, co-worker or subordinate—has a *different* function in helping the troubled worker, based upon his or her distinct strengths, degree of access, and organizational role. The helping effort represents a truly collaborative venture among equals. We need to recognize that the foreman's value to the organization, for example, lies in his functional differentiation from human service personnel, and thus his *different* knowledge, skills, and values.

Therefore, the usefulness of the collaboration among the organizational actors lies in their difference and not in their similarity to one another. However, the strength of the collaboration comes from their mutual ability to recognize and respect their symbiotic and reciprocal relationships to one another with regard to the needs of the individual and to the primary goals of the organization. Their ability to make manifest this latent symbiosis will be based as much on their differentiation of function and philosophy as on their common commitment to the individual and the organization.

Considerable organizational acumen is desirable, since building trust and gaining sanction from informal systems are essential to organizational survival. One must be able to create ties to the key subsystems and to the formal *and* informal leadership within the organization in order to gain ongoing support for the social work service. Responsiveness to referrals and a respect for the significance of concrete requests are among the several homily dicta that undergird the successful social work program. In short, one must be organizationally sophisticated in planning and sensitive to the system in style and substance of intervention.

Clients presenting problems of alcoholism and drug abuse utilize industrial social work programs. The social work staff, therefore, must ensure that the policy of the employing organization recognizes, responds to, and covers substance abuse as an illness—a disease. Under these conditions, workers' jobs are likely to be protected while they receive help, and they can be eligible for short-term disability benefits and health care coverage for treatment. The social worker also needs to recognize that alcoholism or drug abuse does not appear as a separate problem in itself, but generally as a symptom or a portion of the client's broader problems in coping with personal and social situations on and off the job.

The workplace provides an excellent opportunity to do training as an integral part of the program. One must be prepared with sufficient small group and instructional skills to do training *regardless* of the specific nature of one's function. Therefore, social workers must see their role in training others within the organization not as a tangential or serendipitous responsibility, but rather as a core function within the larger system that is central to program interpretation, goal attainment, and thus organizational survival.

The initial goal of training may be to define and interpret the nature of the social work service, and then to move toward transmitting information about mental health in order to dispel myths and preconceptions that workers may have, due to stereotype and misinformation. Training programs then normally proceed toward identifying an appropriate division of labor, whereby the trainees such as foremen, supervisors, union business agents, and shop stewards become comfortable and skillful in recognizing troubled workers, talking to them, winning their trust, and referring them to the social work service. In this way, the division of labor becomes clear, and the actors within the system play supportive roles, consistent with their job responsibilities and areas of expertise. Training may serve, as well, to increase the sensitivity of participants to human needs and to the ways in which the system may support or interfere with those needs. Observers have reported that training often has an organizational development outcome.

Once a program is operating relatively smoothly, and initial training has been completed, an option to expand the social work role to include consultation may be present. In labor settings, such consultation may be around new health and welfare arrangements, suggestions for collective bargaining, or service programs for particular groups of members; in management settings, consultation may involve changes in benefits or personnel practices, company policy, and community relations. The consultation role, however, is seldom a point of entree but rather comes out of respect for the primary policy or service role that social workers are playing in the organization, and thus represents a kind of laying-on of hands that sanctions input toward systems change. Leeman notes an example of movement toward a consultation role in a management-sponsored service.

> As the counselor developed a successful "track record," and as rapport within the setting increased, he was consulted on broader questions affecting a larger population rather than a specific individual. In several instances this led to significant changes in the work environment that were beneficial to workers. These changes included the removal of physical hazards, enhancement of supervisors' communication with employees, better utilization of employees' abilities, and modification of company policies concerning retiring employees and employees who abuse alcohol and other drugs.[34]

Social work recommendations can be based upon the statistics of service and on first-hand knowledge of unrecognized opportunities, inequitable policies, or unmet needs. An example of such impetus for a program innovation in a trade union setting is illustrated in *Labor and Industrial Settings: Sites for Social Work Practice,* which highlights the creative use of consultation by the social work staff in recommending and helping to design a legal services program for a major trade union.[35]

Two points of caution must be noted. First, social workers must be clear about the nature and boundaries of their expertise. We are not physicians, actuaries, or F. W. Taylor-style efficiency experts. The consultation and organizational development route can have a life of its own, and can deflect us from the important but sometimes less glamorous role we share as providers of service. Consultation can be sufficiently intoxicating to risk cooptation by the organizational leadership, who may look to the social work staff to sanction or legitimate policies solely in the profit (or survival) needs of the organization and its leaders—rather than in the interest of its workforce and the community. One must recognize the blinding quality that may occur when one has access to and influence with persons in power. A social worker's essentially human service role in an alien setting may be a reminder of his relative instability within the organization and may lead him to see the organizational development role primarily as an opportunity for mitigation of marginality—rather than an occasion to blend cause with function.

Focal Practice Issues

All professionals who practice under an administrative auspices (as opposed to private practice) must deal with the dilemma of reconciling individual client need with the organizational vested interests of their sponsors. In reality, the balancing of one's organizational responsibility with the specific needs of the client population often is no greater in industrial social work settings than in the typical primary or host settings in which we practice, but the *potential* for dissonance is greater, given the primarily non–human-service objectives of management (and even labor) institutions. The question conceptually is: "Whose agent are you?" What impact will the nature of the auspices have on defining social work function in relation to client and organization, when their interests may not always be the same?

The social worker's point of reference here is threefold. The practitioner's mandate comes in part from the organizational subsystem (for example, medical, personnel, community affairs) that is the home base for the service and may be perceived by workers and supervisors as having a special human service role within the larger organization. However, medical departments often play a monitoring role with regard to worker illness and absenteeism, and personnel departments are responsible for maintaining records crucial to decisions on retention and promotion. Therefore, the issue of confidentiality (discussed below) is pivotal in terms of ensuring clients that they will not be jeopardized by coming for service.

A second point of reference is the client. "Beginning where the client is" and a "client's right to self-determination" are fundamental principles of our profession and must be respected in labor and management settings. Contract setting must make explicit the consonance and dissonance between the client's needs and the rules of the organization, the nature and boundaries of confidentiality, and the options open to the client for in-house service or referral. Any external demands of the organization that might conflict with the client's best interests or jeopardize the nature of the contract must be shared with the clients, so that they may select the routes or the sets of options that they feel are in their best interests. Such situations are not frequent. When they occur, they must be handled with conceptual and procedural clarity that maintains maximum options for the clients and preserves their right to self-determination in the face of the organizational imperatives that may influence the situation. Ultimately, social workers, too, must retain the right to leave—however personally and organizationally difficult this might be—if they feel unable to resolve client and organizational interests. Spiegel, in his study of services at the worksite, notes the experience of the counselor in a medium-size trucking corporation. The worker's departure apparently was self-initiated, when "he found the role conflict between management agent and employee advocate too difficult to resolve. There were problems of who really was his client—the person needing help or his superiors."[36]

A third point of reference for the social worker is his profession. The initial contract that the professional establishes when entering the world of work has far-reaching effects in his ability to protect himself and/or his clients from inappropriate or unprofessional practices. The profession's value system represents a key component of the professional expertise that is deployed in practice. Underpinning one's professional use-of-self and conditioning—even clarifying—the resolution of apparent conflicts between loyalty to client and sponsoring organization is one's commitment to the Code of Ethics of the profession.[37] These values may inform a particular situation, where client and agency dictates appear to be in conflict, by providing an external reference comparable for practice in all settings.

The question of confidentiality (that is, its abuse) may appear more problematical in a management-sponsored program than in one being hosted by a trade union. Workers hold allegiance to and identification with their union as an advocate vis-à-vis the employing organization. The union represents their interests with respect to collective bargaining (wages, benefits, and working conditions), and is their defender at times of job jeopardy and grievance hearings. Moreover, the trade union is a fraternal membership organization, where the member helps to select the leadership and to a genuine degree shares a common destiny with fellow members. Generally, it would not be in the interest of a labor union to share information with management that would place a member in jeopardy. In a fraternal climate, moreover, situations often are shared more easily. For example, in reporting on a service sponsored by a trade union for its members, Blanco and Akabas note the "open secret" nature of a worker's troubles at the worksite among co-workers and union representatives. "Interestingly enough," they noted, "when approached at their place of work, patients did not seek confidentiality."[38] They felt free to discuss their problems among union "brothers" and "sisters."

When twenty-one Detroit-area employee assistance programs were surveyed by Erfurt and Foote, sixteen programs (or 76 percent) indicated that they had no problem in maintaining confidentiality of client records (and these were overwhelmingly management-sponsored programs). Almost half of the programs surveyed reported, however, that confidentiality was *perceived* as a problem by employees in the organization out of their concern for job security and career advancement.[39]

To resolve this dilemma, we should explicitly recognize and respect the client's perceptions and feelings as a reality that will condition utilization of the social work service. Over time, client suspicion will be allayed by actual respect for confidentiality and contract. A sense of trust, then, will build up and will permeate the formal and informal network of the functional community of work in a way that will enhance clients' confidence in the service.

Such dilemmas also may be influenced by the way in which clients come for service. Frequently, the cause for referral is the presence of serious job jeopardy, where a client has openly violated the rules or routines of the workplace (through excessive lateness or absenteeism, for example) or evidenced declining job performance (such as persistent substandard quantity or quality of task performance). This is particularly characteristic of situations caused by abuse of alcohol or drugs. At such times, when a client's denial is pervasive, acceptance and use of the social work service has a quasi-compulsory nature, since the outcome of refusal to accept help may be termination of employment. There are parallels in this situation to social work practice in authoritarian settings (such as probation and parole), where client options are constrained by the serious consequences of noncompliance. As the literature indicates, the client's right to self-determination in the absolute sense is modified, and the client-worker contract is conditioned by the organizational imperatives of the situation by which they are *mutually* bound.[40] The ability to be skillful in marshaling the strengths inherent in an authoritarian setting may depend on the practitioners' ability to understand the limitations that these situations pose on client options. The analogy is relevant to community organization and planning practitioners as well. They, too, face instances where the options for intervention are influenced by authority other than their own. For example, when he is responding to enforcement in the arena of occupational safety and health or affirmative action, the social worker's relationship to his labor or management sponsor is affected by the limitations of the options allowable and/or imposed by government regulations and their enforcement. These may be positive aids or negative hindrances to the goals of the social worker. The particular situation will determine the impact, just as the compulsory nature of services for the alcoholic may be the only way to overcome initial denial or may constitute the final step in isolating the alcoholic from the helping system he needs.

The nature of the setting and one's assessment of the factors contributing to the presenting problem make additional impact on options and interventions as well. Not all troubled workers have the kind of "intrapsychic" problem that suggests a treatment approach. What they may need is service referral or systems negotiation. Parker, for example, notes a common dilemma of the working class.

A single call to a lawyer may cost $25 nowadays, and minor litigation seldom costs less than several hundred dollars. For the rich and the affluent, this may be expensive but not burdensome; for the poor, the State may often pay the bill. But the worker may be discouraged by the fees from seeking any help at all. In such cases, the lower middle class has little protection from the hucksters, loan companies, and dishonest merchants that are regular features of life on a marginal income.[41]

The basic assumption, adds Weissman, must be that people need assistance. This does not necessarily mean that they need psychiatric treatment.[42] Nor is service delivery in the workplace restricted to the working class. One of the great advantages of locating services in the workplace—with easy access—is that it is equally available to meet the needs of executive personnel. Highly paid technical and managerial workers have become an appropriate target for a gamut of service interventions, particularly as a result of our increased awareness of the negative effects of excessive job stress on productive functioning and general well-being. It is interesting, however, to note that the preferred modalities of intervention for this group are often euphemistically called "wellness programs" and may encompass meditation, stress reduction, weight moderation, and smoke-enders' efforts as well as direct service for individual troubles.[43]

Social workers also must be able to distinguish between the "troubled" and the "troublesome" worker upon referral. In the latter instance, they must be prepared to assess the responsibility of the organization—its policies, its working conditions, and its actors—as they affect a given worker or a class of workers in the workforce. The "troublesome" worker's acting-out or protest may be the manifestation of a problem of his own, not shared by other workers; it may also be an early warning sign of a systemic inequity, where the client is victim and where a social worker's professional use of self must address the organizational policies or procedures that are the causal agents.

One is led, therefore, to a phenomenon which we might term the "troubled organization." To meet their own organizational maintenance needs in the face of external constraints and competition, an institution's leaders may condone or even support conditions that jeopardize large groups of workers. Workplace hazards, toxic agents, and speed-ups may be common in some situations, while evidence of bias or discrimination toward portions of a workforce may occasion victimization of and protest from workers in other settings. Unions, as well, may ignore the legitimate concerns and demands of workers. Complaints of sexual abuse made by women workers are an example of an issue that has required attention for a long time but is just beginning to receive it.

The social worker must assess each situation, to distinguish among the factors described above, recognizing that a given presenting problem may reflect aspects of all. Therefore, unless professionals are willing to use themselves in a multi-faceted way, they may treat symptoms rather than cause, or cause alone—without proper regard for the compelling quality of the present pain that clients are facing. In sum, differential assessment and a sensitive use of self, which reflects one's sensing of the environment, are essential in order to fulfill the social policy and social service components of professional practice.

We also must transcend our own biases and life experiences to understand special blue-collar *and* white-collar issues, as well as working-class issues in general.[44] Their requests, as we have noted, are often for concrete services; for systems negotiation in lieu of referral; for linkage instead of what we generally term information; for action rather than reflection. These positions are noted in the working-class expression of and approaches to a problem. Mayer and Timms, in their study of working-class help-seeking behavior, cite a client who came to a traditional agency with a problem. "My husband's gambling was driving me around the bend and I thought maybe the Welfare could help me do something about it. But all the lady wanted to do was talk—what was he like when he gambled, did we quarrel, and silly things like that. She was trying to help and it made me feel good knowing someone cares. But you can't solve a problem by *talking* about it. Something's got to be done!"[45] Values, life style, and world view may be different, as well as the clients' feelings about the extrinsic and intrinsic rewards derived from a helping situation. Our ability, therefore, to honor, dignify, and feel professionally fulfilled by meeting a client's concrete requests (which may or may not have broader treatment implications) may be a litmus test of our ability to serve workers well in these settings.

There is a wide range of practice being provided by social workers in labor and management settings, although the present emphasis is on services to workers and their families. A smaller number of programs focus principally on community relations, social responsibility, and organizational development, and a few programs encompass social work involvement in both organizational and service arrangements.[46] While most labor and industrial sponsors chose to establish their own in-house programs, some have negotiated contract or purchase-of-service arrangements with family service agencies, community mental health clinics, or private consultation firms directed by social workers.[47] Among the in-house programs, one division frequently encountered is between those that are primarily information and referral, and those that also do extensive direct service.[48] Factors conditioning these decisions include the size of staff (relative to the demand) and the nature of the third-party coverage provided for workers in personnel practices or in collective bargaining arrangements.[49] In industries like auto and steel where third-party coverage for out-patient mental health care is present, referral to community-based services may be more viable than in the majority of organized and unorganized worksites where such benefits are not available.[50]

An additional demarcation for industrial social work programs is between those that service all personal and emotional problems of the workforce and those that are functionally specific. While specificity may be around any single issue, experience to date has been that such programs generally tend to focus on alcoholism and drug abuse. These programs grew in response to definite need and the availability of funds for them from governmental sources. Many of the programs, however, have moved on to a comprehensive ("broad-brush") approach, offering a full range of social services to all employees, rather than substance abuse services alone. Roman notes that nationwide data on occupational programs show a "decreasing emphasis throughout the country on employee *alcoholism* programs, and that the employee *assistance* model with its broad implications for comprehensive mental health programs, is coming to dominate the scene."[51] Labor and management recognize that workers are plagued by a host of situations that can profit from social work knowledge and skill. In fact, in the health arena alone, it is widely recognized that alcoholism represents only one of many emotionally and physically disabling conditions with which social workers and clients must deal, because of the tremendous effect of on-the-job and off-the-job disabilities in the lives of workers in our society.

It is also recognized that alcoholism may be the cover or the coping mechanism for deeper difficulties with which a person has not yet come to terms. Further, even when alcoholism is "cured," its residue in family conflicts, co-worker distrust, and the individual's sense of worthlessness may remain. In work situations, it is often possible for co-workers and supervisory personnel to see the manifestations of the alcohol problem, in part, because they are so visible and because they may explicitly affect work performance. A resulting job jeopardy situation may precipitate the crisis that helps pierce the alcoholic's denial and bring a request for help from a worker who has never sought professional mental health care services before. The need, however, is for a broad range of services.

Most industrial social work programs have evolved the "broad-brush" approach because, as Feinstein notes, this model is "most effective and most consistent with good social work practice."[52] Erfurt and Foote note, from their study of twenty-one Detroit-area employee assistance programs, that six of ten programs concentrating on alcoholism or substance abuse were dissatisfied with their focus, indicating that it created serious problems for their program. *All* of the "broad-brush" programs indicated satisfaction with and commitment to their focus. "There is general agreement in the Detroit area," the authors note, "that occupational programs should be of the *comprehensive* type, rather than focus on specific types of employee problems."[53]

Implications of the Setting for Professional Behavior

Industrial social work practice in many ways is an experience in isolation. When the first national conference was held for social work practitioners in labor and industrial settings (June 1978), the sponsors noted the sheer joy of the participants in being together. One participant remarked that she believed that this was the first time she had ever been in the same room with more than four or five colleagues who were doing the same things and facing the same issues as she was in practice.

In order to maintain one's sense of identity and equilibrium it is essential that one have access to colleagues. Several strategies can be mapped out to build this support into one's corporate or trade union experience. Providing field instruction for students from a school of social work ensures not only the stimulation that comes from student supervision but also regular contact with faculty from the setting, who serve as faculty advisors and field liaisons. Participation in selected activities of the local chapter of the professional association affords stimulation and the fellowship of peers who share a common identity with the social work profession. Such activity keeps one current with contemporary issues in policy and practice and in touch with new developments in program. In addition, one may wish to take courses or institutes provided by agencies, schools, or the professional association, in order to stay in the mainstream with respect to practice innovations. New models of short-term intervention, advancements in administrative theory and program design, the significance and impact of new government regulations—all may be inviting offerings for the labor- or industry-based practitioner who does not have access to the in-house training and teaching programs that are commonly provided by social agencies and host institutions.

Because our competence is derived from our professional training, the profession (in all of its ramifications) represents an anchor for our expertise and our judgment. The profession's Code of Ethics, for example, can provide external support and legitimization for one's ethical positions within the industrial setting, as one seeks boundaries for professional function. Such points of reference are necessary, in order to ensure that our judgments are well founded in decision-making situations—especially when one may not have a network of colleagues with whom to discuss the situation.

However well one may establish outside support and stimuli, one also must work at building intraorganizational guideposts and supports. Co-workers in the corporate personnel, medical, or community relations departments or in the benefit plan or education division of a trade union can become part of an informal network of workers in human service positions. Conscious development of peer support systems may be warranted, where workers who share goals in common within the organization maintain alliances with one another. Formal and informal exchanges that are mutually supportive may establish a fraternal order, which comes to understand the tangible and intangible rewards of social behavior as exchange.[54]

One of the other pressures that social workers may feel in these settings is the value placed on the variable of "time." The urgency of the referral agent is underscored by the foreman's statement: "I want him back at work tomorrow—he's essential," or the shop steward's plea, "We're going to second-step hearing tomorrow; the member's job is on the line—you've got to do something." The ideas of engagement, setting contract, and building trust as components of "beginnings" do not always wash easily with the urgency of the moment and the demands of the gatekeepers. At times it feels as though what they want is our assessment, prognosis, and evidence of progress in treatment by tomorrow (if not yesterday). We may resent this constraint as an imposition on our intervention, but these are the realities of the workplace, where saving a person's job means loyalty, and where getting him back to work means meeting a production deadline. Comparably, for nonclinical practitioners, the quick assessment of community situations, interpretation of occupational safety guidelines, speed and initiative in negotiating new service arrangements for workers/members—all of these add up to helping the organization maintain a competitive edge. Timing may not be everything, but without it social work may not be accepted.

One more pressure is provided by the nature of the internal political system. As the newest profession in the organization, social work must expect to have to negotiate the rituals of acceptance, as others have done before. There is no basis for expecting that organizational leadership will give full sanction to social workers—*even* to perform their designated functions—until they have had an opportunity to judge how appropriately and how well the social workers fit into the larger system. What is extremely important, however, is that, whatever the specific nature of the social work function, the initial contract specify that the social work leader must have access to top-level decision-makers, even if only to be used on a periodic, as-needed basis.

Other actors within the organization may be uncomfortable or even threatened by a social work presence, wondering how our work will affect their function. Whether in clinical or organizational development positions, we are seldom the first (or the only ones) in the organization who have tried to cope with the assigned problem (or are doing so at present). Turf issues may arise, and other actors may wonder whether our success could expose their prior failure or whether our work will involve a rewarded function. A union business agent may be worried that social work success in treating a member (or saving his job) will mean that the member's appreciation and loyalty will switch to the social work unit. A foreman may wonder if social work's effectiveness with his worker may be regarded by senior management as his own counseling ineffectiveness as a supervisor. A union health and benefit plan clerk (with a somewhat routine job) may derive her real job satisfaction from comforting and counseling members when they apply for disability benefits; and now, this is to be somebody else's function, and she has a diploma!

An awareness of the nature and meaning of an organization's prior coping mechanisms and of the individuals' investment in them thus becomes an essential component of winning trust with one's colleagues and obtaining sanction and support from the *informal* system. One must, therefore, be sophisticated in understanding the nature of the informal networks and the behavior of the reward systems and in assessing and honoring existing organizational arrangements. A respectful entry will assist in mitigating the severity of the customary rites of initiation and will help win indigenous support within the formal and informal systems for current and future functions. Then, as Miller notes, through competent and sensitive performance of one's core (counseling) function, one can understand what is going on in the company and take on the role of "sensing the environment" as a service to the organization.[55]

Colleagues in other parts of the labor or management organization, as well as clients coming for service, may not be certain as to who social workers are and what they do. Visions of people handing out welfare checks or supervising basketball games in a community center are not uncommon among the uninitiated. Problems of identification may be obscured further by the strange titles we carry as "personal service workers," "employee counselors," or "community affairs officers." In the same sense that we needed to maintain external ties to our own profession, it may be important that our identity *within* the organization be clear as well. Social workers in labor and management settings have found it important to display their state licenses and diplomas, even though they may never previously have done so in traditional social work settings. Social workers here have consciously signed their correspondence with "C.S.W.," or "A.C.S.W.," and have made similar notations of profession and professional title on letterheads, nameplates, and in the staff directory. Clients and co-workers seem to appreciate such explicit reference to profession. In this way, role ambiguity may be reduced, and clients and co-workers may develop clarity and reassurance about the qualifications of the person with whom they will be sharing intimate personal or organizational problems. Since such clarity never has been a question when organizational personnel have conferred with the company (or union) lawyer, accountant, or physician—why should the same clarity not be encouraged when they refer to a social worker?

Whatever limitations may be implied by the issues of isolation, time pressures, and search for organizational acceptance, it is equally important that we understand a special strength that these auspices bring to our practice. Labor and industry are major forces within our economic system, and they have enormous power to effect change on a national or local basis. When a major trade union (such as the United Auto Workers or Steel Workers) negotiates a new contract that adds on a benefit for out-patient mental health care coverage, more than a million workers and their family members suddenly are enfranchised. If a large corporation decides to locate its production in a new city, the economy of the area may be transformed overnight. When an industrial social worker negotiates new job accommodation options (such as flexitime) for the workforce, opportunities may be opened for a whole new sector of the population, such as working mothers. If internal arrangements can be made toward sheltered employment for older workers, disabled workers, or those under acute situational stress, they may be *maintained* in the workforce, instead of quietly slipping out of it.

Being located in such a setting has many implications, even from the relatively modest vantage point of a local social work practitioner. A social work corporate social responsibility officer may influence a bank to open a new branch in a transitional community, thereby helping to stabilize the neighborhood and revitalize its economy. A union personal services worker may identify and win support for the unmet needs of the retired membership and thereby stimulate a new program of benefits or services.

Corporations and trade unions are major purchasers of health and welfare services in the community. Where workers and members choose to go for service often is determined by the kind of support and publicity these services receive from the worker's membership or employing organization, as much as by the nature of the third-party reimbursement arrangements negotiated or approved for payment. Unresponsive agencies or vendors must be willing to deal with the power that social workers, representing labor or management, can have to affect their contracts and intake. The payroll deductions of workers represent 60 percent of the more than $1 billion raised by the local United Way. The AFL–CIO has come to recognize that it has great clout in the social welfare sector. Agencies that unreasonably impose barriers to workers through "lengthy waiting lists, inconvenient days and hours, and inaccessible office locations," may face the prospect of trade union resistance.[56] Organized labor's dissatisfaction with the performance of many social agencies that are supported by the United Way has led to the development of Labor Agencies, which give concrete services to their members and direct them for mental health services only to those agencies which are responsive to the interests and the service needs of working people.

Both unions and corporations also represent a political force in the community. Trade union support may include not only persuasion of its membership to vote for specific candidates but also activity by union staff on election day to get out the vote and man the polls. Corporations may use their status as major employers and taxpayers in the community to influence political decision-making and may release management staff on a *pro bono* basis to support selected community projects.

Seldom have social workers been employed by such powerful organizations! While the prospect may seem a bit intoxicating, the ability to harness this clout on behalf of workers, their families, and their communities is worth noting. Social agencies to whom one makes referrals may feel constrained to be responsive, since a call from IBM or the United Steel Workers cannot be taken lightly. On behalf of both an individual client and the needs of the worker population as a collective, an industrial social worker's conscious use-of-self can be made to achieve systemic change. One is in a position to document unmet needs, unresponsive service systems, and discriminatory practices or legislation. The labor- or industry-based social worker also is in a strategic position to gain access to the boards and commissions in the community that influence social policies and support new service arrangements. Social workers in mental health clinics, family agencies, hospitals, and school systems, who have always wished to have this access and clout, may be intrigued by the realm of the possible that is offered by industrial social work practice.

The industrial social worker's effectiveness depends on her ability to harness information on the needs of the work force. Systematic research and data collection, usually from the experience of providing ongoing services to workers or members, provide the grist for the mill of program development and social change. Arguments based on opinion or intuition are seldom as persuasive in labor and industrial circles as recommendations based on evidence and data. The responsibility to document and record becomes translated into an opportunity to influence systems with power. The result can be felt not only in the social welfare community but also in the way work and its rewards are organized and allocated to workers and to those outside the labor force. Seldom has the occasion been so opportune for translating "private troubles" into "public issues" and achieving an authentic degree of unity between cause and function.[57]

To the Future

In sum, we have tried to convey the thoughts that work and work institutions are not foreign bodies, but rather mainstream institutions in the life of our society and that they must become so in the professional practice of social work. We believe that staying on the sidelines not only will rob the profession of a future opportunity but may actually rob the profession of its future. A new concern about the nature of the workplace and work activities is evident throughout the country. Industrial society has moved away from Taylorism, under which philosophy workers were viewed as integral parts of the operation of machines and were expected to be used in the most efficient manner in concert with the machines. The present view is that the quality of society is instrumentally influenced by the world of work. This new situation invites the kind of contribution in the workplace that the social work professional is capable of making.

The abundant opportunities and challenges available to the industrial social welfare specialist define just what is so special about this professional role. They are scary—and rewarding. They are experienced on unfamiliar ground, yet they call forth the very skills and knowledge that are at the core of social work. When there is a place where people are in need of services, social workers ought to be there. When there are organizations in need of change in their social welfare functioning, social workers ought to be there. When there are allocation decisions in need of social welfare input, social workers ought to be there. Needs of this kind abound in the world of work. They offer the opportunity to influence not only the quality of work life but the quality of life for workers—and for all Americans. They are the legitimate turf of the industrial social welfare specialist. We encourage—indeed we urge—our professional colleagues to enter into this territory, where social workers can achieve their primary professional mission: service delivery and social change.

Notes

[1] See, for example, Paul Pigors and Charles A. Meyers, *Personnel Administration* (New York: McGraw-Hill, 1973) or Michael J. Jucius' *Personnel Management* (Homewood, Ill.: Richard D. Irwin, 1971), for a relatively complete discussion of different aspects and standards of the personnel function.

[2] This complexity and uncertainty, as well as strategies for rationality in boundary-spanning positions, are discussed extensively by James D. Thompson, *Organizations in Action* (New York: McGraw-Hill, 1967).

[3]The situation is not markedly different from one reported by Ann S. Frangos and Donna Chase in "Potential Partners: Attitudes of Family Practice Residents Toward Collaboration with Social Workers in Their Future Practices," *Social Work in Health Care*, 2, no. 1 (Fall 1976), 74-75. Noting that these residents preferred collaborating with social workers to teaming up with other professionals on the psychosocial problems of patients, the authors conclude:

> Perhaps one reason why the physicians were so positive in their attitudes to social work services is because of the broad range of intervention strategies social workers offer. These residents saw psychologists and psychiatrists as filling a much more narrow role than that of social workers. . . . This multiplicity of function makes social worker services attractive and is seen as a major strength by physicians.

[4]See Sheila H. Akabas and Susan Bellinger, "Programming Mental Health Care for the World of Work," *Mental Health*, 61, no. 1 (Spring 1977), 4-8.

[5]For up-to-date figures on labor unions and their membership, see *The World Almanac & Book of Facts* (New York: Newspaper Enterprise Association, 1979), p. 125.

[6]The question of who is and who is not in the labor force, and particularly the handling of the "discouraged worker" in that definition, has significant effects on both the numbers counted and the social issues suggested by a population view of this practice area. See, for example, Robert L. Stein, "National Commission Recommends Changes in Labor Force Statistics," *Monthly Labor Review*, 103, no. 4 (August 1980), 11-21.

[7]Sheila H. Akabas, "Labor: Social Policy and Human Services," *Encyclopedia of Social Work*, 17th ed. (Washington, D.C.,: National Association of Social Workers, 1977), p. 743.

[8]For a discussion of many aspects of stress in the workplace, see Alan McLean, ed., *Reducing Occupational Stress* (Cincinnati: National Institute for Occupational Safety and Health, 1977).

[9]Richard M. Titmuss, *Commitment to Welfare* (New York: Pantheon Books, 1968).

[10]Hyman J. Weiner, Sheila H. Akabas, John J. Sommer, and Eleanor Kremen, *The World of Work and Social Policy* (New York: Columbia University School of Social Work, 1971), p. 6.

[11]We acknowledge the role of Dr. Irving Miller in bringing this tension to our attention.

[12]From *Annual Report*, Association for Improving the Condition of the Poor, as quoted in Elaine Gorson, Beverly Kalter, and Richard Nann, (New York: New York School of Social Work, Masters thesis #4899-2, 1959), p. 17.

[13]A. G. Wagner, S. A. Queen, and E. B. Harper, *American Charities and Social Work*, 4th ed. (New York: Thomas Y. Crowell, 1930), p. 38.

[14]Foster Rhea Dulles, *Labor in America* (New York: Thomas Y. Crowell, 1949), p. 257.

[15]Paul A. Kurzman, *Harry Hopkins and the New Deal* (Fairlawn, N.J.: R.E. Burdick Publishers, 1974).

[16]Bertha Capen Reynolds, *Social Work & Social Living*, (Washington, D.C.: NASW Classics Series, 1975).

[17]The analogue is one often alluded to by the late Dr. Hyman J. Weiner, to whom both authors are indebted for his early leadership in this field.

[18]Leo Perlis, "The Human Contract in the Organized Workplace," *Social Thought*, no. 1 (Winter 1977), 29-35.

[19]W. W. Rostow, *The Stages of Economic Growth* (Cambridge, Mass.: Cambridge University Press, 1960).

[20] Sheila H. Akabas, Paul A. Kurzman, and Nancy Kolben, eds., *Labor and Industrial Settings: Sites for Social Work Practice* (New York: Columbia University, Hunter College, Council on Social Work Education, 1978).

[21] We are indebted to Ms. Mallory Pepper, a research associate at the Industrial Social Welfare Center at Columbia University School of Social Work, for her analysis of the questionnaires.

[22] See, for example, Alice H. Collins and Diane L. Pancoast, *Natural Helping Networks* (Washington, D.C.: NASW, 1976), and Joan Shapiro, "Dominant Leaders among Slum Residents," *American Journal of Orthopsychiatry,* 39, no. 4 (July 1969), 644–50, for discussions of the significance of self-help and mutual aid.

[23] Thomas A. Kochan, Lee Dyer, and David B. Lipsky, *The Effectiveness of Union Management Safety and Health Committees* (Kalamazoo, Mich.: W. E. Upjohn Institute for Employment Research, 1977), pp. 5–6. Of course, many joint union-management committees predate OSHA, while others continue to function satisfactorily despite, rather than because of, OSHA.

[24] Mitchell Sviridoff, *Human Resources and the Pendulum of Power* (New York: Ford Foundation, 1976).

[25] William J. Reid and Laura Epstein, *Task-Centered Casework* (New York: Columbia University Press, 1972), chapter 2; and, Reid and Epstein, eds., *Task-Centered Practice* (New York: Columbia University Press, 1977), chapters 16 and 17.

[26] Howard J. Parad and Libbie G. Parad, "A Study of Crisis-Oriented Planned Short-Term Treatment," *Social Casework,* 49, nos. 6, 7 (June & July 1968), 418–26.

[27] See, Lydia Rapoport, "Crisis Intervention as a Mode of Brief Treatment," in Robert W. Roberts and Robert H. Nee, eds., *Theories of Social Casework* (Chicago: University of Chicago Press, 1970) chapter 7; and Howard J. Parad, ed., *Crisis Intervention: Selected Readings* (New York: F.S.A.A., 1965).

[28] See Collins and Pancoast, *Natural Helping Networks.*

[29] Jack Rothman, "Three Models of Community Organization Practice," in Fred M. Cox and others, eds., *Strategies of Community Organization: A Book of Readings,* 3d ed. (Itasca, Ill.: F.E. Peacock, 1979), chapter 1.

[30] Carel B. Germain, "An Ecological Perspective in Casework Practice," *Social Casework,* 54, no. 6 (June 1973), 327.

[31] Stephen E. Goldston, "An Overview of Primary Prevention Programming," in *Primary Prevention: An Idea Whose Time Has Come,* Proceedings of the Pilot Conference on Primary Prevention, April 2–4, 1976, Department of Health, Education and Welfare, Public Health Service (Washington, D.C.: Superintendent of Documents, 1977), p. 27.

[32] Lillian B. Rubin, *Worlds of Pain: Life in the Working-Class Family* (New York: Basic Books, 1976), p. 164.

[33] A recent issue of *The Community,* a publication of the Department of Community Services of the AFL–CIO, notes, "There is a race to assist members in solving their 'off the job' problems and the prize is loyalty. Organized labor cannot afford to lose this one." (September–November 1978), p. 16.

[34] Cavin P. Leeman, "A Demonstration Project in Occupational Mental Health Services," *Psychiatric Quarterly,* 47, no. 3 (1973), 425–26.

[35] Regarding the development of the Muncipal Employees Legal Services (MELS) Program at District Council 37, see Akabas, Kurzman, and Kolben, eds., *Labor and Industrial Settings,* Pt. I.

[36] Hans B. C. Spiegel, *Not for Work Alone: Services at the Workplace* (New York: Urban Research Center, Hunter College of the City University of New York, 1974), p. 116.

[37] For a copy of the current NASW Code of Ethics, see *NASW News,* 25, no. 1 (January 1980), 24–25.

[38] Antonio Blanco and Sheila H. Akabas, "The Factory: A Site for Community Men-

tal Health Practice," *American Journal of Orthopsychiatry,* 38, no. 3 (April 1968), 547.

[39] John C. Erfurt and Andrea Foote, *Occupational Employee Assistance Programs for Substance Abuse and Mental Health Problems* (Ann Arbor: Institute of Labor & Industrial Relations, University of Michigan, 1977), pp. 45–46.

[40] For reference to social work practice in authoritarian settings, see Irving Weisman and Jacob Chwast, "Control and Values in Social Work Treatment," *Social Casework,* 41 (November 1960) and Elliot Studt, *Education for Social Workers in the Correctional Field* (New York, C.S.W.E., 1959), 451–56.

[41] Richard Parker, "Those Blue-Collar Blues," *New Republic* (September 23, 1972), p. 19.

[42] Andrew Weissman, "A Social Service Strategy in Industry," *Social Work,* 20, no. 5 (September 1975), 402.

[43] See, for example, Alan A. McLean, *Work Stress;* Leon J. Warshaw, *Stress Management;* Arthur Shostak, *Blue Collar Stress;* all in Addison-Wesley Series on Occupational Stress (Reading, Mass.: Addison-Wesley Publishing Co., 1979).

[44] To understand the similarity and difference between blue-collar and white-collar workers and their frequent misclassification by the Bureau of Labor Statistics (DOL), see Andrew Levison, *The Working Class Majority* (New York: Coward, McCann & Geoghagan, 1974), chapter 1.

[45] John E. Mayer and Noel Timms, *The Client Speaks: Working Class Impressions of Casework* (Chicago: Atherton Press, 1970), p. 1. See also Teresa Donati Marciano, "Middle Class Incomes, Working-Class Hearts," *Family Process,* 13, no. 4 (December 1974), 489–502.

[46] Paul A. Kurzman and Sheila H. Akabas, "Industrial Social Work as an Arena for Practice," *Social Work,* 26, no. 1 (January 1981), 52–60 and Akabas, Kurzman, and Kolben, eds., *Labor and Industrial Settings: Sites for Social Work Practice.*

[47] For example, see Elizabeth Mills, "Family Counseling in an Industrial Job-Support Program," *Social Casework,* 55, no. 10 (December 1972); Paul R. Brooks, "Industry-Agency Program for Employee Counseling," *Social Casework,* 56, no. 7 (July 1975), 404–10; and Donald Boone, "Human Effectiveness Systems," in Akabas, Kurzman, and Kolben, eds., *Labor and Industrial Settings: Sites for Social Work Practice.*

[48] See, for example, Hyman J. Weiner, Sheila H. Akabas, and John Sommer, *Mental Health Care in the World of Work* (New York: Association Press, 1973). Here we are discussing programs staffed by professional social workers. There are a number of Employee Assistance Programs, staffed exclusively by the employing organization, that do not have persons with formal mental health training. In these instances, the emphasis generally is on information and referral. Often the staff are "recovered" personnel, and, therefore, the program emphasis may be on alcoholism and substance abuse.

[49] Paul A. Kurzman, "Third Party Reimbursement," *Social Work,* 18, no. 6 (November 1973), 11–22.

[50] For an example of such an arrangement, see Judson L. Stone and Virginia Crowthers, "Innovations in Program and Funding of Mental Health Service for Blue-Collar Families," *American Journal of Psychiatry,* 128, no. 11 (May 1972), 375–89.

[51] Paul M. Roman, "Dimensions of Current Research in Occupational Alcoholism," Tulane University, unpublished manuscript, March 1977, p. 9. Also reported in Alan R. Cutting and Frank J. Prosser, "Family Oriented Mental Health Consultation to a Naval Research Group," *Social Casework,* 60, no. 4 (April 1979), 239.

[52] Barbara B. Feinstein, "Social Services in the Work Place," in *Social Welfare Forum—1977* (New York: Columbia University Press, 1978), p. 31.

[53] Erfurt and Foote, *Occupational Employee Assistance Programs,* p. 3.

[54] See George C. Homans, "Social Behavior as Exchange," *American Journal of Sociology,* 63, no. 6 (May 1958), 597–606 and Peter M. Blau, *Exchange and Power in Social Life* (New York: Wiley, 1964).

[55] Leo Miller, "A Counseling Program in Industry: Polaroid," *Social Thought*, 3, no. 1 (Winter 1977), 42.

[56] See John J. McManus, "The Labor Agency," paper presented at the 21st Annual Program Meeting of the C.S.W.E. (March 3, 1975), p. 6.

[57] See William Schwartz, "Private Troubles and Public Issues: One Social Work Job or Two?" *Social Welfare Forum—1969* (New York: Columbia University Press, 1969), p. 38.

Indexes

Author Index

Subject Index

Responsiveness to diverse constituencies, 154-56
Retirement:
of federal and civil service employees, 47
mandatory, 97
money, importance of, 86
as process, 87
psychological factors in, 87
research on, 122-23
service needs of, 132-33
as social event, 85-86
social factors in, 87
as status, 86
Right-to-work lobbies, 22
Robiotics, work implications of, 28
Role models, occupational choice and, 82
Role segregation, in labor force, 140

Scientific management, 16
Segmented labor market, theory of, 39
Self-actualization, 6, 23, 35, 41, 43, 74, 101, 112
Self-esteem, 74, 82, 122
Self-help groups, 192
labor and management sponsored, 216
support for, 140
Service delivery:
in industrial social work, 215-17
nature of, 158-60
patterns, alternative, 133-38
style of, 187
Sex-role expectations, 140
Shop stewards, 22, 218
Significant others, 72-73
of clients, 114
Silberman Fund, 2, 3
Single persons, in labor force, 40
Slavery, 11
Aristotle's definition of, 101
in ancient world, 9
Slowdown, 22
Social confirmation, 74
Social insurance: (*See also* Occupational Social Welfare Systems)
federal, 33
private, 33
programs, 43-46
Social learning, work as, 69-70
Social planning, 190-92
corporate social responsibility, 191
industrial development and planning, 191
mental health and personal services, delivery of, 190
Social policy:
family value in, 34, 55-57
issues, 138-42
Social Security, 48, 215
Social Security Act (1935), 18, 85-86
Social Security Administration, 51, 52, 124
Social services, planning and organizing, 190-91
Social welfare administration, norms for, 150-62
commitment through participation, 156-58
decentralizing treatment authority, 158-60
evaluation to improve performance, 160-62
responsiveness to diverse constituencies, 154-56
subdominate values, 152-54
Social welfare agency:
environmental relationships of, 152-54
goals and, 155
membership, 156-58
objective standards and, 156
task environment of, 154-56
Social work:

and community of work, separation between, 179
intervention, outcomes of, 129
values of, 194
Social work administration, guidelines for assessing managerial technology and, 154, 156, 158, 160, 162
Social worker(s):
major concern of, 109-10
work attitudes and experiences, 125
as workers, 126
Social work research:
guidelines for, 123-25
reasons for gap in, 120
Speenhamland Law (1795-1832), 13, 18
Staff development and training, 191
Status:
change, 205-206
and social recognition, 71-73
from work, 92
Stratification, 139
Stress, 26
Strike(s), 15, 22
Structural variables, occupational attainment and, 37-38
Subdominate values, agency advocacy of, 152-54
Sweden:
family policy in, 140
social policy of, and family-work relationship, 51-52
Systems negotiation, 199, 223, 225

Taylorism, 16, 17, 42
Temporary Disability Insurance, 43, 45
Time-demands, of work in modern world, 100-101
Time-and-motion, study of workers, 16
Trade associations, 9
Trade union(s), 179, 182, 190
and social action, 177
Training:
on-the-job, 19, 25
programs, 219-20
Transactional issues in social work research, 124
Treatment effectiveness, decentralized authority and, 159-60
Triple community theory, 181
Troubled organization, as client, 188

Underemployment, 132
Unemployment, 141-42
as deliberate policy, 54
elderly, 47
reduction of, 49
service needs of, 132-33
Unemployment insurance, 215
Unionism:
AFL craft, 18
rise of, and meaning of work, 22
Unionism, industrial, 18
social insurance and, 19
Unionization, sense of solidarity and, 22
Unions, 15, 185. *See also* Trade unions, AFL, AFL-CIO, CLUW
labor, 9
as natural focus for social action, 193
and social bonding, 104
United Way, 46, 191, 192, 193, 210, 230
Utopia, 101

Variables, in assessing worker problems, 126-27
Vocational Rehabilitation Act (1973), 46, 52, 122
Volunteers, in social work field, 185